Halsey R Stevens

Faith and reason: heart, soul, and hand work

A concise account of the Christian religion, and of all the prominent religions

before and since Christianity

Halsey R Stevens

Faith and reason: heart, soul, and hand work
A concise account of the Christian religion, and of all the prominent religions before and since Christianity

ISBN/EAN: 9783744741712

Printed in Europe, USA, Canada, Australia, Japan

Cover: Foto ©Lupo / pixelio.de

More available books at **www.hansebooks.com**

FAITH AND REASON:

HEART, SOUL, AND HAND WORK.

A CONCISE ACCOUNT

OF

THE CHRISTIAN RELIGION,

AND OF

ALL THE PROMINENT RELIGIONS

BEFORE AND SINCE CHRISTIANITY.

BY

HALSEY R. STEVENS.

By their fruits ye shall know them.—MATTHEW vii, 20.

NEW YORK:
CHARLES P. SOMERBY,
139 Eighth Street.
1879.

CONTENTS.

	PAGE
PREMISE...	7

PART I.
RELIGIONS BEFORE CHRISTIANITY.

CHAPTER I.
ARYAN RELIGIONS, MYTHS AND LEGENDS................... 19

CHAPTER II.
ETHNIC AND CATHOLIC RELIGIONS........................... 32

CHAPTER III.
RELIGION OF CHINA—CONFUCIANISM....................... 47

CHAPTER IV.
BRAHMANISM AND HINDUISM................................. 58

CHAPTER V.
BUDDHISM... 81

CHAPTER VI.
ANCIENT RELIGION OF PERSIA AND ZOROASTER.:........... 96

CHAPTER VII.
Religion and Sacred Books of Egypt 113

CHAPTER VIII.
The Gods and Religion of Greece 132

CHAPTER IX.
The Gods and Religion of Rome 148

CHAPTER X.
Teutonic and Scandinavian Religion 160

CHAPTER XI.
The Jewish Religion 172

PART II.
CHRISTIANITY.

CHAPTER I.
History and Geography of Palestine 193

CHAPTER II.
Introductory to Christianity 214

CHAPTER III.
Chronology, Birth of Jesus, and Our Era 227

CHAPTER IV.
The New Testament 235

CHAPTER V.
Evangelical and Apostolical Authority 249

CHAPTER VI.
Correctness of Gospel History 291

CHAPTER VII.

Instruction, Direction, and Admonition........................ 327

PART III.
RELIGIONS SINCE CHRISTIANITY.

CHAPTER I.

Mohammedanism, or Islam.................................. 379

CHAPTER II.

Hegelianism and Other Systems............................ 397

CHAPTER III.

The Book of Nature....................................... 410

CHAPTER IV.

Prayer... 417

Index.. 425

FAITH AND REASON.

HEART, SOUL, AND HAND WORK.

PREMISE.

The following work is intended to be a fair, candid and charitable consideration of the subjects of which we speak, without pretending to high attainments or superior wisdom, or omitting to pay proper respect to what others have said and believed. We repeat here what we said in a previous volume: that the timidity of many men has kept back much of importance to the world, not thinking that the little light they could shed would be of any particular value. This is not only neglect of duty: it is a sin. Frankly, honestly and liberally to speak out is the only true way. Under all circumstances, at all times, we should realize that we are in the presence of God our Father, who knows all we do, and our motives in the doing. God also controls all events, substantially governs the world and all things in it, and none can stay his hand. This world is a place for sober thought, for serious and solemn things; and by that we do not mean we are without satisfaction, joy and comfort. God gives us all things richly to enjoy.

Our desire is not only to engage the attention of men, but to feel the approbation of God. To please all is what we do not expect. Every man does not see the same thing in the same light; hence there are honest differences of opinion. We have high and low churchmen, both parties intending to be honest and godly. The former class are pretty likely to condemn much that we say, and think it irreverent, calculated to do harm and open the way for a low estimate of religion. Our lack of belief in Jesus as an atoning sacrifice—which belief many consider most precious—connected with the theory that Adam sinned for himself and all his posterity, making a vicarious atonement all-important, and many other things we say, will draw down upon our head a very large amount of indignation. Our faith is dualistic. Two opposing forces have been plainly observable in man's nature from the first; one inclining to good, the other to evil. We are happy in the thought that we have one spiritual father, God, whom we intend to honor and obey. So we are all begotten of God, heirs to an inheritance that is eternal. Considering this, we ought to be obedient children, thus showing that we realize our sonship. If we look to God as our loving Father, we naturally incline to love him. His laws we are not to learn solely from a printed book, as they are ineffaceably written on our hearts and consciences, so that they cannot be blotted out. All human acts are open before God's all-seeing eye, however well we may succeed in hiding them from finite observation. The way of the transgressor is hard, in the nature of things; a just recompense of reward is in every case meted out. Hence, nothing can possibly be gained by wrong-doing, while much is lost.

In the teachings of our Great Master, Jesus, are many things of importance; but no creeds, no sectarianism, no dogmatism. All is so plain that there is no occasion for the least mistake. The traveler along the pathway of life can read as he goes, and, honestly considering, be in no danger of making mistakes. There is, therefore, no real occasion for sin, no excuse. With the shortest possible teaching we can understand. Jesus said the summing up of man's whole duty was to "deal justly, love mercy, and walk humbly before God." To love God is to love truth, to love righteousness, to love all the creatures God has made, all the works of his hand.

We believe in glorified spirits, in holy angels, in a spiritual life after this mortal life, and that those who are designedly, obstinately and carelessly wicked and bad, are continually suffering here, and cannot be happy at death; but, at the same time, we cannot think it possible that God will punish and confine any of his creatures in endless hell. He is all-wise, as well as all-powerful and good; such a thing as eternal damnation would in no sense benefit any one. But there is no excuse for the willful wrong-doer, who sins against light and knowledge, who treasures up wrath against the day of wrath and the righteous indignation of Heaven, while God is all the time caring for us as a father careth for his son.

Our theological views are of the broadest kind, embracing universal nature, all creatures, all worlds, all immensity; all that we can conceive of or know; all that is unseen, unknowable or unthinkable. All started from the same source, call it what we will; all is governed by the same laws, which we know exist, though we cannot comprehend how they came. About this first beginning of all beginnings we have made some mention in a former volume, and may refer to it again in another chapter.

In regard to special providences, we do not think they are gotten up for every trifling case, or at the solicitation of every man who changes his desires and wishes as the wind happens to blow. If it were so, universal harmony would be disturbed. Through controlling minor events, the sun would be made to rise earlier or later, to suit the convenience of some whimsical mortal; winter delayed, or summer hastened. Better it is by far to submit resignedly to the order of events.

With a belief in the mediatorial power and influence of Jesus, we have also faith in ministering spirits; and to that extent, if no more, we are Spiritualists. Many who claim to be Spiritualists are grossly misrepresented by ignorance or design. Spirit-rapping and table-turning may be a very different thing from the science of Spiritualism, when rightly considered. Many parts of the New Testament cannot be logically explained without the theory assumed in this doctrine.

We read in the New Testament, as plainly as words can express it, that our bodies are of the earth, earthy; that our earthly house must be dissolved and go back to mingle again with other common earth, but, from an inner growth that is not describable to our finite understanding, there comes a spiritual body, adapted to spirit life, that can exist without the old clay body, above and beyond which it is to soar and live for a term of time we have no language to describe. This we call resurrection, or the second birth. However much we may talk about this new birth, here it is not possible. While we are subject to moral infirmity and death, how can it be? Much curious and interesting speculation has been started about the duties, business and enjoyment of a soul when freed from the stage of mortality, though but little, if anything, is really known. Nor can we know aught of the powers a spiritual body may possess. Some believe that in heaven our chief business will be psalm-singing of praises to God for salvation and redemption; others, that our time will be occupied in visiting friends with whom we are to be finally united there, with an occasional coming back to earth to see how it fares with those left behind. That we shall meet our friends in another world is among the natural thoughts. There is much upon which to build the theory that in the next state we shall recognize and be recognized by our relatives, friends and acquaintances, and that the meetings we may have there will be enjoyable beyond all description. We may lay up a stock of comfort in that way, which we may enjoy with all the rest; but any conjecture we can possibly have of such a condition of things is at most but vague and uncertain. Human thought cannot conceive of such a condition, human imagination cannot reach it, human sight cannot penetrate the thick mist that hangs between it and us. Nor can we have any more correct notion of the place denominated Paradise: where it is; the terms of admission; whether we shall, when there, be dormant or active; whether we shall all be happy there, or only part of us.

We read some, and probably imagine more, about a general judgment (an old idea derived from the most ancient times), which, like many other matters, we know nothing about. John the Revelator (vii, 9) tells us about the gathering of an immense throng, that no man could number, of all nations, kindred, people and tongues, clothed in white robes, and palms in their hands. From this and other passages we gather the comforting belief that all the human family will eventually come to a better state. It may be that all will not be equal there; they are not so here, in the full sense of that term: some minds are capable of far greater expansion than others; gifts differ here, and, we have no doubt, will differ in the next life; but we have no idea that God will take pleasure in the infliction of endless hell torments on any of us because we did or neglected to do certain things under certain circumstances that surrounded us. To suppose that God cherishes a wrathful feeling toward mortals who commit sin, would be to suppose him a God of arrogance instead of a God of kindness, long-suffering and mercy. We do not admit there is such a thing as divine wrath. God is not wrath—he is love and kindness. Attributes ascribed to God should be reasonable. So when the Israelites believed God was angry with them, they judged him by the natural feelings of humanity. In our great anxiety to know what cannot be known in this life, we overlook much that we might and ought to understand; much in the way of duty to God and man and our own souls. Instead of trying to talk the best and to make the loudest professions, why not set up a rivalry in good works, in noble actions, in charity for our erring friends, in care for the destitute and downtrodden? Religion is no vain show, no outside putting on, or outward cleaning of the cup and platter; it is the inner man that gets defiled and wants washing.

Evil exists only by God's permission; and that it has existed from all eternity is so self-evident that no argument is necessary. How and why it came into existence, and by what agency, is among the hidden mysteries. God governs the world and all things in or about it; and governing means something. It is the power to will, to accomplish, to place, and to carry out; the power to say this shall and that shall not be. The old notion that there was no sin in the world until Adam's time ought to have been laid aside long ago; at any rate, it should be now. The question may well arise whether it is possible for truth to exist without error, or virtue without vice. Everything takes its character by comparison. All that is good must be compared with something that is bad—with its opposite. In law, no one can be found guilty of counterfeiting when there is nothing to counterfeit. Good and evil, in comparison with each other, never had a beginning within the range of our comprehension, and, to our present conception, can have no end. This conclusion gives no license to the wrong-doer, who is in duty bound to act up to the full extent of his knowledge in pursuing the right and avoiding the wrong. But, it must be remembered, where there is no light there is no sin. A wrong act may be done ignorantly, constituting no sin, which, if done by another knowingly, would be a most glaring sin. All are accountable for what they know, and for their ignorance of duty if the proper means to gain information be neglected. A lazy soul is always condemned. Placed in the world for action, wasting time is not excusable.

Without going into particulars in regard to the New Testament, we will say that it is the best book the world has ever seen or is ever likely to see, and yet we do not consider it a perfect book. A portion of it is the work of men whom we consider good, honest and true men; and, in a certain sense, they, with all other good men, were inspired in regard to many utterances, but not all.

To infuse into a finite being infinite perfection would be but little short of constituting him a God. The power of God is his alone, and cannot be possessed by another while clothed with flesh and blood, if indeed it can be or has been given to another. Jesus, while on the earth, never was by any of his intelligent followers or himself spoken of as equal to the everlasting Father. To say that Jesus was the Son, and the Father also, is too absurd for acceptance by even the weakest minds. So, too, if Jesus was begotten of the Father about two thousand years ago, he was not with God when the worlds were made, or when matter began to aggregate. He either existed before he was begotten, or else he was not at what is called the world's foundation-laying. The New Testament writers, in their eagerness to tell all they knew, at least, would naturally be led to go a little beyond; and then, in believing, the apostles and early Christians were in a constant worry lest they should believe too little. One new convert to Christianity declared he did believe, but, in the same breath, fearing there might be some mistake, asked that his unbelief might be "helped."

To question the birth of Jesus somewhere about the beginning of our era seems to us unwarranted; but when asked to say that he was begotten of God, any more than thousands of other children, would, in our opinion, be straining the truth. Jesus said truly that God was his Father, and it is clearly stated that the Eternal Jehovah is the God and Father of all our spirits, or "the God and Father of us all."

The following work will be treated under three heads, which seem naturally to present themselves. First, comprehending the most prominent and the most extensively embraced religions before the promulgation of Christianity; second, Christianity; and lastly, Mohammedanism, the Hegelian Philosophy, the Book of Nature, and Prayer.

To show our appreciation of some particular portions of the New Testament, we have quoted some parts exactly as they are. The reader will not find them wearisome. There is too much value in it all, and all the truths are too self-evident, to be uninteresting to any but the indifferent. Considered as a whole, we think the conclusion naturally arrived at will be that goodness, purity and truth existed in the world before Christianity, and that God was manifesting himself and has been at least dimly seen by man ever since he existed on the earth. Plainly enough, also, we discover that Christianity is superior to all other religions before or since its development, and that, with all the defects that have been incorporated into its history, by its ardent and enthusiastic followers, we accept it with joy and gladness, and embrace the faith in all its important parts.

PART I.

RELIGIONS BEFORE CHRISTIANITY.

CHAPTER I.

ARYAN RELIGIONS, MYTHS AND LEGENDS.

"The Childhood of Religion" has received particular attention in a highly interesting work, written by Edward Clodd. He says (page 53), it is believed that the birthplace of man was in some part of the earth where the climate was mild, but exactly where it was we may never know: recent information points to a land now submerged beneath the Indian Ocean. His theory is that the early inhabitants became scattered, from a desire to see more of the world, or on account of increasing numbers and lack of food. In their wanderings, the way to Europe was discovered, while they were yet in a savage state, and subsisted by hunting and fishing; for man first of all became a hunter, then he conceived the idea of taming the wild animals, and adopted the life of a shepherd. From that he became a tiller of the soil, a farmer with a family, and discarded his nomadic habits. Then the family grew into a tribe; then succeeded the nation.

The people of whom we are about to speak were not the first civilizers, but were young as compared with those of China or Egypt. In chapter vi, Mr. Clodd says, the Aryan tribes, thousands of years ago, were scattered over the wide plains east of the Caspian sea, and northwest of Hindustan, in Central Asia, but united together by the same manners and customs, though speaking somewhat different dialects of a common tongue — in reality, the offspring of one mother nation. These tribes consisted of two great branches, from one of which came the races that have peopled nearly the whole of Europe: that is to say, the Celts (whom Julius Cæsar found in Britain when he invaded it), the Germans and Slavonians, the Greeks and Romans; while from the other branch the Medes, Persians and Hindus, with some lesser peoples in Asia, have sprung. A learned German has called this the discovery of a new world. And it is certainly a great revelation that the Hindu and the Icelander, the Russian and the Italian, the Englishman and the Frenchman, are children whose forefathers lived in one home.

Arya is a Sanskrit word, meaning *noble*, of a *good family*. It is believed to have come from the root *ar*, to plow, which is found in *era*, the Greek word for *earth;* *earth* meaning that which is *eared* or plowed. *Aryan* was the name given to the tillers of the soil and to householders, and the title by which the once famous Medes and Persians were proud to call themselves. It became the general name for the race who obtained possession of the land, and survives in *Iran*, the modern native name of Persia, and in other names of places; even, as some think, in Ireland, which is called *Erin* by the natives. The name *Indo-European* is sometimes used instead of *Aryan*, and is a better name, because it conveys a clearer idea of the races included therein.

We will inquire more fully into the old life of this interesting people, about their legends of the past, and their arts and customs. In the Zend-Avesta, or sacred book of the Persian religion, only fragments of which have been preserved, there are some statements about the country peopled by the Aryans which seem to hold a little truth:

Sixteen countries are spoken of as having been given to Ormuzd for the Aryans to dwell in, each of which became tainted with evil. The first was named Airyanem-Vaego, and it was created a land of delight; but, to quote the ancient legend, the evil being Ahrieman, full of death, made a mighty serpent and winter, the work of Devas' (or bad spirits). In this Persian legend we have one of the many traditions which have come down from the past concerning disaster and ruin befalling fair lands where men once dwelt in peace. Concerning the Deluge, there are two Chaldæan accounts, one of which belongs to a series of legends on tablets found among the ruins of Nineveh, and resembles that now given. It is said the god *Ilu* warned Xisuthrus of a flood by which mankind would be destroyed, and commanded him to write a history of all things and to bury it in the City of the Sun. He was then to build a ship, and take refuge in it with his relatives and friends, every kind of beast and bird, and food for them. This he did, and, when the flood came, sailed as he was bidden "to the gods." Birds were sent out three times, to ascertain whether the waters were abated. Looking out from a window, he found the ship had stranded upon the side of a mountain, and he at once left it with his wife and daughter. After worshiping the earth and offering sacrifice to the gods, he was translated, and, as he arose, told the friends he left behind to return to Babylon and dig up the books he had buried. This they did, and taught from these books the true religion to the Chaldæans. The Babylonians and Jews were members of the same race, hence the likeness in their traditions. The Chaldæan records speak of the building of the Tower of Babel, the legend of which has just been found on another tablet from Nineveh, and the tower was said to have been overthrown by the wind, and man's language confused by the gods. The Chaldæan history speaks of ten kings whose reigns added together amounted to four hundred and thirty-two thousand years. The likeness between the Hebrew Bible tradition and this is very striking, showing them to be children of one parent. The Aryans, says Mr. Clodd, have left behind them no ruins of temples or tombs, no history stamped on pieces of baked clay, or cut on rocks; historic traces of them are derived from language alone. The Aryans were an inland race, and knew little or nothing of the wide waters that laved the distant coasts. Their skiffs were small, only suited to river use. The Aryan and Semitic languages represent language in its third and highest stage. First, the Supreme is *like-God;* second, *God-like;* third, *God-ly.*

It is one of the few *facts* of history that, before the Hindus crossed the mountains that lay between Bactria and India, before the Celts and other tribes left the west, their common ancestors spoke the same language—a language so firmly settled that Sanskrit, Persian, Greek, Latin, German, Slavonic and Celtic words are simple alterations of its words, and not additions to it.

The Aryan got beyond the lower beliefs of his ancestors in his idea of the gods, though he had not reached the height to which man can climb. At first man explained the movements of Nature by his own.

He knew that he moved because he lived, and willed to do whatever he did, and that the dead moved not. The Aryan spoke of the earth as *Mother*, and invoked her blessing; and yet she appeared to depend, like himself, upon some greater powers, who could shroud her in darkness or withhold the rain. So he looked up to the broad heaven that arched in the earth at every point, and from whence came each morning the light that cheered his life and removed the fear which filled his heart. There, in the heavens, he naturally thought, lived and moved in strength and majesty the great Lord of all, whom he named *Dyaus*, from the root *div*, or *dyu*, which means *to shine*. This was the most ancient of the names by which the Aryans spoke of him who seemed the god of gods, as we now speak of one God in whom we believe. This idea was borne away by all the tribes wherever they went. The name "heaven" above was a never-fading record all could read. *Dyaus* is the same as *Zeus* in Greek, *Jovis* and *Deus* in Latin, and *Tiu* in German. From *Deus* comes our word *Deity*, which, therefore, means the God who is light. In their hymns in the Rig-Veda, or chief sacred book of the Brahmans, the gods are called *diva*, meaning *bright*. Dyaus, the god of the bright sky, and chief deity among the Aryans, was only one of the names by which they invoked the moving powers of Nature. Hence, *Jupiter* (in the Veda, *Dyaus-pitar;* in the Greek, *Zeu-pater*) means

Heaven-Father. These two words form the basis of all prayer, and constituted the oldest prayer man ever offered up—uttered to the unknown God before Sanskrit or Greek was known. Thousands of years have passed since the Aryans separated to travel to the north and the south, the west and the east. Each branch have formed their languages, founded empires and philosophies, built temples and razed them to the ground; but now, with all the wisdom they have learned, there is no name so exalted, so dear to each and all of us, so expressive of awe and love, the infinite and the finite, as the selfsame words uttered in the primeval Aryan prayer—Heaven-Father—in that form which will endure forever, "Our Father which art in heaven."

Sacrifice is the oldest of all rites, for man's first feeling toward the gods was that of fear. They ruled over all things; life and death were in their hands; hence the effort to win their favor. When he saw blessings were greater in number than ills, fear gave place to love, and thank-offerings were made. Realizing that the gods were stronger, their forgiveness was desired for bad deeds done and for good deeds left undone, which led to sin-offerings. Thus we see that the first conception of a God (or, as the Eastern terms were, *the gods*) did not at the start come from a written book, nor from a legend: he showed himself in the heavens, in his laws controlling matter, by his spirit in the heart of man.

The places where these sacrificial altars stood were revered, and temples raised on the same spots. A class of men claiming to be in favor with the gods presided and directed at all public gatherings. Hence originated religious rites, and the order of priests, who pretended to know more about unseen things than the common people; which class, the priests said, need have no concern about religious matters except to do the latter's bidding; therefore many ceased to think for themselves, and laid aside this great privilege that, more than anything else, made them men. How well, by the aid of that priestly order, this arrangement has been maintained, we all know too well. We are too much in the way of forgetting that the voices of God are around us, speaking in thunder tones, if we would but listen. His secrets, if secrets he have, are with no particular class of men, but with those who fear him, with those who are true to what they feel to be highest and best.

The belief that certain buildings are sacred is common to us now. So we speak in our time about God's house, God's temple, God's holy hill, just as they did. Many think a great work has been done when they have erected a house *for God's* worship on some hill, and consecrated the former to his use, if not the latter; and, more important than all, obtained one of God's accredited agents to tell all who will listen how to conduct themselves to secure an entrance into heaven. Mr. Clodd says: The belief that certain buildings are more sacred than others, and one kind of work holier than another, has caused people to think that God is more with the priest than with the peasant, more in a church than in a house or shop. The Psalmist knew better than that, for he asked, "Whither shall I go from thy spirit? or whither shall I flee from thy presence?" And so did Jesus, when he told the people that to the pure in heart there was some showing of God's blessed face, and that not on mountain or in city only, but everywhere, he could be worshiped. The whole earth is a temple, and every hill on it is God's hill, where all honest work is service.

Nor is the position in which our bodies may be fixed to worship God important. Whether kneeling, sitting, standing or reclining, if in our hearts we look up to God and long for mercy and forgiveness, a gracious answer of peace will be given; our souls will be refreshed. Sacrifice was an important part of the Aryan religion. One of the chief offerings to the gods was the fermented juice of the *soma* or moon-plant, a strong and exciting drink. It was thought to aid in the working of miracles, and in time became one of the chief gods among the Hindus.

The Veda contains hymns and prayers used at these sacrifices, and *Vach*, or the goddess of speech, who taught the people to worship in spirit as well as in form, is praised in words much like those about Wisdom in the eighth chapter of Proverbs. We shall all along see that in the Aryan and other religions of the early nations much was common to them all, and that a portion at least of what is now the Christian religion was derived from them, so that in the starting of Christianity it was far from being all new, though a great improvement on anything before it.

Myths have been, to a greater or less extent, incorporated into nearly every form of religion. We may say that what is called mythology is found among every people, and comes from the Greek *muthos*, a fable, and *logos*, a word. Under this name may be classed all legends, traditions and fairy tales. Myths and folk-lore containing stories of the loves and quarrels of gods and goddesses, the feasts they ate and the foes they slew, heroes fighting with monsters for the rescue of maidens from dark dungeons and enchanted castles, lovesick princes, cunning dwarfs that killed stupid giants, elves, satyrs, fauns and pigmies, and a whole catalogue of others we will not name.

There are also legends that people the air with spirits of the dead, such as vampires, witches, and the like; that tell of men changed to bears, maidens to swans; of magic horns and lamps; of flasks that fill the ocean; of hidden stores of gold and gems. Just as the Aryan language shows itself in the language of the

English, Russians, Hindus, and other Aryan nations, so do these myths, legends and fairy tales. . Mr. Clodd remarks ("Childhood of Religion," page 99) that in consequence of the discovery of a strong likeness in all nursery tales, some light is thrown on the common origin of all nations. Sure it is that grandams in Northern Europe did not learn their tales from Hindu books or story-tellers: we must therefore suppose that the Aryan tribes carried from their *one* Aryan home a common stock of stories as well as a common speech and common name for Heaven-Father.

This legendary and mythical chapter will be brought to a close with a few more strange stories. It is said of Kronos (which is a Greek name only), who was a son of Ouranos, with whom the race of gods began, that he swallowed his first five children soon after the birth of each. Kronos means *time;* and Ouranos, *the heaven*. *Ouranos* is the same as the sky-god *Varuna,* invoked in the Veda, whose name comes from the root *var, to veil*. Tantalus was said to be king of Lydia, and when Zeus and all the gods came and sat down to a feast which he gave, killed his own son and set the roasted flesh before them, for which act the assembled gods sent Tantalus to Tartarus, where all are banished who sin against the gods. Among the names given to the sun in the Veda, he is called the golden-handed. A story grew up that at a sacrifice he cut off his hand, which was replaced by the priests with one of gold.

In looking at the Greek, Norse, German and other myths by the light of the Veda, we find the full, fresh thoughts of the mind of man when there were no bounds to his beliefs and fancies. These myths having forced their way into history, came in time to pass as veritable facts. The story of William Tell, that has for many centuries passed for true history, Mr. Clodd says is merely an old Aryan myth, and nothing more. In every country it is not exactly in the same words and the same relation, but evidently sprang from the same stock in each case. Cinderella, about whom so much has been written, is spoken of in the Veda, and is merely a myth. There is seemingly no end to these old myths and fables. In the Jataka, an ancient collection of Buddhist fables, Buddha is said to have had five hundred and fifty births before he attained Buddhahood.

Those who want more of such stories as these can avail themselves of Æsop's Fables and other works of the kind. Great caution is necessary to avoid estimating fiction as the truth of history, and, worse than that, as classing it with the revelations of God to man. An excessive leaning that way has done great harm, and minds are drawn away from substantial facts, personal experience and actual knowledge, into figurative realms, from the real to the fanciful. Instead of examining into the works of Nature—the evidence of God's power—they wander into mysticism. Imagination is given a loose rein, to float at will in the region of fancy. The moment anything, however absurd and foolish, gets mixed with the religious faith of a people, then, in their estimation, it becomes the Word of God, not to be controverted by evidence, be it ever so strong.

CHAPTER II.

ETHNIC AND CATHOLIC RELIGIONS.

We are indebted to the able and learned writer James Freeman Clarke for a work entitled "Ten Great Religions," in which are contained many highly important and interesting religious, historical and geographical facts, set in order with great care and labor, from which we make liberal extracts of matter suited to our purpose.

Without an analytical consideration of the various religions that have obtained favor from large portions of mankind, we can form no correct estimate of the comparative value of them. Christianity has nothing to lose by such an examination. The good and the true will always bear close scrutiny without detriment.

What we call Ethnic, Gentile or Heathen religions will, on candid examination, all be found to contain much good. They had only a dim light, it is true, but at no time in the world's history was there total darkness with respect to religion. In going back to the very early times, proper allowance must be made for the state of things then existing; otherwise, great injustice will be done and a false estimate made.

Corruptions found their way into all the old religions, and care must be taken that corruptions do not creep into the Christian religion also, and that its beautiful simplicity and harmony be not destroyed or laid aside, for formalism. Supernatural religion and mystery were in the world many thousand years before Adam's time, and in a lively condition up to the full dawn of Christianity, if indeed it can be said that Christianity is free from it. We may take them to be natural to a certain degree of development of the human mind.

Spirituality now is not easily kept alive. In the earlier religions it was but faintly discernible; though hearts were then drawn upward in adoration of a power not fully seen or comprehended. But few are so arrogant now as to say they comprehend Omnipotence. In the old religions they did not pretend to know God. Then, as now, they were feeling after him.

How many think the best service they can render true religion is to keep up a constant clamor about everything that is not Christian, and stigmatize the wisest and best of men as cold philosophers. Mosheim says: "Before Christianity, all the nations of the world, the Jews excepted, were plunged in the grossest superstition. Some nations went beyond the others, but all stood charged with irrationality and gross stupidity in matters of religion. The greater part of the gods of all nations were ancient heroes, famous for their achievements and their worthy deeds—kings, generals, and founders of cities; to these some added the more splendid and useful objects in the natural world, as the sun, moon and stars; some were not ashamed to pay divine honors to mountains, rivers and trees. The worship of these deities consisted in ceremonies, sacrifices and prayers, for the most part absurd and ridiculous, and, throughout, debasing, obscene and cruel. The prayers were truly insipid and devoid of piety, both in their form and matter. The priests who presided over this worship basely abused their authority to impose on the people. The whole pagan system had not the least efficacy to preserve and cherish virtuous emotions in the soul, because the gods and goddesses were patterns of vice, the priests bad men, and the doctrines false." This view of the heathen religion is quite exaggerated. If the priests among the idolatrous nations were bad, so they were among the Jews, if we can credit the great prophets before, during, and after the Captivity. So, also, were many who pretended to exercise prophetic powers denounced by those of their own class as bad men, liars, and wicked in many respects.

It is not only easy, but very natural, to think all are out of the way but ourselves; that all creeds are wrong but ours; that our own nation, country, institutions, government and laws are vastly superior to all others; that all the Divine wisdom shed abroad in the world, everything that tends to promote morality, goodness and piety, is included in the only really catholic religion, the Christian. Such a position is not tenable. God, in his kindness, love and mercy, did not leave the world in utter darkness for many thousands of years before the birth of Jesus, or before Abraham left his native country—which many learned writers say was near to the place of Zoroaster's birth. Puffing up and inflating one thing, so as to belittle and disparage all else, is not necessary.

The crude religions of antiquity have been giving way before the light of Christianity, and yielding to the constant force of progression and evolution. But they are not devoid of interest. The voice of prayer then was directed toward God, if it did not reach him. Had there been nothing but unmixed evil in idolatry, could it have been maintained so long? It partially satisfied the natural longing of the human heart. Man is not the easy and universal dupe of fraud; though it is more than the best of us can do to distinguish truth from error; hence, the designing are ever ready to impose upon our credulity. In all ages men have suffered by fraud and deception. Nor are we rid of them now. Christian catholicity has not yet had the power to abolish them among the most faithful adherents of Christianity. A decent respect for the wild opinions, and charity for the erring portion, of mankind, forbid us to ascribe the pagan religions entirely to priestcraft or jugglery. Reverence for Divine Providence would not admit of it.

Is it reasonable to suppose that God was without a witness in the world before Abraham, before Jesus? Away with the narrow thoughts that exclude God from communication with man at any and all times since man's existence! Has not God's favor been continually manifested, as far back as our thoughts can range? Had he no care over us, no compassion for us, before the dawn of Christianity? Must we continue to think our God-Father neglected everything until he could contrive some plan of salvation by which the damning sin of Adam would be wiped out? No one ever believed in or heard of a spiritual deliverer other than God our Father till about the time of Jesus' death. How must it fare with those who died with no faith in an atonement except by the blood of beasts? Some of our modern religionists represent God as electing to pour abundant light on a portion of those he created, and leaving all the rest in darkness; not only to perish and die in their errors without seeing the light, but to be tormented in indescribable agony unendingly. Many were born ignorant and lived so by no fault of theirs. Who can infuse into stupid beings the fire of intellect? God has appointed the times and fixed the bounds of every habitation. Those who were born in India where they could only hear of him through Brahminism, or in China through Buddha or Confucius, did not select their birthplaces: God put them there, knowing that light could get to them through only one channel, and that through him. Must they be tormented in hell for being in a region of error, where God put them? They were feeling after God, seeking him with all their power, if haply they might find him; trying to see him partially, if they could not fully.

Pagan religions are only the efforts of man to find God. Every insect, every animal, is provided with food, is cared for by the God-Father. Can it be, then, that he has left his human children without the nutriment of truth? Such a view tends to atheism. In fact, if atheism has a hold anywhere among men, it is engendered by false notions of God and his orderings. Everywhere we see progress, higher forms of life succeeding lower. Heathen religions are stepping-stones to Christianity. The latter did not start up and grow from nothing, any more than a tree can grow without materials to grow from; "first the blade, then the ear, afterward the full corn in the ear." Thus we can understand why the coming of Christ took place as it did, instead of sooner or later; we can see why all religions have more of the true in them than the false; why they do more good than harm; instead of degenerating into something worse, they come to prepare the way for the better. It was the will of God that Christianity should grow out of Judaism, and in the fitness of time develop into a universal religion. That is not yet accomplished, but it will be.

Jesus virtually taught that many good men were found among those called heathen, though they never heard of him. The word "heathen," occurring in the New Testament one hundred and sixty-four times, is in ninety-three cases translated "gentiles," four or five times "heathen," and in most other cases "nations." Jesus plainly recognizes among the ethnic or heathen people some as belonging to himself, while he speaks of others shut out of the Jewish fold. Paul, who was the especial apostle to the Gentiles, did not regard their religion as wholly false and valueless, for he declared the God they ignorantly worshiped was the true God; while, on his missionary travels in Greece, at the same time, he saw the city filled with idols. Paul said, "I see that ye are, in all ways, exceedingly pious," thus recognizing them as going beyond the idols to the true God. In his subsequent remarks he does not teach them that there is but one Supreme Being, which he assumes as something already believed; and whom he designates as omnipotent, "Lord of Heaven and Earth"; spiritual, "dwelling not in temples made with hands"; absolute, "not needing anything"; but the Creator and Source of all things. He then declares that the different nations of the world have a common origin, belong to one family, with a providential place in space and time, and each left to seek the Lord in its own way. Those who do not think there is anything good in heathenism admire the speech of Paul above referred to, and call it a masterpiece of ingenuity and eloquence. Paul did not tell the Athenians they were worshiping the true God when, in his opinion, they were not. While placing God above the world as its ruler, he placed him also in the world as an immanent presence, in whom we live and move and have our being. He takes the same ground in writing to the Romans: that the Gentiles had a knowledge of the eternal attributes of God (chap. i), and saw him manifested in his works (chap. v); they also had in their nature a law of duty which taught them to do the things contained in the law, and this he calls the law written in the heart. He blames them not for ignorance, but for disobedience; thus recognizing that the heathen religion contained essential truth along with their errors.

Clement of Alexandria refused to consider either the Jewish religion or the Greek philosophy as the only divine preparation for Christianity. Tertullian declared the soul to be naturally Christian. The Sibylline books were quoted as good prophetic works, worthy to be classed with those of the Jewish prophets. Socrates was called by the Fathers a Christian before Christ. The extravagant condemnation of the heathen religions has in a measure subsided within the last few years. To suppose that almost the entire human race had been fed on error for long centuries was too disparaging, too dishonoring, to a God of light. This has led to the placing of some of those old religions on a level with Christianity, thus showing how easy it is to go from one extreme to another. The Vedas are spoken of by many as superior to the Old Testament, Confucius is quoted as equal to Paul or John, and admiration is expressed for the sacred books of the Buddhists and Brahmans. Good sense calls for a candid examination and comparison of these systems.

The question may properly be asked whether Christianity is the only revelation from God to man, and if miracle is necessary to prove the communication of divine truth. Can we justly regard the record of Jesus' life and teaching as all strictly true only on account of the miracles which he performed; because many things were done which the people eighteen hundred years ago thought were real, but which are not credited by us now? Believing implicitly in Jesus as a Messiah does not involve the necessity of believing in the genuineness and authenticity of the whole New

Testament. The real question is not whether our religion is or is not supernatural; whether Christ's miracles were or were not violations of natural law; nor whether the New Testament as it stands is the work of inspired men. It is better to examine and see if the principal ethnic religions of the world are not local, incapable of catholicity, and defective, while Christianity is progressive and capable of universal expansion. In explanation, it may be said that by ethnic religions we mean those which have always been confined within the boundaries of a particular race or family of mankind, and have never made converts, except accidentally, outside of it. This, we know, is the case with most of the religions of the world outside of Christianity.

Ethnic is the Greek for the Latin word *Gentile:* that which "belongs to a race." We find that each race, beside its special moral qualities, seems also to have special religious qualities. Brahmanism is confined to that section or race of the great Aryan family which has occupied India for more than thirty centuries. It belongs to the Hindus; to the people taking their name from the Indus, by the tributaries of which stream it entered India from the northwest, and has never extended itself beyond these people. Its sacred books are more than three thousand years old; it has been held by this race as their religion from a period so remote in the history of mankind that we cannot estimate it. From one hundred and fifty millions to two hundred millions of people are supposed to accept Brahmanism as their faith. It is strictly ethnic, having no tendency to become the religion of mankind. The same may be said of the religion of Confucius—it belongs to China. The Chinese have observed it as their state religion for more than two thousand years, but a Chinese form of Buddhism is the religion of the masses. But out of China Confucius is only a man. With the system of Zoroaster it is the same. It was for a long period the religion of one Aryan tribe, who became the ruling people among mankind. The Persians extended themselves through Western Asia, and, although they conquered other · nations, they never communicated their religion, for it belonged only to the Iranians and their descendants, the Parsees. The same may also be said of the religions of Egypt, Greece, Scandinavia; the Jewish, Islam, and Buddhist: they are all ethnic; those of Egypt and Scandinavia decidedly so. The Greeks are said to have borrowed the names of their gods from Egypt, but the gods themselves were entirely different ones. So, also, some of the gods of the Romans were borrowed from the Greeks, but their life was left behind.

If the aim of Judaism was to be catholic, there was no prospect that it would ever become so. Judaism, Islam and Christianity all aimed to become universal. By seeking to proselyte without making converts Judaism failed; Islam, because it sought to make subjects rather than converts. Its conquests were over a variety of distinct races: the Arabs, a Semitic race; the Persians, an Indo-European race; the Negroes; and the Turks, or Turanians. In a true sense, Islam is a heretical Christian sect; Islam is a kind of John the Baptist, crying in the wilderness, "Prepare the way of the Lord." Mohammed is a schoolmaster to bring us to Christ. Mohammedanism does for the nations what Judaism did: that is, it teaches the Divine unity. Buddhism has extended itself over the eastern half of Asia, thus showing a tendency to catholicity.

Brahmanism is not lacking in spirituality; it is full as regards the infinite, recognizing eternity, but not time; God, but not nature. It is a vast system of spiritual pantheism, in which there is no reality but God; all else is illusion. Its followers are particularly pious, but singularly immoral. It has no history, for history belongs to time. When the sacred books of the Brahmins were written, when their civilization began, or aught of its progress and decline, no one knows. They strangely enough combine the most ascetic abstraction and self-denial with voluptuous self-indulgence. The tendency of their peculiar belief is to see God as the infinite, and disregard the finite.

Buddhism is a revolted offspring of Brahmanism, with opposite truths and opposite defects. It recognizes man, not God; morality, not piety. Its only God is Buddha (figuratively), who, they believe, passed through innumerable transmigrations, until, by reason of exemplary virtues, he reached the lordship of the universe. Nirvana is its heaven—the world of infinite bliss. The Buddhists' notion of an infinite God, if they have any, is exceedingly faint. The system of Confucius is a kind of moral conservatism, prosaic and reverential. China has but a vague idea of progress. Repose and earthly comfort is the ever-present desire. By the system of Confucius the state was organized on the basis of the family; so also is the Roman Church. The word Pope means "the father": he is the father of the whole Church; every bishop and every priest is the father of a smaller family; so all born into the Church are children. This is one of the most beautiful tenets of the Catholic Church. Only in China and in Christendom is family life thus sacred and worshiped. As the idea of the kingdom of heaven is centered in Christianity, so it is in the religion of Zoroaster.

The Zend-Avesta makes every man a soldier fighting for light or for darkness, as in the Gospels; good and evil are perpetual foes. Dualism is discernible in all the New-Testament scriptures and the teachings of the Church. God and Satan, heaven and hell, are constantly held up before us. Dualism is fully as prominent in the Gospels as it is in the Zend-

Avesta; the doctrine of an everlasting punishment in hell is not recognized in the Avesta; but, on the other hand, it teaches universal restoration—the ultimate triumph of good over evil.

That evil is a formidable enemy of good must be universally conceded. The monotheism of Christianity renders dualism harmless in one sense—that is, ultimately: for evil must yield to good in order to render a heaven possible, or to give safety to those who love and obey God. Christian monotheism differs from Jewish and Mohammedan monotheism in that it recognizes God *in* all things as well as *above* all things. We see God in Christ, with his fullness of sympathy for our nature; God with us all, in nature and providence; above all, and through all. By examination thus far we see a great lack in all the ethnic religions that nothing but Christianity can fill. The former supply this lack only in part, the latter fully.

It may be said, with some truth, that the religions of Persia, Egypt, Greece and Rome came to an end with their national civilizations. The religions of China, Islam, Buddha and Judea remain unchanged, though they are further and further behind the spirit of the age; while Christianity is ever on the advance. Passing out of its old Jewish body into its new and beautiful body, under the teaching of Jesus, who came as the true light to lead us safely to the kingdom of God, it can never cease, nor its luster be dimmed. Hope, faith and love constitute the deep fountain from which we can draw forever. Christianity is alone the fullness of truth: not come to destroy, but to fulfill; not to annul previous religions, but to supply what they had omitted. Christianity is not a system, but a life; not a creed, but a spirit feeding the life of man at its roots by fresh supplies of faith in God, faith in man.

CHAPTER III.

RELIGION OF CHINA—CONFUCIANISM.

CHINA is admitted to be the oldest nation in the world, though how long it has existed no one can tell. Herodotus, in his travels about 450 B.C., found monuments that denoted a great antiquity. On the soil of this vast empire we find a very considerable portion of the human race. China proper alone is estimated to contain nearly three hundred and fifty millions. Its total area is five millions of square miles. This is not a land of golden romance or song, but of sober fact. Everything points to permanence; the same old pattern is followed. Slight changes in politics and social customs take place at long intervals, but the main features continue unaltered.

Enterprise and skill must have been displayed by the Chinese at an early period in their history, for the mariner's compass, printing, gunpowder and other inventions were known to them long before they were known in Europe. They printed books from wooden blocks as early as 958, about five hundred years before Gutemberg invented the art of printing. The authentic history of China dates back over two thousand years B.C. The same language has been spoken for more than thirty centuries. Canals were common in China long before they were constructed in Europe. The great canal, like the great wall, is unrivaled by any similar work of modern times. Wells were sunk at great depths, to obtain salt water, at a time far remote in the past. Bronze money was made there eleven hundred years B.C. Men rise to the highest political stations, not by artful electioneering devices and smooth words, but by real merit, sound sense, and ability. No attention is paid to birth; the lowest can rise on his merits.

A state worship, says Mr. Clodd, is kept up by the Emperor and his court, in which sacrifices are offered to heaven and earth, to the spirits of sages, rulers and learned men, and also to mountains, fields and rivers. The best-furnished houses contain a camphor-wood coffin, to be seen by all visitors. Every household has its family spirits, to whom honor and reverence are paid. But behind all these, and above all, the Chinese recognize a Supreme Power, lord of the sky, "ancestor of all things"; their notions of him, however, are extremely vague.

China may be said to have three national religions:

Buddhism (which was admitted as a religion of the state A.D. 65), Tao-ism, and Confucianism. All of these are frequently professed by the same person, and there is none of that bitter feeling between the believers of different creeds which exists among Christians, Mussulmans and others. Lao-tse, the founder of Tao-ism, lived between five hundred and six hundred years B.C. Unlike Confucius, he was a thinker, and not a worker; he endeavored to explain what Buddha could not—spirituality. Confucius is said to have visited him for the purpose of gaining information in this respect which he much desired, but did not obtain. Tao-ism has become so mixed up with magic and other wild and foolish ideas that it is but little regarded now in China. K'ung-Foo-Tse, whose writings and life have given direction to Chinese thought, bears the Latinized name of Confucius. He is their patron saint, and his descendants are held in especial honor. The most famous temple in the empire is built over his grave, hundreds of other temples are dedicated to his memory, and thousands of animals are sacrificed to him on the two great yearly festivals. Confucius was born B.C. 551, and was, therefore, contemporary with the Tarquins, Pythagoras and Cyrus. There are at the present day nearly forty thousand of his descendants. His family is the oldest in the world, unless we consider the Jews as a single family of Abraham. The influence of his writings and teachings has been greater than that of any other man who ever lived.

To recount all that Confucius did for the benefit of the Chinese people would occupy too much of our space. Through his teaching came the reverence for family ties, especially for parents; the love of order, and a recognition of literary merit. Such extended influence could only have been produced by great worth and ability. To suppose that a man of low morals or ordinary intellect, an impostor or enthusiast, could have so signally impressed millions of people, is simply absurd. There must have been a solid foundation, a real manifestation of God in man, in a life so productive of noble results. His light was not a fitful meteor, but an emanation from the Light of all lights. Confucius, like other great and good men, labored for moral elevation. While his life and teachings visibly lack the spirituality inculcated by Jesus, his morality was pure and his aims lofty, exhibiting much that is worthy to take rank with Christianity.

He was born the same year that Cyrus became king of Persia. His ancestors were men of eminence in the country now called the province of Loo. At fifteen he had studied the sacred books of the Kings, and was married at nineteen. From his only son's son descended his immense posterity.

Disciples collected around him to the number of three thousand, and they successfully spread his doctrines among the common people. He lived to the age of seventy-three, and devoted the last years of his life to the publication of his works and editing the sacred books. Records extending back 2,357 years before Christ are considered authentic, and the Chinese philosophy is said to date back to 3327 B.C. Confucius edited the Yih-King, the Shoo-King, the She-King, and the Le-Ke, which constitute the whole of the literature of ancient China that has come down to posterity. One of these is called the "Immutable Mean," the object of which is to show that virtue consists in avoiding extremes. Another, the Lun-yu, or Analects, contains the conversation or table-talk of Confucius.

China was divided into a number of petty kingdoms in the time of Confucius, and, being without a well-established federal head, these factions were in continual disagreement. Confucius endeavored for a long time to harmonize these differences, and, failing to do so, he resigned a place of high public trust and retired to another part of the country. But, not content to remain idle, he devoted himself to the inculcation of moral truth and the study of self-government. He gathered around him many of the thoughtful and good. In time he returned to his native place, Loo, and for some years lived in retirement. In his fiftieth year he became minister of state, and for a while met with great success. On account of the wild excesses of the court, however, he was finally obliged to resign his place. To add to his afflictions, poverty and other ills came upon him. His words of wisdom were not heeded by the people, and he again returned to his native land, a despised and poor man.

Mr. Clodd says the system of Confucius can scarcely be called a religion, and yet that is the best name for it, because it teaches men how to live. He taught four things in particular: learning, morals, devotion of soul, and reverence. All were required to be sincere, just, loving, careful of duty to themselves and to others. Concerning God or a future life he had little, if anything, to say. His ideas of heaven were vague. In the sky he could see an emblem of power, but did not discern God as the one great Cause of all, to whom we should render praise unceasing. This was not because Confucius was an unbeliever, for he was not; above all men he reverenced the unknown power that underlies all things; but because his nature was so beautifully simple and sincere that he would not pretend to a knowledge of that which he felt was beyond human reach and thought. To his credit let it be said, his life was devoted to teaching a few great truths which he believed would bring happiness to man. He thus speaks of himself: "At fifteen I had my mind bent on learning; at thirty my mind was fixed in the pursuit of it; at forty I saw clearly certain principles; at fifty I knew the decrees of heaven; at sixty I understood all I heard; at seventy the desires of my heart no longer transgressed the law." In saying this, and feeling that it was true, he declared what few who ever lived could honestly and truly declare. But he goes on to say: "If in the morning I hear about the right way, and in the evening I die, I can be happy." He says of himself: "He is a man who, through his earnestness in seeking knowledge, forgets his food, and in his joy at having found it, loses all sense of his toil, and, thus occupied, is unconscious that he has almost reached old age." Again: "Coarse rice for food, water to drink, and the bended arm for a pillow—happiness may be enjoyed even with these; but without virtue, both riches and honor seem to me like a passing cloud." "Worship as though the Deity were present. If my mind is not engaged in my worship, it is as though I worshiped not. Formerly, in hearing men, I heard their words, and gave them credit for their conduct; now I hear their words and observe their conduct." Confucius was humble; he said: "I cannot bear to hear myself called equal to the sages and the good. All that can be said of me is, that I study with delight the conduct of the sages, and instruct men without weariness therein. The good man is serene," said he; "the bad is always in fear. The good man regards the root; he fixes the root, and all else flows out of it. The root is filial piety; the fruit, brotherly love. There may be fair words and an humble countenance where there is little virtue. I daily examine myself in a threefold manner: in my transactions with men, if I am upright; in my intercourse with friends, if I am faithful; and whether I illustrate the teachings of my master in my conduct."

The great principles which he taught were chiefly based on family affection and duty. Kings were to treat their subjects as children. Can we doubt the desire of Confucius to do right, and, as far as he could discern, to honor God? Is it possible that he had a bad heart, or was a deceiver? His industry, above all things, was commendable. His whole life was filled with commendable actions. Nothing that he said or did could encourage vice or immorality. In the darkest hour he had faith, in the midst of danger he had courage; in the highest position of honor he had humility. No less than sixteen hundred and sixty temples have been erected to the memory of this illustrious character by his devoted followers; while the purity of his life, the worthiness of his motives, and the extent of his attainments are conceded by the wisest and best men of every creed.

The sacred books, or classics, of the Chinese, as given by Dr. Legge, are the Five King and the Four Shoo. The Five King are the five canonical works, containing truths upon the highest subjects from the sages of China, and which should be received as law by all generations. The term *Shoo* means simply, *writings*, or *books*. The Five King are the *Yih*, or "Book of Changes"; the *Shoo*, or "Book of Historical Documents"; the *She*, or "Book of Poetry"; the *Le-ke*, or "Record of Rites"; and the *Ch'un Ts'eu*, or "Spring and Autumn": annals extending from B.C. 721 to 480.

Confucius made some additions to the Yih, Shoo, and She, but the Ch'un Ts'eu is the only one of the "Five King" which can, with an approximation to correctness, be described as of his own "making." The four "Books" are the *Lun-yu*, occupied chiefly with the sayings of Confucius; the *Ta-Hio*, or "Great Learning," by *Tsang-Sin*, a disciple of Confucius; the *Chung-Yung*, or "Doctrine of the Mean"; and the *Works of Mencius*, the "Master's" most illustrious disciple. These books Confucius studied with great care and attention, making such corrections as were necessary to their complete understanding. It would appear that the philosophy of the Tao-te-king is that of absolute being, or the identity of being and not-being. It teaches that the absolute is the source of being and not-being. Being is essence, not-being is existence. The first is the noumenal; the last, the phenomenal.

The philosophy of the Confucians, though an ultimate principle, is not identical with a living, intelligent and personal God. In speaking of Teen, or

Heaven, Confucius did not express faith in such a being, nor did his worship and prayers fully imply it. There was obviously reverence for an unknown power conceived of, but only in a measure understood. What that power was Confucius did not pretend to understand. In the She-King a personal God is addressed. The oldest books recognize a Divine Person, and teach that there is one Supreme Being, who is omnipresent, who sees all things and has an intelligence which nothing can escape; that he wishes men to live together in peace and brotherhood; that this Being demands not only pure desires, but right actions. Humility is declared to be the solid foundation of all virtue. The teachings of these Kings may be safely set down as the oldest production of the human mind now in existence. When these books of Kings were revised by Confucius, his own explanations and comments were added, and these constituted the last acts of his life. To close all, he made a solemn dedication of these books to Heaven. Placing them on an altar of his own erection, he returned thanks for being allowed to finish his work.

Something should perhaps be said about "The Ti-Ping Revolution" (published in London, 1866), written by an Englishman, which gives correct accounts of many observances, forms and ceremonies quite as solemn and impressive as any among the Protestant Christians in Europe and America. We have not room to speak of these at length, but they show how easily Christianity may have been ingrafted into this old Gentile stock, giving an earnest of the time, that will eventually come, when a better and more real knowledge of God than the heathen world could in their time possibly attain shall cover the earth as the waters cover the deep.

CHAPTER IV.

BRAHMANISM AND HINDUISM.

BRAHMANISM and Hinduism include many Hindu sects that differ greatly from each other in belief and form of worship, but all receive the Vedas as the inspired word of God. They comprise altogether a large proportion of mankind. Unlike the religions founded by Jesus, Zoroaster, and Mohammed, the history of Brahmanism, says Mr. Clodd, does not gather round a person. A thorough study of all its sacred books would be the work of an ordinary lifetime. Hence this religion is difficult to explain. We know less about it than we do concerning the old Aryan religion. It may be not improperly styled a body of shapeless things, which can be formed into an orderly whole only with great labor and difficulty; yet it is rich in the profoundest thoughts of a deeply religious people. It teaches that the end of every life should be to shut its ears to the call of duty; to be unmoved by pleasure or pain, and to sit down to dreamy thinking. It has caused the Hindus to fall into the grossest and most loathsome superstitions, and to obey the most foolish priest-made rules about food and cleansing, and other like matters.

Brahmanism, says Mr. Clarke, with all the late aids, is a difficult study. Its source is not in a man, but in a caste. It is not the religion of a Confucius, a Zoroaster, a Mohammed, but the religion of the Brahmans. We call it Brahmanism, but it can be traced to no individual as its founder or restorer. It is a vast world of ideas, but wanting in the unity which is given by the life of a man as its embodiment and representative. It is a system so vast, so complicated, so full of contradictions, so various and changeable, that it is impossible to do it justice. From the earliest times India has been a mystery. Away back in the world's history, India is heard of as being the most populous of nations, full of barbaric wealth and strange wisdom. Conquering armies have been attracted to it. Semiramis, Darius, Alexander, Mahmud, Tamerlane, and the Duke of Wellington have all given it attention, and left traces of war's devastating power. The British Mercantile Company have plundered India no less ruthlessly than invading armies; yet there remains the same marvelous country as before. It is the same land now that it was in the time of Alexander: a land of grotto temples dug out of solid porphyry; of social distinctions as fixed as the earth itself; the land of one of the most ancient pagan religions of the world; of the sacred Ganges; of the idols of Juggernaut and its bloody worship; the land of elephants, tigers, fields of rice and groves of palm; of treasuries filled with chests of gold and heaps of pearls and diamonds. But, above all, it is a land of unintelligible systems of belief, of puzzling incongruities and irreconcilable contradictions.

While the Hindus have sacred books of great antiquity, and a rich literature extending back nearly thirty centuries, they have, in one sense, no history, no chronology, no annals. Their philosophy is acute, profound and spiritual, mixed with the coarsest superstitions. With a belief so abstract as to be almost beyond the grasp of the most speculative intellect, the notion is maintained that sin can be atoned for by bathing the body in their sacred river, the Ganges. They had an ideal pantheism resembling that of Hegel, united with the opinion that Brahma and Siva can be driven from the throne of the universe by the sacrifice of wild horses.

To be, if possible, abstracted from matter; to renounce, in a degree, all gratification of the senses; to macerate the body, is by the zealous Hindu thought to be the true road to felicity; and yet by some licentiousness and the gratification of the appetites is carried to the extreme. A code of laws, older far than the Christian era, fixes the rights and privileges of ruler and subject. Their constitution is like a house without a foundation, without a roof. The Hindu religion forbids the killing of a worm, or the treading on a blade of grass, for fear of injuring life; while the torments, cruelties and bloodshed inflicted by Indian tyrants would shock a Nero.

Mr. Clarke says: "Half the best-informed writers on India will tell you that the Brahmanical religion is pure monotheism; the other half as confidently assert that they worship a million gods. Some teach us that the Hindus are spiritualists and pantheists; others, that their idolatry is more gross than that of any other living people." There really seems to be no way of reconciling the inconsistencies that meet us at every step in our study of this peculiar people. Their life is a mighty maze, seemingly without a plan. But we must remember that the whole tendency of thought in India is ideal; the whole religion, spiritualism. The God of Brahmanism is an intelligence absorbed in the rest of profound contemplation. The good man of this religion is he who withdraws from an evil world into abstract thought, and this is just what explains the Hindu character. So we have no definite way of obtaining light on the dark subject of Hinduism.

Sandracottus, a contemporary of Alexander, became king B.C. 315, at which time Buddha, according to

Hindu traditions, had been dead one hundred and sixty-two years. Buddha may have died B.C. 477; and thus a single date from Greek history may have been incorporated into that of India. This is all the light that can be obtained as to the vague antiquity of the Hindu race.

Going back to the condition of family life among this great people of Central Asia before their dispersion, we find them included under the general name of Aryans, who occupied the land called *Ar-ya-vesta;* or, *inhabited by honorable men.* The people of Iran receive this same appellation in the Zend-Avesta, with the same meaning of *honorable.* Strabo mentions that in the time of Alexander the whole region about the Indus was called *Ariana.* In modern times, *Iran* for Persia, and *Erin* for Ireland, may be reminiscences of the original family appellation. Long before the age of the Vedas or the Zend-Avesta, the Aryans were living as a pastoral people on the great plains east of the Caspian Sea, and we may be pretty sure that they lived in houses, and knew something of nautical affairs.

It is also very clear that, some 3000 years B.C., the Aryans were not yet divided into Hindus, Persians, Kelts, Latins, Greeks, Teutons and Slavi, but were living in Central Asia, in a region of which Bactria was the center. They were a pastoral, but not a nomad, people; they had oxen, horses, sheep, and other domestic animals, and fowls. Herds of cows found pasturage, and stables to shelter them when the weather was inclement. They had fields of barley, and, probably, other cereals, and mills for grinding their grain; the plow, hatchet, hammer and auger; and among the metals, gold, silver, copper and tin. They understood spinning and weaving, and the making of pottery. We have no knowledge as to the construction of their houses, except that they had doors, windows and fireplaces. In cooking, they broiled and roasted meats. They had cloaks and mantles; lances, swords and shields, but no armor. They had family life, simple laws, games, the dance, and wind instruments. They worshiped or paid homage to heaven, earth, sun, fire, water, and wind: but there are traces of an earlier monotheism, from which this nature-worship proceeded. Their year was 360 days.

Treating of this people historically at such great length may seem out of place, but we have felt warranted in so doing, as from this Aryan race so many nations have originated, and also on account of their great antiquity.

The Vedas, the oldest works extant in Hindu literature, are fifteen hundred years more recent than the time we have been describing. The Aryans have separated, and the Hindus are now in India, occupying the region between the Punjaub and the Ganges, where was accomplished the change of habits from warlike shepherds to agriculturists and builders of cities. Saint Martin says the last hymns of the Vedas were written after the Hindus had migrated from the Indus to the Ganges, and while they were building their oldest city at the confluence of that river with the Jumna. Their complexion was then white; the race they conquered were afterward called *lowest caste*, blacks.

In the Vedic age there were five principal gods: *Indra*, god of the atmosphere; *Varuna*, god of light, or heaven; *Agni*, god of fire; *Savitri*, god of the sun; *Soma*, god of the moon. *Yama* was the god of death. There were also many other inferior gods, but, among all the divinities, Indra and Agni were the chief. Behind this incipient polytheism lurks the original monotheism, for each of these gods in turn becomes the Supreme Being. The Universal Deity seems to reveal himself first in one form of nature, and then in another. Such is the opinion of Colebrooke, who says that the ancient Hindu religion recognizes but one God, it not having yet sufficiently discriminated between the creature and the Creator. Max Mueller says the hymns celebrate Varuna, Indra, Agni, etc., and each in turn is called supreme. He adds: "It would be easy to find, in the numerous hymns of the Veda, passages in which almost every single god is represented as supreme and absolute. Indra is celebrated as the strongest god, and in one hymn it is said that Indra is stronger than all. Of another it is said that he is the conqueror of every one.

The following hymn is from one of the oldest Vedas (Rig-Veda, x, 121):

"In the beginning arose the Source of golden light. He was the only born Lord of all that is. He established the earth and the sky. Who is the god to whom we shall offer our sacrifice?

"He who gives life. He who gives strength; whose blessing all the bright gods desire; whose shadow is immortality, whose shadow is death. Who is the god to whom we shall offer our sacrifice?

"He who through his power is the only king of the breathing and awakening world. He who governs all, man and beast. Who is the god to whom we shall offer our sacrifice?"

This is a fair sample of the hymns of the Rig-Veda, all of which seem to breathe the true spirit of devotion; to recognize a Supreme God as the governor, as well as the former, of all matter, of all beings. God was found by these Vedic worshipers, the sincerity of whose faith none of us ought to question. Where shall we find authority for condemning such as strive with all their powers to live as well as they can according to the light given them?

Colebrooke and other eminent writers say that the oldest and most striking account of the Creation is contained in the tenth chapter of the thirteenth book of the Rig-Veda, as follows:

"Then there was no entity, nor non-entity; no world, no sky, nor aught above it; nothing anywhere, involving or involved; no water, deep and dangerous. Death was not, and therefore no immortality, nor distinction of day or night. But THAT ONE breathed calmly alone with Nature, she who was sustained within him. Other than He, nothing existed since. Darkness there was; the universe was enveloped with darkness, and was indistinguishable waters; but that mask which was covered by the husk was produced by the power of contemplation. First, desire was formed in his mind; and that became the original productive seed, which the wise, recognizing it by the intellect in their hearts, distinguished as the bond of non-entity with entity.

"Did the luminous ray of these expand in the middle, above, or below? That productive energy became providence and matter; Nature, who is sustained within, was inferior; and he who sustained was above.

"Who knows exactly, and who shall in this world declare, whence and why this creation took place? The gods are subsequent to the production of this world: then who can know whence it proceeded, or whence this varied world arose, or whether it upholds or not? He who, in the highest heaven, is the ruler of this universe—he knows, or does not know."

The following hymn, says Mueller, would sound well in a Christian liturgy, leaving out the word "Varuna":

1. "Let me not yet, O Varuna, enter into the house of clay; have mercy, almighty, have mercy!

2. "If I go along trembling, like a cloud driven by the wind, have mercy, almighty, have mercy!

3. "Through want of strength, thou strong and bright god, have I gone to the wrong shore; have mercy, almighty, have mercy!

4. "Thirst came upon the worshiper, though he stood in the midst of the waters; have mercy, almighty, have mercy!

5. "Whenever we men, O Varuna, commit an offense before the heavenly host; whenever we break thy law through thoughtlessness; have mercy, almighty, have mercy!"

Is it possible that words like these could have had their origin in any source but in the God whom we Christians worship? Will any one dare to say that the people who uttered them had no devotional feeling? Call them gentiles or heathens, as we may, they were feeling after God, looking up to the great Heaven of heavens. They constitute a tree whose roots started from the great Source of all things. What is wanted in their case is not to be cut down, cast off, thrown away, but to be built upon, to be indoctrinated with a faith in Christianity, to have all the Christian graces added to the good which they now possess.

The space we allotted to this subject has been pretty well taken up, but we will give a part of one more hymn addressed to "Indra":

1. "Let no one, not even those who worship thee, delay thee far from us. Even from afar come to our feast! or if thou art here, listen to us!

2. "For those who here make prayers for thee sit together near the libation, like flies round the honey. The worshipers, anxious for wealth, have placed their desires upon Indra, as we put our foot upon a chariot.

3. "Desirous of riches, I call him who holds the thunderbolt with his arm, and who is a good giver, like as a son calls his father.

4. "These libations of soma, mixed with milk, have been prepared for Indra; thou, armed with the thunderbolt, come with the steeds to drink with them to thy delight; come to the house!

5. "May he hear us, for he has ears to hear. He is asked for riches: will he despise our prayers? He could soon give hundreds and thousands; no one could check him if he wishes to give."

13. "Make for the sacred gods a hymn that is not small, that is well-set and beautiful! Many snares

pass by him who abides with Indra through his sacrifice."

Mueller says that Indra is here clearly conceived as the Supreme God; and we can hardly understand how a people who had so exalted a notion of the Deity, and embodied it in the person of Indra, could at the same sacrifice invoke other gods with equal praise.

It was the business of every Brahman to learn by heart the Vedas during the twelve years of his student life. None of the ordinary modern words for *book*, *paper*, *ink*, or *writing* have been found in any ancient Sanskrit work. In a book relating to Buddha, translated into Chinese A.D. 76, he is represented as teaching somewhat as Jesus did; but the first authentic inscription in India is of Buddhistic origin, belonging to the third century B.C. The Vedic age, according to Mueller, may be reckoned as follows:

Sutra period, from B.C. 200 to B.C. 600.
Brahmana period, from B.C. 600 to B.C. 800.
Mantra period, from B.C. 800 to B.C. 1000.
Chhandas period, from B.C. 1000 to B.C. 1200.

Dr. Haug considers the Vedic period to have been from B.C. 1200 to B.C. 2000, and the very oldest hymns to have been composed B.C. 2400. The principal deity in the oldest Vedas is *Indra*, god of the air; who in the Greek becomes *Zeus;* and in the Latin, *Jupiter*. The hymns to Indra are somewhat similar to the Psalms of the Old Testament. Indra was the most ancient god whom the Fathers worshiped; next came *Agni, fire,* derived from the root *Ag, to move.* Fire was worshiped as the principle of motion on the earth, as Indra was worshiped as the moving power above.

Mr. Maury quotes from Gotama: "Aditi is heaven; Aditi is air; Aditi is mother, father and son; Aditi is all the gods and the five races; Aditi is whatever is born and will be born; is, in short, the heavens and the earth, the heavens being the father, and the earth the mother, of all things."

Brahmanism did not begin till long after the age of the elder Vedas. "The Manu of the Vedas and he of the Brahmans are very different persons. The first is called in the Vedas the father of mankind. He also escapes from a deluge by building a ship, which he is advised to do by a fish which grows to a great size, and, when the flood comes, acts as a tow-boat to drag the ship of Manu to a mountain." This is according to the account in the Brahmana. The name of Manu seems to have been given by the Brahmans to the author of their code.

The following are extracts from the first book, on the Creation:

"The universe existed in darkness, imperceptible, undefinable, undiscoverable, and undiscovered; as if immersed in sleep.

"Then the self-existing power, undiscovered himself,

but making the world discernible, with the five elements and other principles, appeared in undiminished glory, dispelling the gloom.

"He whom the mind alone can perceive, whose essence eludes the external organs, who has no visible parts, who exists from eternity, even he, the soul of all things, shone forth in person.

"He having willed to produce various beings from his own divine substance, first with a thought created the waters, and placed in them a productive seed.

"The seed became an egg bright as gold, blazing like the luminary with a thousand beams, and in that egg he was born himself, in the form of Brahma, the great forefather of all spirits."

"The waters are called Nara, because they were the production of Nara, or the spirit of God; and hence they were his first ayana, or place of motion; he, hence, is named Nara yana, or moving of the waters.

"In that egg the great power sat inactive a whole year of the creator, at the close of which, by his thought alone, he caused the egg to divide itself.

"And from its two divisions he framed the heaven above and the earth beneath; in the midst he placed the subtile ether, the eight regions, and the permanent receptacle of waters.

"From the supreme soul he drew forth mind, existing substantially, though unperceived by sense, immaterial; and before mind, or the reasoning power, he produced consciousness, the internal monitor, the ruler.

"And before them both he produced the great principle of the soul, or first expansion of the divine idea; and all vital forms endued with the three qualities of goodness, passion and darkness, and the five perceptions of sense, and the five organs of sensation."

"The very birth of Brahmans is a constant incarnation of Dharma, god of justice; for the Brahman is born to promote justice, and to procure ultimate happiness.

"When a Brahman springs to light, he is born above the world, the chief of all creatures, assigned to guard the treasury of duties, religious and civil.

"The Brahman who studies this book, having performed sacred rites, is perpetually free from offense in thought, in word and in deed.

"He confers purity on his living family, on his ancestors, and on his descendants as far as the seventh person, and he alone deserves to possess this whole earth."

For want of space we omit quotations from Book II, "On Education and the Priesthood"; also from Book IV, "On Private Morals"; and from Book V, "On Diet." The Sixth Book of the Laws of Manu relates to "Devotion." Brahmans were inclined to asceticism. A Brahman, or twice-born man, becomes an ascetic; he abandons his family, and goes to live in the forest; makes roots and fruits his food, and a bark garment or skin his clothing; he must bathe morning and evening, and allow his hair to grow. He must spend his time in reading the Veda, with a mind intent on the Supreme Being; he must be a perpetual giver, but no receiver of gifts, and be imbued with a tender affection for all animated bodies. He is to perform various sacrifices, with offerings of fruits and flowers; practice austerities by exposing himself to heat and cold; and, for the purpose of uniting his soul with the Divine Spirit, he must study the Upanishads: "A Brahman, having shuffled off his body by these modes, which great sages practice, and becoming void of sorrow and fear, is exalted into the divine essence."

"Let him not wish for death. Let him not wish for life. Let him expect his appointed time, as the hired servant expects his wages.

"Meditating on the Supreme Spirit, without any earthly desire, with no companion but his own soul, let him live in this world seeking the bliss of the next."

The anchorite is to beg his food, and that only once in a day; if none be given him, he must not be sorrowful; and if he receive it, he must not be glad; he is to meditate on the subtle, indivisible essence of the Supreme Being; he is to be careful not to destroy life, even of the smallest insect; and he must make atonement for the death of those which he has ignorantly destroyed by repeating in a particular way the traditional syllable A U M.

The Seventh Book relates to the duties of rulers. One of these is to reward the good and punish the bad. The Eighth Book relates to civil and criminal law. The Ninth Book relates to women, to families, and to the law of castes. It states that women must be kept in a state of dependence. The Tenth Book relates to mixed classes and times of distress. The Eleventh Book relates to penance and expiation. "A Brahman who has performed an expiation with his whole mind fixed on God purifies his soul." Intoxicating liquors are prohibited; a Brahman who tastes them sinks to the low caste of a Sudra.

The last book of Manu treats of transmigration and final beatitude. The highest of all virtues is disinterested goodness, performed from the love of God, and based on a knowledge of the Veda. A religious action, performed from hope of reward in this world or the next, will give one a place in the lowest heaven. But he who performs good actions without hope of reward, perceiving the supreme soul in all beings, and all beings in the supreme soul, fixing his mind on God, approaches the divine nature.

"Let every Brahman, with fixed attention, consider all nature as existing in the divine spirit; all worlds as seated in him; he alone as the whole assemblage of gods; and he the author of all human actions."

There are three great systems of Hindu philosophy: the Sankhya, the Nyaya, and the Vedanta; reaching back into a misty twilight, leaving it doubtful when they began or who were their authors. The object of deliverance from all cares, with eternal rest and peace, characterizes them all. These are held by all the Brahmans who consider themselves orthodox. The Vedantists hold that, while in truth there is but one God, the various forms of worship in the Vedas, of Indra, Agni, the Maruts, etc., were all intended for those who could not rise to this sublime monotheism. The great problem to be solved in these philosophies, is, How did all things come? Much that might be said about Brahma, Brahmanism and Hinduism would fail to interest the general reader, as we fear may be the case with a portion of what has been given.

According to Mr. Wilson, the works known as *Puranas* were promulgated in their original form about one hundred years B.C. Of these there are now eighteen in all, the greater portion of which are devoted to the worship of Vischnu. Brahma, who is in one place called "the cause of causes," proclaims Vischnu to be the only pure, absolute essence, of which the universe is the manifestation.

Hinduism was widely different in its early history

from what it is now, having of late become much corrupted—as there is reason to fear may be the case with the Christian religion in time. Too often the substance of things is lost sight of in a wild pursuit of the shadow; so ritualistic forms and ceremonies are in many instances practiced as a substitute for pure religion of the heart, which consists in works alone. Devotion is an inward work, without regard to external show. The idea that God manifested himself to Moses for the first time on the earth, in a way in which mortals could discern him, and that he continued to so reveal himself to the Hebrew leaders until the advent of Jesus, is a mistaken one, and is about as far from the truth as it would be to say there was no God before the commencement of what is so improperly denominated the Mundane Era. Independent thinkers can see that a change is all the time going on for the better, though with a degree of slowness that is painful. Superstitions instilled into young minds grow with their growth and strengthen with their strength, until the importance of good works is lost sight of and formalism depended on to gain eternal rest.

High-Church Christians think the forms of worship in early Brahman days were most abominable. God's light was then as well as now discernible. The ray, though but feeble, can be distinguished. How can it be otherwise, when we look closely? God is light, and the author of light. We should not look for perfection in mortal man. Good thoughts are apt to get mixed with bad ones. Just ideas of God and his providences do not come to us in our imperfect state. Purity can hardly be contained in an impure vessel. The Brahman undoubtedly acted as honestly in matters of religion as the Christians do now.

Women in India worship a goddess friendly to little babies. They bring the infants to be blessed by some venerable woman before the image of the goddess, whose messenger is a cat. This is just as truly believed to be efficacious as many other ceremonies. How many infants that are said to be regenerate and grafted into the body of Christ's Church turn out to be devils in conduct, and totally unfit to form any part of Christ's Church or any other!

June in India is devoted to the bath of the god called Juggernaut, who is considered one of the incarnations of Vischnu. Worship is also paid to the Ganges during this month. Important festivals for worship are also held during most of the other months.

This religion and its offshoots, says Dr. Ward, is professed by more than half the human race. The Veda is known throughout India; the religion of Boodh, a Hindu incarnation, prevails in the Birman Empire and Ceylon; and Lamaism, in Tartary, of Egyptian origin.

The elaborated work of Mr. Maurice gives a full

account of the Hindu nation and their religious systems. Mr. Maurice maintains that the first migration of mankind took place from the region of Ararat, where the Ark rested, before the confusion of tongues at Babel, and that Noah himself or some of the descendants of Shem led on this journey to the western frontiers of India, with a pure religion, which they continued to practice until the descendants of Ham invaded and conquered India and corrupted their ancient religion. We have the authority of Sir William Jones for saying that the supreme god Brahma in his triple form is the only self-existent divinity acknowleged by the philosophical Hindus. When they consider the divine power as exerted in creation, they call the deity *Brahma;* as a destroyer or changer of forms, they call him *Mahadeva, Siva,* and various other names; as the preserver, he is called *Vischnu.* This triad they suppose to be *always everywhere,* not in substance, but in spirit and energy. According to the before-mentioned authors, there is a perpetual recurrence of the sacred triad in the Asiatic mythology. It is also said that the doctrine of a trinity was promulgated in India in the Geeta fifteen hundred years before the birth of Plato, it having originated with the ancient patriarchs.

The Hindu system teaches the existence of good and evil genii, who are eternally in conflict, filling creation with uproar continually. This doctrine teaches, also, that degenerate spirits falling from rectitude migrate through various spheres in the bodies of animals. They also suppose that there are fourteen spheres, or *bobuns*—seven below and seven above the earth. The spirits above are continually ascending, and reach to the residence of Brahma and his particular favorites. After the soul transmigrates through various animal mansions, it ascends up the great sidereal ladder of seven gates, and through the revolving spheres, which are called in India the bobuns of purification. The Brahmans believe that man is a fallen creature. Metempsychosis was designed to restore the fallen soul to the pristine state of perfection and blessedness. Deity was represented as only punishing to reform his creatures. Nature itself was considered one vast field of purgatory. Their sacred writings represent the whole universe as an ample and august theater for the probationary exercise of millions of beings who are supposed to be so many spirits degraded from the high honors of angelic distinction, and condemned to ascend through various gradations of toil and suffering to an exalted sphere of perfection and happiness, which they enjoyed before their defection.

These ideas, so well understood by Plato, were, beyond a question, in existence long before his time, and came down, possibly, from nations of higher culture than any then on the earth.

One great branch of the business of our age is to

bring to light a knowledge of the past. In so doing, it will appear plain that a great portion of what we call new in religion, in science and art, is but uncovering the past. The Hindus hold to punishment after death, but that ultimately the whole family of man will be happy. Sacrifices and offerings were not uncommon with them. Their ancient books, the Vedas, are filled with religious precepts, prayers and hymns—used as books of devotion as well in the primitive days of their religion as at present.

CHAPTER V.

BUDDHISM.

BUDDHISM, which is thought by Mr. Clodd to number more followers than any other faith, is younger by many hundred years than the old Hindu religion, and yet learned men differ as to what much of it really means. This is not strange, when we consider that the Christian believers are at a loss to tell the meaning of much contained in the Scriptures, though comparatively of recent date, and hence are divided into more than a thousand sects. Buddhism is a reformed successor to Brahmanism. The founder of Buddhism, of royal parentage, was born not less than 628 years B.C., in Kapilavastu, the capital city of a kingdom north of Oude, in India. He was called *Gautama*, from the tribe to which he belonged. His father gave to him the name of *Siddartha*, or, "he in whom wishes are fulfilled," but in after years he was called *Buddha*, the enlightened. His future greatness was revealed to his mother in a dream, soon after which she died. Max Mueller tells us he used to say that all on earth was unstable and life transitory. Therefore he resolved to leave his palace and retire from the world to escape all that was unreal in it. Leaving his wife and son, he decided not to see them again till he had become the Buddha.

Fergusson says that Buddhism is many centuries older than Christianity, and that *topes*, or shrines for relics, of very great antiquity, exist in India, Ceylon, Birmah and Java. Many of these topes belong to the age of Asoka, the great Buddhist emperor, who ruled all India B.C. 250, in whose reign Buddhism became the religion of the state and held its third Œcumenical Council. The ancient Buddhist architecture is very singular, and often beautiful, consisting of topes, rock-cut temples, and monasteries. Some of the topes are monolithic columns more than forty feet high, with ornamented capitals; some are immense domes of brick and stone containing sacred relics. A piece of ivory or bone about two inches long, said to be a tooth of Buddha, was conveyed, A.D. 311, from India to Ceylon, where it is kept in six cases, the largest of which is five feet high, and of solid silver. The other cases are inlaid with rubies and precious stones. The "left collar-bone relic" is contained in a belt-shaped tope, built by a Hindu rajah, B.C. 250, beside which two others were erected, the last being eighty cubits high.

Besides the rock-cut temples in India, the rock-cut monasteries are numerous, though the latter have long been deserted. One of the former, at Karli, excavated from solid rock, resembling in form the Roman Catholic churches, with a nave, and both aisles terminating in an apse, or semi-dome, is one hundred and twenty-six feet long and forty-five feet wide. It has fifteen richly-carved columns on each side, separating the nave from the aisles. More than eight hundred of these are known to exist, most of them having been excavated between 200 B.C. and 500 A.D. Buddhist monks then, as now, took the same three vows of celibacy, poverty, and obedience.

Though given to constant and intense thought, Gautama Buddha lived happily with his wife. He said: "There must be some supreme intelligence in which we can find rest. If I attained it, I could bring light to men. If I were free myself, I could deliver the world." Departing from his wife and child, he went among the Brahmans, to see if, by their teachings, his burthens could be lightened. In the performance of their ceremonies and attendance to their rites he found no relief. Retiring to a small village and practicing severer rites, attention was drawn to his austerities, and five disciples joined him. In a few years, a recluse life becoming distasteful and unlikely to lead to that state of perfection so much desired, he sought again the comforts of social life and the opportunities it afforded for the spread of a new doctrine, as really the only way such a work was possible.

One day, while seated in deep meditation under the shade of a tree, the knowledge burst upon him by which he became Buddha — that is, the man who knew. Under this same tree he is said to have fasted seven times seven days and nights, subject all the time to attacks from the demon of wickedness, the demon at last using force, though he suffered defeat in the end, and Buddha succeeded by aid of the ten great virtues. The weapons of the evil one were changed into beautiful flowers, falling upon Buddha. Even rocks became nosegays. Whereupon, as Mr. Clodd says, "the spirits who had watched over his birth, and who now followed his life on the earth, rent the air with shouts of joy at his victory. Afterward the tempter sent his three daughters, one a winning girl, one a blooming virgin, and one a middle-aged beauty, to allure him, but they could not. Buddha was proof against all the demon's arts, and his only trouble was whether it were well or not to preach his doctrine to men." Feeling how hard to gain was that which he had gained, and how enslaved men were by their passions, and that they might neither listen to nor understand him, he was almost inclined to be silent, and was moved only by deep compassion to tell his secret to mankind, that they might also be free. Thus he became the founder of one of the most popular religions of ancient or modern times. Though encountering strong opposition from the Brahmans, he steadily made converts of the high and low until the time of his death, in his eighty-fifth year, which occurred while he was seated under a tree. His remains were burned and the fragments divided into eight portions, over each of which a tope was built. Many stories were told about the miracles wrought by him, though he told his disciples the true miracle was to hide their good deeds and confess their sins.

Very soon after his death his disciples held a general council to fix doctrines and rules of their religion. Buddha had left no writings of his own, and his disciples wrote only from memory. Mr. Clodd says: "It is interesting to note that among these were two men, one of deep earnestness and zeal, the other of most sweet nature, loving Buddha much, and most beloved by him; reminding us of two of Christ's disciples—Peter and John. Two other councils were held afterward for the correction of errors that had crept into the faith, and for sending missionaries into other lands. The last of these councils is said to have been held 251 years B.C. So that, long before Christianity was founded, we have this great religion, with its sacred traditions of Buddha's words, its councils and its missions, besides many things strangely like the rites of the Roman Catholic Church.

Is it not probable that the Catholic Christians copied their monastic institutions, their bells, their rosary, their confession, and much else from the Buddhists? Buddhism has, with some propriety, been characterized by Mr. Clarke as Eastern Protestantism, because it accepts nature and her laws, and makes a religion of humanity as well as of devotion. Brahmanism is a system of sacrifices. Protestantism and Buddhism save the soul by teaching. Buddhism in Asia is a natural revolt of humanity against caste; of individual freedom against the despotism of an order; of salvation by faith against salvation by sacraments. In Buddhism the Creation and Creator are left out. But the Buddhists believe in an intelligent and free obedience to divine laws. Mr. Hodgson says: "The one infallible diagnostic of Buddhism is a belief in the infinite capacity of the human intellect." The name Buddha means the Intelligent One, or the one who is wide awake.

DENOMINATIONAL ESTIMATE.

The following is made up from the estimates by Perkins for Johnson's "American Atlas," 1863:

WHAT MAY BE CALLED CHRISTIANS.

	Protestant.	Catholic.	Greek.	Other Den's.	Total Christ'n
America....	27,738,000	38,759,000	31,000	....	66,527,000
Europe......	65,850,000	138,103,000	74,633,300	....	278,586,300
Asia........	428,000	7,167,000	3,000,000	7,853,000	18,448,000
Africa......	719,000	1,113,000	5,000	3,191,000	5,028,000
Australia and Polynesia.	1,100,000	280,000	....	....	1,380,000
Total.....	95,835,000	185,422,000	77,669,300	11,044,000	369,969,300

DENOMINATIONS NOT CALLED CHRISTIANS.

	Mohammedan	Pagan.	Jews.	Total.
America......	....	3,899,000	Some.	3,899,000
Europe.......	9,823,000	....	Some.	9,823,000
Asia..........	50,000,000	666,251,000	6,000,000	722,251,000
Africa........	100,000,000	94,972,000	....	194,972,000
Australia and Polynesia	1,000,000	1,220,000	....	2,220,000
Total......	160,823,000	766,342,000	6,000,000	933,165,000

In all there are 1,000 different religions; 3,642 languages. We may estimate 300,000,000 Caucasians, 552,000,000 Mongols, 190,000,000 Ethiopians, 176,000,000 Malays, 1,000,000 Indo-Americans. Prof. Newman estimates the number of Buddhists at 369,000,000; the "New American Encyclopedia" at 290,000,000. The whole population of the world is from 1,300,000,000 to 1,400,000,000.

Denominational estimates have been made by different writers, but we do not know how much they can be depended on, as we have no reliable data. Mr. Clarke, in his work entitled "Ten Great Religions," has the following:

Cunningham, *Bhilsa Topes.*
Christians..................................270,000,000
Buddhists....................................222 "

Hassel, *Penny Cyclopedia.*
Christians..................................120,000,000
Jews..4 "
Mohammedans................................252 "
Brahmans....................................111 "
Buddhists...................................315 "

Johnston, *Physical Atlas.*
Christians..................................301,000,000
Jews..5 "
Brahmans....................................133 "
Mohammedans................................110 "
Buddhists...................................245 "

Perkins, *Johnson's American Atlas.*
Christians..................................369,000,000
Mohammedans................................160 "
Jews..6 "
Buddhists...................................320 "

Buddhism, though expelled from India, and unable to maintain its control over any Aryan race, converted to its creed a majority of the Mongol nations, and, according to the tables just given, embraces somewhere about three hundred millions of human beings. It is the popular religion of China, the state religion of Thibet and of the Birman Empire. It is the religion of Japan, Siam, Anam, Assam, Nepaul, Ceylon, and nearly all Eastern Asia. Of this extensive religion we have had until lately but very limited information. There is the best authority for believing that Buddhism was the state religion of India in the fourth century before Christ. Buddha is not a proper name, but a title: as we say Jesus the Christ, so Siddartha the Buddha, or Sakya-muni the Buddha, or Gautama the Buddha.

The fundamental doctrine of Buddhism is contained in the four sublime truths, namely:

1. "All existence is evil, because all existence is subject to change and decay.

2. "The source of this evil is the desire for things which are to change and pass away.

3. "The desire, and the evil which follows it, are not inevitable; for, if we choose, we can arrive at Nirvana, where both shall wholly cease.

4. "There is a fixed and certain method to adopt, by pursuing which we attain this end without possibility of failure."

To this way there are eight steps:

1. "Right belief, or the correct faith.

2. "Right judgment, or wise application of that faith to life.

3. "Right utterance, or perfect truth in all we say and do.

4. "Right motives, or proposing always a proper aid and aim.

5. "Right occupation, or outward life not involving sin.

6. "Right obedience, or faithful observance of duty.

7. "Right memory, or a proper recollection of past conduct.

8. "Right meditation, or keeping the mind fixed on permanent truth."

Then follow certain commands and prohibitions, five of which apply to all men, and five to the novices, or monks, only. The first five are: "1. Do not kill. 2. Do not steal. 3. Do not commit adultery. 4. Do not lie. 5. Do not become intoxicated."

The other five are: "1. Take no solid food after noon. 2. Do not visit dances, singing, or theatrical representations. 3. Use no ornaments or perfumery in dress. 4. Use no luxurious beds. 5. Accept neither gold nor silver."

In reference to these, comments have been made almost without number, as they were in after time concerning what was said and done during the life of Jesus, of whom we have so many minute and unimportant details from Saint Thomas. The monks have their Golden Legends and their Lives of Saints, full of miracles and marvels. Much of this literature is entertaining and instructive. Buddhism has a rationality and humanity interwoven with it as a system. It appeals to human reason, proposing to save, not from a future, but from a present, hell. As Buddha preached many sermons, so his missionaries went forth preaching. The great influence exerted was through these sermons. Buddha never used force, but made all his appeals in a rational way to human understanding. Buddhism was not propagated by force: only one religious war happened in which its followers took part, during twenty-three centuries. It has not been without its superstitions, nor in all respects free from errors; but it has no prejudices against those who profess another faith, nor has it maintained any inquisitions. With a zeal that has converted kingdoms it has combined full toleration.

A Buddhist in Ceylon sent his son to a Christian school, out of respect to Christianity, not deeming it improper to profess both Christianity and Buddhism. All men are respected by those of this faith, for it is really a religion of humanity. Men of every rank can enter its priesthood. It has unbounded charity for all souls. Buddhism has abolished human sacrifices among the Mongols, and all bloody rites, and its innocent altars are crowned with flowers and leaves.

Mr. Malcom, the Baptist missionary, who traveled and spent some time in Birmah, speaks of many excellent traits of character common to the Birmese, and noticed very little in the way of vice or intemperance. He continues: "A man may travel from one end of the kingdom to the other without money, feeding and lodging as well as the people. I have seen thousands together, for hours, on public occasions, rejoicing in all ardor, and no act of violence or case of intoxication. During my whole residence in the country I never saw an indecent act or immodest gesture in man or woman. I have seen hundreds of men and women bathing, and no immodest or careless act. Children are treated with great kindness, not only by their mothers, but also by their fathers. A widow with male and female children is more likely to be sought in marriage than if she have none."

Saint Hilaire says: "Buddhist morality is one of endurance, patience, submission and abstinence, rather than action, energy and enterprise. Love for all beings is its nucleus, every animal being our possible relative. To love our enemies, to offer our lives for animals, to abstain from even defensive warfare, to pay obedience to superiors, to reverence age, to provide food and shelter for men and animals, to dig wells and plant trees, to despise no religion, show no intolerance, not to persecute, are the virtues of the people. Polygamy is tolerated, but not approved. Monogamy is general in Ceylon, Siam and Birmah; somewhat less so in Thibet and Mongolia. Woman is better treated by Buddhism than by any other Oriental religion." Buddhism lacks the all-important, distinctive idea of God; hence, their devotion, worship and prayers are spiritless. The God of Buddhism is the Buddha himself, the deified man, who has become infinite by entering Nirvana; and to him prayer is addressed. Plenty of prayers are made. Prayer-meetings are held in the streets of Thibet. Huc says: In the evening, just before sundown, all the people leave their work and meet in the public squares. All kneel and chant their prayers in a low, musical tone, producing an immense and solemn harmony, deeply impressive.

Thirty-five or more Buddhas preceded Sakya-muni, who are conceived to have power to take away sin, and are called "Buddhas of Confession"; some lamas are reckoned with them, as Tsonkhapa, born A.D. 1555. The mendicant priests of Buddha confess at every new and full moon. *Karma* means the law of consequences, and is considered the most essential property of all beings, the cause of all good and evil. This religious law operates till one reaches Nirvana.

The following account of "Nirvana" is taken from the Pali Sacred Books: "Again the king of Sagal said to Nagasena, 'Is the joy of Nirvana unmixed, or is it associated with sorrow?' The priest replied that it is unmixed satisfaction, entirely free from sorrow. Again the king of Sagal said to Nagasena, 'Is Nirvana in the east, west, south, or north? above or below? Is there such a place as Nirvana? If so, where is it?' Nagasena: 'Neither in the east, south, west, nor north; neither in the sky above, nor in the earth below, nor in any of the infinite sakwalas, is there such a place as Nirvana....There is no such place as Nirvana, and yet it exists."

The Buddhist asserts Nirvana to be the object of all his hope, yet if you ask him what it is, may reply, "Nothing." This cannot mean that the highest good of man is annihilation. No pessimism could be more extreme than such a doctrine.

Can men of sound reason say that there is nothing good in Buddhism; that it has no good effect, no restraining influence; that the prayers of its adherents do not go up effectually to the Almighty Giver? What mortal being is authorized to tell his neighbor what he shall say in his prayer, or to truly tell whether or not God accepts it? Possibly those who think they understand the best how and what to ask of God, with the expectation of a favorable answer, are the least likely to receive it. If there be anything among us, lowly mortals, that God detests, it is bigotry. A self-righteous feeling Jesus often rebuked. The religion of Christianity is good, all good, but all the good in the world is not embraced in that alone. God only is all wisdom and goodness. Buddhists have one noble quality in a high degree—that is, charity. Better it would be if all those who claim to be followers of

Jesus were, like him, meek and humble, forgiving and gentle, loving and kind, not alone toward those of their particular faith, but toward all. What a poor exhibition those make who put up fences around their church doors and their altars, virtually saying, " We are God's chosen people; our church door is the gate to heaven " ! As Jesus said to those who were puffed up with self-righteous feelings, and made long, formal, heartless prayers, so he will say to many who have lived since : " I never knew you; depart from me, ye workers of iniquity." Those who have said less and done more shall enter heaven before them.

CHAPTER VI.

ANCIENT RELIGION OF PERSIA AND ZOROASTER.

ZOROASTER and the Zend-Avesta, as connected with the ancient religion of Persia, have an important relation to the religious history of the world, and deserve a more extended notice than we have space to give. Mr. Clarke speaks of the lovely valley in the southwestern part of Persia, in the province of Farsistan, called Schiraz. At one extremity of this valley, northwest of Schiraz, stands an immense platform, fifty feet above the plain, hewn in part out of the mountain itself, and partly built up with gray marble blocks, from twenty to sixty feet in length, so nicely fitted together that the joints can scarcely be detected. This platform is about fourteen hundred feet long by nine hundred feet broad, and is reached by marble steps. In the vicinity are found many inscriptions, which all the learning of Europe could not decipher for many years. One was read by Grotefend as follows: "Darius the King, King of Kings, son of Hystaspes, successor of the Ruler of the World, Djemchid." Another, as follows: "Xerxes the King, King of Kings, son of Darius the king, successor of the Ruler of the World." The German Orientalist Benfey deciphered another inscription, as follows: "Ahura-Mazda (Ormazd) is a mighty God; who has created the earth, the heaven, and men; who has given glory to men; who has made Xerxes king, the ruler of many. I, Xerxes, King of Kings, king of the earth near and far, son of Darius, an Achæmenid. What I have done here, and what I have done elsewhere, I have done by the grace of Ahura-Mazda." Diodorus Siculus says that at Persepolis, on the face of the mountain, were the tombs of the kings of Persia, and that the coffins had to be lifted up to them, along the wall of the rock, by cords.

Many things point to a great Iranic religion as the religion of Persia, centuries before—the religion of which Zoroaster was the great prophet, and the Avesta the sacred book. Zoroaster was mentioned by Plato, about four hundred years before Christ. The worship of the Magians is described by Herodotus before Plato, and a minute account is given of their religious rites B.C. 450. According to Plutarch's account of Zoroaster and his precepts, some believed in two gods: one the author of good things, the other of bad—a god and a demon. Oromazes is said to have sprung from purest light, and Arimanius, on the other hand, from pitchy darkness, and therefore to be continually at war with each other. It is said that Oromazes made six gods: one the author of benevolence, one of truth, one of justice, one of wisdom, one of wealth, and one of pleasure; and that Arimanius likewise made the like number to confront them. After this, Oromazes, having first trebled his own magnitude, mounted aloft as far above the sun as the sun is above the earth, and studded the firmament with stars.

Anquetil du Perron, born at Paris in 1731, devoted himself early to the study of Oriental literature. The French East India Company gave him a passage to India in 1755. He returned to Europe with one hundred and eighty valuable manuscripts, and published his great work in 1771. His death occurred in 1805. For many years after the publication of the Avesta, its genuineness and authenticity were a matter of dispute among the learned men of Europe, Sir William Jones especially denying it to be an ancient work, or the production of Zoroaster. Mr. Rhode says: "There is not the least doubt that these are the books ascribed in the most ancient times to Zoroaster." Of the Vendidad he says: "It has both the inward and outward marks of the highest antiquity, so that we fear not to say that only prejudice or ignorance could doubt it." As to the age of these books, and the period at which Zoroaster lived, there is a great difference of opinion. Mr. Clarke thinks the date may with propriety be fixed at twelve to thirteen centuries B.C., and refers to many authors of the highest repute in proof; but, as all know, there is great difficulty in fixing dates so remote. Nothing is known with certainty of the place where he lived or the events of his life. Some writers suppose he resided in Bactria. Haug maintains that the language of the Zend books is Bactrian. "The language of the Avesta," says Max Mueller, "is so much more primitive than the inscriptions of Darius, that many centuries must have passed between the two periods represented by these two strata of language." These inscriptions are in the Achæmenian dialect, which is the Zend in a later stage of linguistic growth.

Mr. Clodd, who is a few years' later authority than Mr. Clarke, says that Zoroaster was the founder of an ancient religion in Persia, but that we have *no trustworthy* account of him. "He was probably born in Bactria, and his name implies that he became one of the priests who attended upon the sacred fire. We are sure that he lived more than three thousand years ago, because his religion was founded before the conquest of Bactria by the Assyrians, which took place about twelve hundred years before Christ. It has been argued, chiefly from the strong likeness between Jewish and Persian legends, that he was a neighbor of Abraham; but of this the proof is far too slender." To him was given the message of one who was Lord of all. *Ahura,* "Spiritual Mighty-One"; *Mazda,* "Creator of All." *Ahura-Mazda* (corrupted into *Ormuzd*) is thus spoken of in the Zend-Avesta: Highest of all, Ahura-Mazda was said to have below him angels who did his bidding.

Those who clung to the older faith and those who adhered to Zoroaster were bitter against each other, so that the gods of the Vedic hymns became demons in the Zend-Avesta. In that book Indra is an evil being; in the Vedic belief Ahura is a demon.

That Zoroaster believed in one God is generally admitted. He, through the Zend-Avesta, expresses faith in a good place where the pure and faithful find a home after death, and a bad place where the wicked are to suffer in the regions of Ahriman. The rites and ceremonies adopted into his religion were copied in part from the Aryans when together, and were mainly the offering of *Homa* and of *fire.*

Mr. Clarke says that, though absolutely nothing is known of the events of Zoroaster's life, there is not the least doubt of his existence or of his character. He has left the impress of his commanding genius on great regions, various races, and long periods of time. Like Buddhism, his religion is eminently moral. The glaring defects of each, however, as compared with Christianity, are too plain to be overlooked. The method of salvation, as expounded by Zoroaster, is that of an eternal battle for good against evil; according to Buddha, it is that of self-culture and virtuous activity.

The religion of the Avesta all centers in Zoroaster (or Zarathustra), who in some of the sacred books is called the *pure* Zarathustra. He, alone, it is said, knows the precepts of Ahura-Mazda (Ormazd), and that he shall be made skillful in speech. Meditation led him to conclude that all the woe of the world had its root in sin, and that the origin of sin was in the demoniac world.

It is maintained by some that about the period of Zoroaster the climate of Northern Asia was changed in temperature from that of the tropics to severe cold. At some date far back in the past, but probably long before Zoroaster, this change beyond a doubt happened, but exactly through what agency has not yet been satisfactorily explained. The slowly-acting causes or the violent convulsion that changed a summer climate into the present winter of ten months' duration is entirely beyond our comprehension.

This Aryana-Vaejo, Old Iran, the primeval seat of the great Indo-European race, is supposed by Haug and Bunsen to be situated on the high plains northeast of Samarcand, between the thirty-seventh and fortieth degrees of latitude, north, and the eighty-sixth and ninetieth of longitude, east. This region has exactly the climate described in the old writings translated by Spiegel and Haug — ten months of winter and two of summer. The same will apply to Western Thibet and nearly all of Central Siberia. Malte-Brun says that the winter is nine or ten months long throughout almost the whole of Siberia. June and July are the only months entirely free from snow. Geologists have calculated that great oscillations of climate occurred immediately antecedent to the period when the earth was peopled by man. In Central and Northern Asia there are traces of such changes at a more recent date.

It is thought that about the time of some great convulsion Zoroaster developed his belief in the dualism of all things, which now has much logical ground to rest on, in the opinion of many thinkers. Pantheistic optimism, as it was taught in India, could not satisfy his mind. He could not say all that happened was right, because he feared evil sometimes prevailed over good and the right was made to suffer. The world is not rid of this foolish notion, that whatever is is right, even now. But, if God and light do not hold control over error, where is our safety?

To Zoroaster the world was a scene of war, not of peace and rest. Life to the good man was not sleep, but battle. While he saw a good God presiding over all, he also saw a spirit of evil continually rising up against God's will and works. In the far distance he saw the spirit of good triumphant.

The Zend-Avesta does not give a system of theology or philosophy. It is, rather, a liturgy—a collection of hymns, prayers and invocations. Among the deities, Ormazd is always counted supreme. "I worship and adore," says Zarathustra (Zoroaster), "the Creator of all things, Ahura-Mazda (Ormazd), full of light!...I worship the body of the primal Bull, the soul of the Bull! I invoke thee, O Fire, thou son of Ormazd, most rapid of the immortals! I invoke Mithra,...the pure, the sun, the ruler, the quick Horse, the eye of Ormazd! I invoke the holy Sraosha!...I praise the good men and women of the whole world of purity!...I praise Sraosha, whom four horses carry, spotless, bright-shining, swifter than the storms, who, without sleeping, protects the world in the darkness!" Though there is much in the forms found in the Avesta that, by our Protestant standard of to-day, might be called a waste of words, there is at least the form of devotion, and, to those who believe in it, there may be a renovating spirit.

The following is from the Khordah-Avesta:

"In the name of God, the giver, forgiver, rich in love, praise be to the name of Ormazd, the God with the name, 'Who always was, always is, and always will be'; the heavenly amongst the heavenly, with the name 'From whom alone is derived rule.'"

"Offering and praise to that Lord, the completer of good works, who made men greater than all earthly beings, and, through the gift of speech, created them to rule the creatures, as warriors against the Dævas" (or evil spirits).

"All good do I accept at thy command, O God, and think, speak, and do it. I believe in the pure law; by every good work seek I the forgiveness for all sins."

"I enter on the shining way to Paradise; may the fearful terror of hell not overcome me!...May I attain Paradise, with much perfume, and all enjoyments, and all brightness."

Confession of sin is not wanting:

"I repent of all sins. All wicked thoughts, words and works which I have meditated in the world, corporeal, spiritual, earthly and heavenly, I repent of, in your presence, ye holiness. O Lord, pardon!"...

"I repent of the sins which can lay hold of the character of men, or which have laid hold of my character, small and great, which are committed amongst men!...The sins against father, mother, sister, brother, wife, child, against spouses, against the superiors, against my own relations, against those living with me," etc., etc., embracing almost every sin that could be named; so that, if the petition was made in sincerity, and the power to whom the request for pardon was addressed had compassion and ability to forgive, there could be no doubt about forgiveness.

The Avesta consists of the Vendidad, of which twenty-two Fargards, or chapters, have been preserved; the Vispered, in twenty-seven; the Yacna, in seventy; and the Khorda-Avesta, or Little-Avesta, which contains prayers for the use of the laity. The Bundehesch is a book still later, though running back to an early period. It says that Ormazd began the creation by bringing forth the Fravashi. Everything which has been created, or which is to be created, has its Fravashi, which contains the reason and basis of its existence. A spiritual and invisible world preceded this visible, material world as its prototype. The order of creation is thus given: "Ormazd first created the firm vault of heaven, and the earth on which it rests. On the earth he created the high mountain Albordj, which soared upward through all the spheres of heaven, till it reached the primal light, and Ormazd made this summit his abode." The monstrous gulf, the home of Ahriman, was placed beneath the earth. Ormazd, who knew that after the first period his battle with Ahriman would begin, armed himself, and created for his aid the whole shining host of heaven—sun, moon and stars—mighty beings of light, wholly submissive to him. First he created "the heroic runner, who never dies—the sun—and made him king and ruler of the material world."

When he had completed his preparations in the heavens the first four ages drew to an end, and Ahriman saw, from the gloomy depths of his kingdom, what Ormazd had done. In opposition to this creation of a world of light, Ahriman created a world of darkness, a terrible community, equal in number and power to the beings of light. Ormazd, knowing all the misery that Ahriman would cause, yet knowing that the victory would remain with himself, offered Ahriman peace: Ahriman chose war; but, overcome by Ormazd, he sank back into the pit of darkness, where he was confined for three thousand years. Ormazd now completed his creation upon the earth, and the earth, or Hethra, was mother of all living. Everything earthly in the world of light of Ormazd had its protecting deity. These guardian spirits were divided into series and groups; had their captains and their associated assistants.

In the second age Ormazd also produced the great primitive Bull, in which, as the representative of the animal world, the seeds of all living creatures were deposited.

While Ormazd was completing his creation of light, Ahriman, in his dark abyss, was perfecting a corresponding creation of darkness, making a corresponding evil being for every good being created by Ormazd. These spirits of night stood in their ranks and orders, with their seven presiding evil spirits, or Daevas, corresponding to the Amshaspands.

The vast preparations for this great war being completed, and the end of the second age now coming, Ahriman was urged by one of his Daevas to begin the conflict. He counted his host; but as he found nothing therein to oppose to the Fravashis, he sank back in dejection. Finally the second age expired, and Ahriman now sprang aloft without fear, for he knew his time had come. His host followed him, but he alone succeeded in reaching the heavens; his troops remained behind. A shudder ran over him, and he sprang from heaven upon the earth in the form of a serpent, penetrated to its center, and entered into everything he found upon it. He passed into the primal Bull, and even into fire, the visible symbol of Ormazd, defiling it with smoke and vapor. Then he assailed the heavens, and a part of the stars were already in his power, and veiled in smoke and mist, when he was attacked by Ormazd, aided by the Fravashis of holy men, and after ninety days and ninety nights he was completely defeated, and driven back with his troops into the abyss Duzahk. But he did not remain there, for through the middle of the earth he built a way for himself and his companions, and is now living on the earth together with Ormazd, according to the decree of the Infinite.

The destruction by all this war was terrible, but

the evil done resulted in good. The original Bull died; and that, too, was a gain, for the first man, Kaiomarts, came out of his right shoulder, and the soul of the Bull became the guardian spirit of the animal race. Kaiomarts was both man and woman, but when he died there came from him the first human pair; a tree grew from his body and bore ten pairs of men and women, of whom Meschia and Meschiane were the first. They were originally innocent, and made for heaven, and worshiped Ormazd as their creator. But Ahriman tempted them. They drank milk from a goat, and so injured themselves. Then Ahriman brought them fruit, they ate it, and lost a hundred parts of their happiness. Only one pair remained. The woman was the first to sacrifice to the Daevas. After fifty years they had two children, Siamak and Veschak, and died a hundred years old. For their sins they remain in hell until the resurrection.

The human race, which had thus become mortal and miserable by the sin of its first parents, assumed nevertheless a highly interesting position. The man stands in the middle between the two worlds of light and darkness, left to his own free will. He is assailed on every side by Ahriman, but succored by Ormazd, who sent him a revelation of his will by Zoroaster. If he obey these precepts he is safe. The command is: "Think purely, speak purely, act purely." All that comes from Ormazd is pure, from Ahriman impure.

The Fravashis of men originally created by Ormazd are preserved in heaven, in Ormazd's realm of light. But they must come from heaven to be united with a human body, and to go on a path of probation in this world, called the Way of the Two Destinies. Those who have chosen the good in this world are received after death by good spirits, and guided, under the protection of the dog Sura, to the bridge Chinevat; the wicked are dragged thither by the Daevas. Here Ormazd holds a tribunal and decides the fate of souls. The good pass the bridge into mansions of the blessed; the bad fall into the gulf of Duzahk, to be tormented. Ormazd will clothe anew with flesh the bones of men, and relatives and friends will recognize each other again. Then comes the great division of the just from the sinners.

When Ahriman shall cause the comet to fall on the earth to gratify his destructive propensities, he will be really serving the Infinite Being against his own will. For the conflagration caused by this comet will change the whole earth into a stream like melted iron, which will pour impetuously down into the realm of Ahriman. All beings must pass through this stream: to the righteous it will feel like warm milk, and they will pass through to the dwellings of the just; but all the sinners shall be borne along by the stream into the abyss of Duzahk. Here they will burn three days and nights, then, being purified, they will invoke Ormazd, and be received into heaven.

Afterward, Ahriman himself and all in the Duzakh shall be purified by this fire, and all evil be consumed, and all darkness banished.

From the extinct fire there will come a more beautiful earth, pure and perfect, and destined to be eternal.

Windischmann, who has made a recent translation of the Bundehesch, says that a close study of this remarkable book and an exact comparison of it with some original texts will give great confidence in it as having been taken from the original, most of which is now lost; so that the more thoroughly it is examined the more trustworthy it will be found.

The reliability of this old record as that of doctrine promulgated long centuries before the time of Moses—from which Moses possibly might have copied or compiled the account of Creation—may be depended upon with tolerable if not entire confidence; but that the Persian record came from the Old Testament account is totally insupposable.

Many other things are set forth in a way to favor the idea that at least portions of the New Testament derived their outward form and materials for construction from various writings, legends and myths in existence when the New Testament writings took their earliest shape.

Having given this brief account of what is known as the Parsi system, in its later development, it cannot be claimed as an invention of Zoroaster, nor of any one else; for, as Mr. Clarke says, "Religions are not invented: they grow. Even the religion of Mohammed grew out of pre-existent beliefs. The founder of a religion does not invent it, but gives it form. It crystalizes around his own deeper thought. So, in the time of Zoroaster, the popular imagination had filled nature with powers and presences, given them names, and praised them in the heavens."

Many adopt the absurd theory that all the ideas contained in the New Testament originated during our first and second centuries. This is entirely wrong. Jesus, with all his apostles, aids, converts and helpers, did not make an entirely new religion. But by his presence and wonderful powers he infused into old truths a vitality and force wholly new. The Bundehesch, with its elaborate theories, came as a natural result from the tendencies of the older portion of the Avesta.

The Zearna-Akerana—in the Vendidad "The Infinite Time," or "All-embracing Time"—is the creator of Ahriman, according to some translations. "Spiegel," says Mr. Clarke, "considers this supreme being, above both Ormazd and Ahriman, as not belonging to the original Persian religion, but as borrowed from Semitic sources. But if so, then Ormazd is the supreme, uncreated being, and creator of all things. Why, then, has Ormazd a Fravashi, or archetype? And in that case, he must either himself have created Ahriman, or else Ahriman is as eternal as he, which latter supposition presents us with an absolute, irreconcilable dualism." The theory, therefore, forces itself upon us that behind the two opposing powers, good and evil, the thesis and antithesis of moral life, remains the obscure background of original being, the identity of both, from which both have proceeded, and into whose abyss both shall return. That monotheism and pure dualism are doctrines of the Avesta is quite plain.

CHAPTER VII.

RELIGION AND SACRED BOOKS OF EGYPT.

The country known as Egypt, though of limited extent (about seven miles in width), derived much importance from being watered by the Nile. If not the earliest, it was among the earliest of inhabited and civilized portions of the globe. Several cities of large wealth and commercial importance were located along the banks of this ancient river. Science and religious culture found a home here. Some of the public works and monuments have no rival in magnificence. In its highest state of prosperity the people numbered seven millions. It was a world's university, where Pythagoras, Herodotus, Plato, and other eminent men went as students. At an early time they had a tolerable knowledge of astronomy, geometry, music, medicine, anatomy, architecture, agriculture, and mining. Looking back five thousand years, we find Menes, a great warrior and scholar, king of this mighty nation. History speaks of him as the builder of Memphis, where he studied the wisdom of the gods and wrote books. This nation was not idle during the Thinite dynasties of several centuries, and the five dynasties of the Memphite kings, down to the time of the Hyksos, or shepherd kings.

We have the authority of Mr. Clarke, as well as of many others, for saying that ancient Egypt has been an object of deep interest to the whole civilized world in all ages, and more especially to the Christian part. Thither it was that Abraham journeyed, and subsequently Jacob followed his son Joseph, who had become one of the chief men of the nation. There it was that the Hebrews increased in number from seventy to two millions, as most historians say. There Moses was found by Pharaoh's daughter floating near the Nilotic shore in an ark of bulrushes, from whence he was taken by her, and educated in all the learning of the Egyptians. In the course of events, Moses journeyed to Midian, and in due time returned to Egypt, by the supposed command of God, to deliver his Hebrew brethren from the bondage they were under to the Egyptians.

Among the evidences of Egyptian enterprise and skill of ancient date may be mentioned the erection of pyramids, temples, and monuments, requiring not only genius, but concentration of labor and persistent toil. The great pyramid of Cheops was built in the midst of the plain. For its erection vast blocks of stone were transported from the upper Nile, and laid into a pyramid covering more than thirteen acres and rising to a height of nearly five hundred feet. This pyramid is nearly solid, and constructed over a huge mound. A passage-way leads to the inner portion, in which are several rooms, at least one of which is supposed to have been a burial-place. Near this pyramid stand two others of about the same size, and many smaller ones at no very great distance. Not far from these is the famous Sphinx, hewn from solid rock, the proportions of which are truly colossal, it being one hundred and eighty feet long. Modern man is not able to move a block so ponderous. The statue of Rameses II still remains at Memphis. It is eighteen feet across the shoulders. The date of the foundation of Thebes is buried in the past. In the time of Menes, fifty centuries ago, it was in existence as a city; how long before that is not known. On the eastern bank of the river still stands the temple El-Karnak. Thothmes II carried his conquering armies into Mesopotamia, brought back the spoil of nations, and commemorated his deeds on the walls of Karnak. Half a mile from Karnak were two obelisks of red granite, upon the apex of each of which were engraved hieroglyphic writings telling of Rameses II, the Sesostris of classic times. Within is an avenue of fourteen columns sixty feet high, with capitals on which are sculptured bell-shaped flowers of the papyrus. The great Hypostyle hall in the temple El-Karnak is the most imposing and extensive in Egypt, or in the world. In length it is 175 feet, in width 329 feet. It is supported by 134 columns, some of which rise to the height of 75 feet and are 36 feet in circumference. In Ramesium, on the edge of the desert, a statue hewn out of a solid rock of red granite, estimated to weigh nine hundred tons, was in some way, to us now unknown, transported from its bed in the quarries of Syene, and placed in the courts of the temple. These temples were approached by Dromos, or paved walks, of great length.

As far back as history reaches, the Egyptians had a religion and a well-developed mythology. The reign of Menes began after the reign of the gods was ended. Manetho computes a time of twenty-four thousand nine hundred years, of which the gods ruled thirteen thousand nine hundred. Then came the dominion of the heroes, or demi-gods.

No attempt will here be made to unravel legends or to make mysteries clear, but we find that for five thousand years they believed in a series of gods depending on one another. They believed in three orders of gods. There were eight of the first order:

1. Ammon, the Concealed God — the god of Thebes.

2. Khem, the husband of Ammon's mother—the generative god of Nature—the god of Panopolis.

3. Mut, the Mother-Goddess, and temple consort of Khem.

4. Num, the ram-headed god of the Thebaid.

5. Seti, or Sate, the consort of Kneph.

6. Pthah—the god of Memphis—the Creator of the World, sprung from an egg, which came from the mouth of Kneph.

7. Net, or Neith, the goddess of Sais (without descent: "I came from myself").

8. Ra, or Helios, the god of Heliopolis, or On, in the Delta.

There were also twelve gods of the second order and seven of the third, and they were represented in sculpture with a beard hanging from the chin, and the common hieroglyphic sign of an egg or of a snake was attached to all of them.

Ammon, or Ammon-Ra, is the chief king of the gods, corresponding with Zeus of the Greeks. Osiris and Isis seem to have prevailed from the beginning, to pervade the whole mythology, and to have been worshiped throughout all Egypt.

According to Plutarch, Apis, the sacred bull of Memphis, was considered the image of the soul of the god Osiris, and on that account the two names were joined. Osiris also represented the living sun.

His enemy was Typhon, who at the autumnal equinox overcame him.

A singular myth was current in Egypt which may be regarded with interest. It is that Osiris was killed by his brother Typhon (the incarnation of evil), his body cut in pieces and strewn over the earth; that in due time they gathered themselves together and were reunited, and then Osiris was resurrected from the dead, and reigned forever. Thus it seems the doctrine of a resurrection and an unending life thereafter is older than the Hebrew race, and as firmly believed by some of the prehistoric nations as by Christians in our age.

Ammon was by the Egyptians conceived not only to be king of all the gods, but their god especially. Like the Israelites, who most likely copied from the Egyptians, they claimed a powerful deity, who at all times supported them as his particular and chosen people. Nor were the Egyptians, any more than the Israelites, without a priesthood. The priests of the former, as well as of the latter, were supposed to hold intercourse with God. They had their Holiest of Holies, into which none but the priests were allowed to enter, and where they alone could hear the voice of God.

Belief in a future life was general with this nation, also in a Day of Judgment, and in a system of rewards and punishments. Their sacred writings not only show this, but the sculpture on their temples, and their estimation of good and bad acts as represented by the figure of a balance.

Their belief was that the good only would be admitted to the presence of their god Osiris. The practice of embalming may have grown out of their faith in a future life.

In regard to the theology of Egypt, the most important information is obtained from the monuments, which contain the names and the tablets of the gods of the three orders. Then came the sacred books of the Egyptians, made known to us by Clemens Alexandrinus, which were numerous, writing having become common among them as early as the dynasty of Menes. The sacred books of Hermes were:

1. The two books containing sacred songs and hymns in honor of the gods, and also in praise of their ancient kings.

2. The astronomical books, of the Horoscopus, which treated of the system of the fixed stars, the solar and lunar conjunction, the phases of the moon, the risings of the sun, moon, and stars.

3. The ten books of the Hierogrammatist, the books of the sacred scribe, which treated of the hieroglyphic art, and of the rudiments of writing, of cosmogony and geography; of the system of the sun and moon and the five planets; of the chorography of Egypt; of the delineation of the course of the Nile within the limits of the Egyptian territory; and of a

general survey of Egypt, with a description, or inventory, of each temple, of its landed property, of its weights, measures, and utensils.

4. The ten ceremonial books of the Stalistes; these were devoted principally to religious worship, and contained "ordinances as to the first-fruits, the sacrificial stamp"; regulations concerning hymns, prayers, festal processions, and ceremonies in honor of the dead.

5. Ten books of the prophets. These were purely sacerdotal, and intrusted to the care of the prophets, or the first order of priests immediately following the high-priests of the temples. They treated of the entire education of the priests. They included the apportionment and collection of taxes, their mythology, and the laws connected with their religious rites and the duties of the priesthood, which was the really privileged class. It assumed to speak with the voice of God, and the recognition and consecration of the king was one of their solemn duties. Into this class the sovereign must be admitted, if he were not a priest already.

Of the sacred Hermaic books, one, which is probably as interesting as any of them, is still extant, dating fifteen to sixteen hundred years before Christ.

Beside these, Diodones tells us they had books of the civil laws. The "Book of the Dead," in manuscript, has been brought to light recently. It is written in hieroglyphic characters, and treats of the ceremonies in honor of the dead, and of the transmigration of souls.

A papyrus is said to lie in the museum at Turin which Lepsius has carefully examined. It contains a history of the adventures of a soul. Lepsius says it furnishes the only example of a great Egyptian literary work transmitted from the old Pharaonic times. A compilation made at various times, probably in various parts of Egypt, the original plan unquestionably belonging to the remotest age, it, doubtless, like other sacred books, was ascribed to Hermes or to Thoth. The figurative authorship is no invention of later times, for in the text of the work itself mention repeatedly occurs of the book, as well as of the book of Thoth. In the vignette to chapter xliv the deceased himself is offering to Thoth the Hermetic book to which these allusions apply.

By this brief reference to an ancient nation, we find that, if natural darkness occasionally covered that part of the earth, they had a fair supply of intellectual light.

Before the first beams of Christianity broke upon the world, the spirit of tolerance appeared at Alexandria, in Egypt, B.C. 356. The founder of this great city, who gave it a name, is more entitled to be called great for his acts of toleration than for all the conquests he made in Egypt or elsewhere. On account of the liberal policy he pursued, a general movement took place to a spot so desirable, and at that time so congenial. There the religion of every caste and nation was secure from assault. Great numbers came from places far and near. Thither flocked the great and the good, the learned and the simple, who loved religious freedom. There each could offer to the powers of heaven such prayers and perform such oblations as seemed to them most proper. It was a bright page in the world's history. To this beautiful oasis in the moral world came prophets, judges and doctors; the princes of On, Memphis and Thebes honoring it with their presence.

According to what Mr. Clarke says, derived from the authority of Bunsen and others, the Egyptians were of all men the most particular in their worship of the gods. The origin of much of the theology, mythology and ceremonies of the Hebrews and Greeks was in Egypt; and the names of almost all the gods came from Egypt into Greece. The Greek oracles, especially that of Dodona, were brought from Egypt. Moreover, the Egyptians were the first who introduced public festivals and solemn supplications, which the Greeks learned of them. They invented the calendar, and connected astrology therewith. Each month and day, says Herodotus, is assigned to some particular god; and each person's birthday determines his fate. The Egyptians were the first to say the soul of man was immortal; that when the body dies the soul transmigrates through every variety of animal. Osiris, the judge, is mentioned in tombs erected two thousand years B.C. Bunsen tells us that the names of all the great gods of Egypt are on the oldest monuments; that in the earlier part of the empire of Menes, on their first appearance in history, the Egyptians possessed an established mythology and a series of gods. M. Maury says that everything took the stamp of religion. Their writings were full of sacred symbols; literature and science were only branches of theology; art labored in the service of worship to glorify the gods. Religious observances were so numerous that those in the common walks of life were scarcely able to perform them. Worship was the great business, and the future fate was constantly brought to mind. Religion became almost a fixed part of the physical organization; an instinct transmitted with the blood. Of all polytheisms it offered the most obstinate resistance to Christianity. The numerous Egyptian feasts were well attended. Every temple had its own particular priests. The priests were of various grades: chief-priests, pontiffs, and others of inferior rank. Priests were exempt from taxes; they paid great attention to diet, as to quantity and quality of food. Swine's flesh was in particular forbidden. They bathed twice a day and twice in the night; shaved the head and body every three days. They offered prayers for the dead. Their dress was a loose linen robe worn over common garments. Sacrifices were made of oxen and other animals, from which the Hebrews first obtained the idea. Shrines were carried in processions, overshadowed by the wings of the Goddess of Truth, much in the same way as the Jews carried the ark, and with the same veneration. The Egyptian prophets were the most highly honored of the priestly order. They studied the ten hieratical books; had only one wife; were circumcised like other Egyptians, as were also the Israelites after them; their lives were full of constant action, of duties and restrictions. The latter, therefore, did not, as many suppose, originate the practice of circumcision. They copied it from the Egyptians, along with many rites and ceremonies of which the Hebrews knew nothing before they came to Egypt as visitors, or to reside at the time of the famine. They came to Egypt ignorant, and ready to adopt, in part at least, the religion of their new home.

Before Swedenborg came, no theology ever indoctrinated an immortality as well-defined as that of the Egyptians. The Greek and Roman hereafter was shadowy and vague; that of Buddhism remote; the Hebrew Beyond was wholly eclipsed by the sense of a divine presence and power immanent in time and space.

The doctrine of the immortality of the soul, Mr. Birch says, is as old as the inscriptions of the twelfth dynasty, many of which contain extracts from the Ritual of the Dead. One hundred and forty-six chapters were translated by him from the text of the Turin papyrus, the most complete in Europe. This Ritual is all that remains of the Hermetic Books, which constituted the library of the priesthood. In it antagonistic deities are represented as contending for the soul of the deceased. At the final judgment some forty-two deities are said to be present to feed on the blood of the wicked. At this great judgment all deny, in full detail, that they have sinned or neglected duty, declaring that they have not denied the truth nor God, but have loved God, given bread to the hungry and garments to the naked.

Funeral ceremonies were imposing. After seventy days of mourning, the body was ferried across the lake in front of the temple, to represent the passage of the soul over the infernal stream. Then came a dramatic representation of the trial of the soul before Osiris. Intercessors plead for him. A pair of scales was set up; in one side his conduct was placed in a bottle, in the other the image of truth. These proceedings are represented on the funeral papyri. One of these, twenty-two feet in length, Mr. Clarke says, is in Dr. Abbott's collection of Egyptian antiquities, in New York. It is beautifully written, and illustrated with careful drawings, one of which represents the Hall of the Two Truths, and Osiris sitting in judgment, with the scales of judgment before him. By this we see that the idea of a Judgment is not only older than Christianity, but far older than the Hebrew or the Jewish name. Brugsch says that a thousand voices from the tombs of Egypt show that the claims they set up for self-justification include many of the Christian virtues which Christians are wont to think to belong to them only; such as, "He loved his father, he honored his mother, he loved his brethren, and never went from home in bad temper; he never preferred the great man to the low one." Another inscription says: "I was a wise man; my soul loved God." An inscription at Sais, on a priest who lived in the sad days of Cambyses, says: "I honored my father, I esteemed my mother, I loved my brothers."

It should not be forgotten that the history of Egypt extends far back in the past. The priests of Egypt told Herodotus that there were three hundred and thirty-one kings from Menes to Meoris, whose names they read out of a book. After him came eleven others, of whom Sethos was the last. From Osiris to Amasis they counted fifteen thousand years. This would make the time of Menes about B.C. 9150. The history of Egypt is divided into three periods: that of the old, the middle, and the new monarchy. The first extends from the foundation of the united kingdom of Menes to the conquest of the country by the Hyksos; the second from that conquest till the expulsion of the Hyksos; the third from the re-establishment of the monarchy by Amasis to the final conquest by Persia.

According to Dr. Brugsch, the Israelites were slaves in Egypt in the fourteenth century B.C., which was in the reign of Rameses II. This goes far toward establishing a synchronism between Jewish and Egyptian history, and to warrant the belief that the Israelites left Egypt somewhere about 1491 B.C.

There is a papyrus in the imperial library at Paris, which M. Chabas considers the oldest book in the world. It is an autograph manuscript written B.C. 2200, or four thousand years ago, by one who calls himself the son of a king. It contains practical philosophy like that of Solomon in his proverbs, and is so much like the proverbs that there is ground for thinking one was copied from the other—at least in part. Mr. Clarke says it is a question how much of the doctrine and ritualism of the Hebrews was taken from that of Egypt. It is evident enough that Christianity adopted some of the heathen customs. The rite of circumcision was certainly copied by the Jews from the Egyptians. Dr. Livingstone found this rite in existence among the tribes south of Zambesi, and thinks it cannot be traced to any Mohammedan source. It still exists in Ethiopia and Abyssinia. Wilkinson affirms it to have been "as early as the fourth dynasty, probably earlier; or long before the time of Abraham." It may have been a sign of the dedication of the generative powers to the service of God, and the first step out of the untamed license of passion. A great deal of similarity might be pointed out between Egyptian and Jewish practices. The Egyptians had in their temples a special sanctuary more holy than the rest, and so had the Jews. The Egyptians had their scapegoat, and so had the Jews. The use of a ring in the ceremony of a wedding was, according to Clemens, a custom derived from Egypt. Four principal doctrines are said by Mr. Samuel Sharpe to be common to Egyptian mythology and orthodox Christianity:

1. That the creation and government of the world is not the work of one being, but of one God made up of several persons. This is the doctrine of plural unity.

2. That salvation cannot be expected from the justice or mercy of the Supreme Judge unless an atoning sacrifice is made to him by a divine being.

3. That among the persons who compose the godhead, one, though a god, could yet suffer pain, and be put to death.

4. That a god, or being half god and half man, once lived on earth, born of an earthly mother, but without an earthly father.

The gods of Egypt appear mostly in triads; sometimes as three gods in one. The triad of Thebes consisted of Ammon-Ra, Athor, and Chouso; or, father, mother, and son.

There were other groups: Isis, Nephthys, and Horus; Isis, Nephthys, and Osiris; Osiris, Athor, and Ra. In later times Horus became the supreme being, and appeared united with Ra and Osiris in one figure, holding the two scepters of Osiris with the hawk's head of Horus and the sun of Ra. The painters of Rome made large gains by painting the goddess Isis as the Madonna of Egypt, which, being imported into Italy, became very popular there.

It appears that the doctrine of the Trinity and that of the Atonement began to take shape in Egypt long before the dawn of Christianity, and the Trinity was symbolized to the Egyptian mind. According to Plutarch, they worshiped Osiris, Isis, and Horus under the form of a triangle, and considered that everything which was perfect had three parts; hence the good god had three parts, while the god of evil remained single.

Egypt not only exercised a powerful influence over the religion of Rome, but over Christianity also. Alexandria was the great center of profound religious speculations in the first centuries. There the doctrine was maintained that God had revealed himself to all nations by his Logos, or Word. The influence of this Alexandrian thought became widespread, from the high culture which prevailed there, and from the book-trade carried on in this growing Egyptian city, where all the oldest manuscripts of the Bible were transcribed. As the Egyptian mind naturally left its impress on Judaism, so it did on Christianity.

Traces of Egyptian speculations are visible not only in the Church doctrines of the Trinity and Atonement, but in the idea of a material resurrection. Egyptian asceticism is also found in the history of Christian monasticism. Looking fully at the large amount the Hebrews and Christians borrowed from the Egyptian and other earlier nations, we are astonished. Not that anything is less valuable because it was borrowed, but what so many Christians feel sure was specially revealed to the well-informed Jews, or the devout followers of Jesus, had been promulgated thousands of years before, in substance, if not in the same words, concerning God, Satan, the angels and devils, heaven and hell, the judgment and the resurrection. The Egyptian religion was strictly ethnic; it never attempting to spread itself beyond the borders of the Nile until after the Roman conquest. The worship of the Divine in Nature, the sentiment of wonder before the great mystery of the world, and the feeling that Duty is in all life, in all form, in all change, as well as in what is permanent, was the great element, the most original part, of Egyptian religion.

We are reminded of the great changes that have been going on, and will continue to go on, when we consider that the vast range of Egyptian wisdom has nearly disappeared; for it was a religion of the priests, who were not willing to communicate freely to the people, but, like many priests in Christian lands, set themselves up as superior in ability, and as having a knowledge of God's will and purposes to which the common people could not attain. Although much good may be done by priests, priestcraft, like most other craft, carries in itself the principle of death. Truth only is immortal—plain, open, frank, manly truth.

CHAPTER VIII.

THE GODS AND RELIGION OF GREECE.

Considering the interest that has been and still is felt in the small but famous country called Greece, or Hellas, something ought to be said about its gods and religion. It makes but little show on the map of Europe, but no other country was ever so well situated for development, or has had a more brilliant career. The climate is remarkably good, quite free from the excesses of heat and cold, dryness and moisture; both healthful and well suited to the growth of many important and necessary productions of its soil.

Thorough examination shows plainly that the Greeks emigrated from Asia, and that they brought with them oxen, cows, horses, dogs, swine, goats and geese; that they knew the use of metals, and lived in houses. The original abode of the race was in Bactria, where they were gradually broken up by emigration—not later than four thousand years before our era—and from whence came also the Hindus, the Persians, the Latins, the Celts, the Teutonic tribes, and the Slavi.

The Hellenic tribes, about the first of the seventh century B.C., were known under four heads, or groups —the Achaians, Æolians, Dorians, and Ionians, with other tribes more or less connected; but another race had preceded them, known as Pelasgians.

Greek writers bear testimony to the early Egyptian influence on their country and its religion. M. Maury also admits this influence on the worship and ceremonies of Greece, and thinks it gave their religion a more serious tone.

Greek religion is unlike all others on account of the human character of its gods. The gods of Greece are idealized men and women, on a larger scale, but still human. "The gods of Greece," Mr. Clarke says, "are persons, warm with life, radiant with beauty, having their human adventures, wars, and loves.... If we suppose a number of human beings, young and healthy and perfectly organized, to be gifted with an immortal life and miraculous endowments of strength, wisdom, and beauty, we shall have the gods of Olympus." The Greeks by their religion are not trying to save their souls; they are intent on having a good time. They live for fighting, feasting, and making love. The Greek religion, unlike many others, had no great founder, no restorer, no priestly caste, no sacred books, no Avesta, no Vedas. In Greece, kings and generals, with the common people, offer prayers and sacrifices, as well as the priests. Their religion was moderate in restraints; their gods did not come down from above, but came up from below. They did not emanate, they evolved. They made their gods to suit themselves, and regarded them as companions rather than as objects of reverence. The gods lived near to them, on Olympus, a mountain snow-capped even in July. They had a most delicious religion, without asceticism, austerity, or terror; a religion filled with forms of beauty, with gods who were never stern, seldom jealous or cruel. It was a heaven near at hand. The Greek religion did not guide; it scarcely restrained. Their Book of Genesis, the Theogony of Hesiod, gives the history of three generations of deities: first, the Uranids· second, the Titans; third, the gods of Olympus.

According to Hesiod, first of all was Chaos. Next, broad-bosomed Earth, or Gaia. Then was Tartarus, dark and dim, below the earth. Next appeared Eros, or Love, most beautiful among the immortals. From Chaos came Erebus and black Night, and then sprung forth Æther and Day, children of Erebus and Night.

Pictet has inferred that the original Aryan tribes worshiped the Heaven, the Earth, the Sun, Fire, Water, and Wind. The oldest hymns in the Vedas mark the second development of the Aryan deities in India. The chief gods of this period are Indra, Varuna, Agni, Savitri, and Soma. Indra is the god of the air, directing the storm, the lightning, the clouds, and the rain; Varuna is the all-embracing circle of the heavens, earth, and sea; Savitri, or Surja, is the Sun, King of Day, also called Mitra; Agni is Fire; and Soma is the sacred fermented juice of the moon-plant—often, indeed, the moon itself.

Herodotus says that Hesiod and Homer lived four hundred years before his time, and framed a theogony for the Greeks, gave names to the gods, assigned them honors and acts, and declared their several forms. But the poets, said to be before them, in his opinion were after them. In Homer, the gods are very human, with few traits of divinity or of dignity. As a family, they live together on Mount Olympus, feasting, talking, making love, deceiving each other, angry, and reconciled. So, in the Iliad, they are at their feasts, with Vulcan pouring out nectar for them all and handing each the cup. Above all these gods there exists a mightier power, a dark Fate, an irresistible Necessity.

Pindar, the Theban, born B.C. 494, in the time of the conquests of Darius, composed one of his Pythian odes in the year of the battle of Marathon. He taught the doctrine of a divine retribution, that the bitterest end awaits the pleasure that is contrary to right. He declared that law was the ruler of gods and men.

One or two centuries before this, Callinus made religion to consist of patriotism.

In the third century B.C. we have much from the poets truly monotheistic as well as devout. Though the tendency is strongly polytheistic and anthropomorphic, there yet existed a faith in one supreme God, ruler of all things. The poets, in giving a human character to the gods, never quite forgot their origin as powers of nature. Jupiter Olympus is still the god of the sky, the thunderer. Neptune is the ruler of the ocean, the earth-shaker. Phœbus-Apollo is the sun-god. Artemis is the moonlight, chaste, pure, and cold.

The Olympic games were celebrated at the temple at Olympia by the united Hellenic race, and occurred every fifth year, lasting five days, calling together all Greece. These were to the Greeks, says Mr. Clarke, what the Passover was to the Jews, blending divine worship and human joy. They formed a chronology. Epochs were reckoned from them. The first Olympiad was seven hundred and seventy-six years B.C. A large part of our ancient chronology depends on these festivals.

Over the gathering, at this festival, within a Doric temple sixty-eight feet high, ninety-five wide, and two hundred and thirty long, covered with sculptures of Pentelic marble, the great Jupiter of Phidias presided. The god was seated on his throne, made of gold, ebony, and ivory, studded with precious stones, and so colossal that, though seated, his head nearly reached the roof.

There arose, five or six centuries B.C., a school of philosophers in Greece, a superior order of educated men, deep, solid thinkers; and, though they did not all entertain exactly the same opinions, they had ideas largely in advance of the Greek mind generally, and of that of other portions of the world. Their thoughts were turned to the truly sublime, to the beginning of things. From this point all grasping minds desire to start. They crave a base line upon which other lines may rest. They want material before starting to build; solid ground for standing. There is too much ephemeral thinking; too much studying results without looking to causes; building up one-sided theories; hewing out broken cisterns that can hold no water; too much narrowness of vision. That great master of thought, Plato, did much to harmonize idealism and realism. What the philosophers of Plato's time were trying to find was a central unity underlying outward phenomena. Thales (B.C. 600) said it was water. Anaximander, his disciple, called it chaotic matter, containing in itself a motive-power for successive creations and destructions. Heraclitus of Ephesus (B.C. 500) said it was fire—not physical fire, but the principle of antagonism. Thales was not a materialist, for he said: "Of all things, the oldest is God; the most beautiful is the world; the swiftest is thought; the wisest is time." He taught, also, that there was a divine power in all things. Anaxagoras (B.C. 494) distinguished God from the world, mind from matter.

To say that Pythagoras, Xenophanes, and other great scholars born about B.C. 600, did not aid in opening the way for greater light, that they were not feeling after God that the breaking light of that time was not the early dawn of the Christian day which came with Jesus of Nazareth, would be unfair, unjust.

Parmenides, a scholar and successor of Xenophanes, at Elea, taught that God, as pure thought, pervaded all nature. Empedocles (about B.C. 460) followed Xenophanes, and, though he introduced dualism into his physics, was a monotheist, declaring God to be the Absolute Being. His idea of an infinite God is quite distinct. Socrates was another great light, radiating from the Great Source—the Brightest Beam. He first taught the science of ethics and the doctrine of divine providence, and declared that we could only know God through his works. The basis of religion he called humanity, and proclaimed the well-being of man to be the end of the universe. He regarded the inferior deities as we regard angels, saints, and prophets. Mr. Clarke says: "Socrates took his intellectual departure from man, and inferred nature and God. Plato assumed God and inferred nature and man. He made goodness and nature godlike, by making God the substance in each. His was a divine philosophy, since he referred all facts, theoretically and practically, to God as the ground of their being. The style of Plato combined analysis and synthesis, exact definition with poetic life. His magnificent intellect aimed at uniting precision in details with universal comprehension." Plato was a strict transcendentalist. He says the life and essence of all things is from God, and his idea of God is of the purest and highest kind. God is spirit, the supreme, real being, the creator of all things, his providence over all events.

Plato avoids pantheism, on the one side, by making God a distinct personal, intelligent will; and polytheism, on the other, by making him absolute. Plato's theology is therefore pure theism. Ackerman says: The Platonic theology is strikingly near that of the Christian in regard to God's being, name, and attributes. It argues the existence of God from the movements of nature, and the necessity of an original principle of motion. But the real Platonic faith in God, like that of the Bible, rests on immediate knowledge. As to the essence of God, Plato gives no definition, but says: "To find the Maker and Father of this All is hard, and having found him it is impossible to utter him." The idea of Goodness, Plato says, is the best expression. The idea of God was the object and aim of his whole philosophy, so he calls God the Beginning and End. The Sun is the image of the Good

Being. In the same way the Scriptures speak of the Father of light. So Aristotle declared that "since God is the ground of all being, the first philosophy is theology." Plato said that no one who did not first look at divine things could understand human things. There is abundant evidence that Plato was a monotheist, and that in speaking of gods in the plural he was only using the common form of speech. The Bible speaks of the God of gods.

More especially during the last centuries we hear much said about a cold philosophy, in contrast with the warmth imparted by Christian religion. At the time the Greek schools were in their glory, Jesus had not appeared as a spiritual guide and teacher, nor was he at any time, by the Jews or any other nation, for a moment thought of as such. When he did come, with the warming power of love, the regenerating, vivifying force of the Christian religion, it opened a new fountain of joy and gladness, of faith and hope. But in the enjoyment of that, why forget the advance made by Greek philosophy? Sound thought, deep and serious reflection, a close watch over all we say or do, with an eye single to God, and a constant effort to better our race, are much more profitable than shouting hallelujahs, without any higher motive than to hear ourselves declare what we cannot feel.

With the Stoics, theism is converted into pantheism. There is one Being, the substance of all things, from whom the universe flows forth, and into whom it returns in regular cycles. The everlasting existence of souls as individuals was denied by the Stoics, who believed that at the end of a certain cycle they would be resolved into the Divine Being. In like manner the Scriptures say the spirit at death shall return to God, from whence it came, and the body to the dust, as it was before being created.

The Epicureans were opposed to religion in all its forms, which they pronounced a curse to mankind. They did not respect the popular faith in gods; denied the care of Divine Providence; rejected prayer, prophecy, divination, and considered that religion was founded on fear; yet, like their master Epicurus, they believed in the existence of the immortal gods.

Such, in brief, were the principal theological views of the Greek philosophers. The ground they took was far higher than that occupied by the poets. It may also be noticed that, from the first account we have of the Greek colony, onward in their history, there was a steady advance in all that constitutes civilization and profound learning, in political economy, in ethics and religion. Many practices still survived quite unworthy of a nation so enlightened, such as burning incense and offering sacrifices, which were very prevalent. On great occasions the sacrifices were large as the hecatomb—which means a hundred oxen. It is a curious fact that holy water was placed at the entrance of the temple, consecrated by putting into it a burning torch from the altar, with which, or with a branch of laurel, the worshipers were sprinkled on entering. The worshipers were also expected to wash their bodies, or at least their hands and feet, before going into the temple—a custom common also among the Jews and other nations. So Ezekiel says: "I will sprinkle you with clean water, and you shall be clean." And, according to this custom, Paul said: "Let us draw near, having our hearts sprinkled from an evil conscience, and our bodies washed with pure water." We can see by this that the use of water as a symbol for cleansing and washing away sin did not originate with the disciples and followers of John the Baptist, or with Jesus. The ceremony was possibly contemporaneous with the Greeks and other nations, and with the prophets. As with the Jews, so with the Greeks, all offerings were made of the best things they had of the kind. An animal, if such was to be sacrificed, without spot or blemish, if possible, was taken. All the Greek festivals were religious, but they were held in honor of almost everything, and for almost every purpose. Such festivals constituted the acme of Greek life. Greek temples were not intended for worship, but chiefly to contain the images of the gods. Along the magnificent peristyle which surrounded the four sides of the Doric temples, the splendid processions could circulate in full view of the multitude.

The office of priest was sometimes hereditary, but not confined to any particular class. Plato recommends that there should be an annual rotation, no one acting as priest for more than one year. No such thing, therefore, as priestcraft existed with the Greeks. They had no hierarchy.

Diviners, however, were common, and much consulted. Alcibiades had augurs and oracles devoted to his interest, who deceived the Athenians. The Delphic oracle took the highest rank. It was thought to be the center of the earth, and revered by the Pan-Hellenic race as a supreme religious court, and believed to be infallible. Döllinger says the whole life of the Greeks was penetrated by religion, so they instinctively and naturally prayed on all occasions. They prayed at sunrise, at sunset, at mealtimes, for outward blessings of all kinds, and also for virtue and wisdom. They prayed standing, with a loud voice, and hands lifted to the heavens. They threw kisses to the gods with their hands. So we see the Greek worship, like their theology, was natural, cheerful, hopeful, and free from superstition.

The early gods of most nations are local. This was the case in Greece. In Athens, down to the time of Alexander, each tribe kept its own divinities. Everything like mystery is foreign to the Hellenic mind. The early home of mystery is thought to have been Egypt, from whence it spread into various other countries. Orpheus is the reputed founder of the Bacchic mysteries, in the island of Samothrace, near the coast of Asia Minor. Another account says that this mode of worship was reformed by Orpheus and a portion of the gross licentiousness abolished. He died a martyr to the purer faith he undertook to establish. The principal mysteries were those of Bacchus and Ceres. The Bacchic mysteries were a wild nature-worship, accompanied with frenzy and many strange and peculiar demonstrations. Mysteries were celebrated at Eleusis every fourth year. They are said to have been introduced B.C. 1356. All persons were required to be initiated, in order to enjoy its privileges. Candidates were crowned with myrtle and admitted by night into a vast temple, where they were purified, and instructed, and assisted at certain grand solemnities. The unity of God and the immortality of the soul are supposed to have been taught. Bacchus was believed to be an Indian god first, and afterward adopted by Greece, to whose use in their early history he seemed well adapted. The Thracian form of Bacchic worship was distasteful to the enlightened class. Plato discarded it entirely. From the last accounts we have of it, the effect was to degrade, not elevate; to demoralize, not enlighten.

Orpheus probably came from Egypt into Greece. The Orphic doctrine may be traced back at least six centuries before Christ. It constituted a mystic and pantheistic theology. The Pythagoreans had much respect for this system. The Orphic doctrine unfolded a system of cosmogony in which Time was the first principle of things, from which came chaos and ether. Then came the primitive egg, from which was born Phanes, or Manifestation. At death the soul escapes from this prison, and passes through many changes, by which it is purified. These notions were not suited to the Greek mind, for the true Greek was not pantheistic nor introspective. The Orphic theology constantly shows its pantheistic character.

What was long known as the Greek oracles has by some been considered as the effect of stupefying gases. Among them the oracle of Apollo, at Delphi, was the most noted, and explicitly confided in among the ancient Greeks. Diodorus Siculus tells us how this was discovered: " Upon Mount Parnassus, where goats were wont to feed, there was a deep cavern, with a small, narrow mouth, which, when approached by the goats, caused them to leap in a most frantic and unusual manner, and utter strange, unheard-of sounds. The goatherd, observing this, and wondering what could be the cause of it, went himself to view the cavern, whereupon he also was seized with a like fit of madness, leaping and dancing, and foretelling things to come."

Archbishop Patten, in speaking of the officiating priestess of this oracle, says that, when inspired, she began immediately to swell, foam at the mouth, tear her hair, cut her flesh, and to appear like one distracted. In some cases the paroxysms were so violent as to cause immediate death. The wisest men of that time believed in these oracles most implicitly, and as honestly as the Jews gave credit to their best prophets, who took strange means to bring out their powers —in some respects in imitation of the Greeks. The latter were more general in predictions than the former, and to that extent wiser. Pausanias informs us that those who desired to consult the oracles of Trophonius' cave, at Lebadea in Bœotia, were obliged to undergo various preparatory ceremonies, which continued through several days; to purify themselves by various methods; to offer sacrifices to different deities; to be anointed and washed; and to drink of the waters of forgetfulness, that their former cares might be buried, and of the waters of remembrance, that nothing of what they saw should be forgotten.

The cave was surrounded by a wall resembling an oven on the inside, being about four cubits wide and eight deep. This was entered by means of a ladder, and those going down carried with them cakes made of honey. Having in all respects complied with the regulations established as necessary by experience, and reached the bottom of this artificial cave, the future was fully opened to them.

Now we may think it strange that a belief so foolishly whimsical could find dupes among a people so highly cultivated and far advanced in civilization. We wonder they were so easily duped. Nevertheless, we are still subject to the same folly, the same weakness. After a little ceremony over an infant and saying that "the child is regenerate and grafted into the body of Christ's Church," we believe it true. The cases where we can, by anything we say or do, gain a knowledge of God's purposes, of what he will or will not do, are few, if any ever happen. No man can tell with certainty what is to be his condition after death, what is to occur, or where he is to go. He may dream about it, may talk about it, but he *knows* absolutely nothing. Vague superstitions and idle dreams draw us on until good sense is all gone.

CHAPTER IX.

THE GODS AND RELIGION OF ROME.

That portion of Europe known as Italy, of which Rome is the capital, extends from the mountain range of the Alps in a southeasterly direction into the Mediterranean sea about five hundred miles. The part of this sea between Italy and the Hellenic peninsula was named the Adriatic; that on the west the Tyrrhenian sea. The great plain in the north extends in a nearly unbroken level from the Alps to the Appenines and the sea. Its principal rivers are the Po, the Adige, the Arno, and the Tiber, of which the last two are navigable.

The best authority on Roman history down to the time of Octavius, first emperor under the name of Augustus, B.C. 27, is Niebuhr. He informs us that the purely mythical history of Rome terminates with Numa. The dawn of reality begins to glimmer during the reign of Tullus Hostilius. He says that the story about the infancy of Romulus and Remus is mythical, and that the War of Troy is so completely mythic that no part can be regarded as strictly historical.

After the beginning of the fifth century B.C., about the time the regal period ended and the republic began, we have a more thorough knowledge of what took place among the Romans. Mr. Clarke says that with the Romans everything was done with a deliberate intention. Their religion was not an inspiration, but an intention. All forms of religion might come to Rome and take their places in its Pantheon, but they must come as servants and soldiers of the state. Rome opened an asylum for them, just as Rome had established a refuge on the Capitoline Hill, to which all outlaws might come and be safe on condition of serving the community. Everything in Rome must serve the state; hence the religion of Rome was a state institution, though nothing is clearly known of it during the mythic period.

There is quite enough of myth and legend interwoven with the religious history of every nation, if, indeed, these traits are wanting in a single case. Considering that the Christian religion started in a Roman territory, we could hardly omit to say something of the religion that prevailed there before the birth of Jesus.

All liberal thinkers can but admire the spirit of toleration displayed in Rome; for, though the state religion was a system of ritualistic worship, it compelled no one to abjure his own faith, nor to adopt theirs, if we can in truth say that they had a faith. The high office of Pontiff was common in the time of Numa, the earliest of their authentic history. It was the business of this priest to superintend divine worship, the offering of sacrifice, and other religious ceremonies. The Romans had a college of pontiffs, or high-priests. The very respect for national law in the Roman mind caused the worship of national gods to be legalized.

The Jews in Rome were not interfered with, but were allowed to worship the Jewish God in which they believed. The Christians were only interfered with when they openly rebelled against the national faith. The Roman nation was derived from various sources: from the Latins, Sabines, Pelasgians, and Etruscans, more particularly. Niebuhr thinks the Sabine ritual was adopted by the Romans, and that Varro found the real remains of Sabine chapels on the Quirinal. The system of divination came from Etruria. Being strongly polytheistic, they had, like many other nations designated as idolatrous, an obscure conception of one Supreme Being. They had also many inferior divinities who presided over small matters. One of the oldest and most original of the gods of Rome was the Sabine god Janus. The opening month of the year, January, received its name from this god. The temple for him had four sides, corresponding to the four seasons of the year; he was god of the year. This temple was open in war, but closed in peace. It is thought by Creuzer and others that the idea of this god, with his characteristics, came from Bactria. The chief feast of Janus was on the Calends (first day) of January. On this day all the Romans put on their best attire, avoided all bad talk and conduct, and made presents of small coin with a Janus-head. Janus was the great god of the Sabines, with a temple on Mount Janiculum.

Mr. Clarke says: "In every important city of Etruria there were temples to the three gods, Jupiter, Juno, and Minerva. In like manner the magnificent temple of the Capitol at Rome consisted of three parts —a nave sacred to Jupiter; and two wings, or aisles, one dedicated to Juno, the other to Minerva." This temple was two hundred and fifteen feet long and two hundred feet wide, and in it immense wealth was accumulated. Jupiter derives his name from the Sanskrit word "Div," or "Diu," indicating the splendor of heaven or of day, which means the same as *Father of Heaven* or *Father of Light*. His whole attention was devoted to the care of the city and state.

The Roman Pantheon contained three classes of gods and goddesses: First, the old Italian divinities, Etruscan, Latin, and Sabine, naturalized and adopted by the state; secondly, the pale abstractions of the understanding, invented by the College of Pontiffs for moral and political purposes; and thirdly, the gods of Greece, imported, with a change of name, by the literary admirers and imitators of Hellas. The genuine deities of the Roman religion were all of the first order. The second class of deities were those manufactured by the pontiffs—almost the only instance in the history of religious affairs of deliberate god-making. The result of this manufacture was not the most favorable. The third class of deities were principally adopted from Greece. Some, like Apollo, were imported, others Hellenized. In their early days the Romans had no statues of their gods; that custom was adopted from Greece.

Besides Jupiter, Juno, and Minerva, the Romans worshiped many others. *Sol*, the sun, a Sabine deity; *Luna*, the moon; *Mater Matuta*, Mother of Day—that is, the dawn; *Tempestates*, the tempests; *Vulcanus* (from *fulgeo*, "to shine"), an old Italian deity, whose temple was in existence B.C. 491; *Fontus*, the god of fountains; *Divus pater Tiberinus*, or Father Tiber, chief river god, etc. There were also gods of human relations: *Vesta*, queen of the hearth and household fire; the *Penates* and *Lares*, who were purely Roman, and were supposed to be the souls of ancestors, which resided in the house and guarded it; the *Genius:* the worship of this god was purely Italian. Each man had his genius, from whom his living power and vital force came.

There were also deities of the human soul: 1. *Mars*—mind, intellect; 2. *Pudicitia*—chastity; 3. *Pietas*, piety, reverence for parents; 4. *Fides*—fidelity; 5. *Concordia*—concord; 6. *Virtus*—courage; 7. *Spes*—hope; 8. *Pallor*—fear; 9. *Voluptas*—pleasure.

Deities of different occupations were common: 1. *Tellus*, the earth; 2. *Saturnus*, Saturn, the god of planting and sowing; 3. *Ops*, goddess of the harvest; 4. *Mars*, originally an agricultural god, dangerous to crops; 5. *Silvanus*, the wood god; 6. *Faunus*, an old Italian deity, the patron of agriculture; 7. *Terminus*, an old Italian deity, the guardian of limits and boundaries; 8. *Ceres*, or goddess of the cereal grasses; 9. *Liber*, god of the vine; 10. *Bona Dea*, the good goddess; 11. *Magna Mater*, or Cybele, a worship introduced early at Rome; 12. *Flora*, who was an original goddess of Italy, presiding over flowers and blossoms; 13. *Vertumnus*, the god of gardens; 14. *Pomona*, goddess of the harvest; 18. *Pales*, a rural god protecting cattle. Besides these the Romans had many other deities, more or less in favor. This classification and arrangement is in most respects copied from Mr. Clarke.

The Roman ceremonial worship was very elaborate, and applied to every part of daily life. They had family feasts in honor of the dead. Between things sacred and profane there was a careful distinction. Festivals were frequent at all seasons of the year. There were five in January, six in February, seven in March, eight in April, four in May, five in June, five in July, five in August, games in September, two feasts in October, and two in December. Religion was prominent everywhere in Rome. All was conducted with system and regularity—prayers and sacrifices as well as daily pursuits. The doctrine of the *opus operatum* was supreme in Roman religion. The intention was not taken into account. The question was, had the thing been done, or the operation performed, according to rule? If not, it must be done over again. Many victims were often killed before priestly etiquette was satisfied.

In law-making and judicial proceedings the augurs were not only consulted, but radical changes were made in obedience to this strange and now seemingly ridiculous authority.

Prayers were made after the manner of our times, but the slightest mistake destroyed all their efficacy. Religious acts were a kind of charm. The supreme god of Rome, in their early history, might with propriety be called law, rule, order, regulation. Organic law was a system of hard, external method. In the oldest Roman time the seat of worship was the Regia, in the Via Sacra, near the Forum. Here was the house of the chief pontiff; here the sacrifices were performed by the Rex Sacrorum. The temple of Vesta stood near. The home of the Latin gods was Palatine Hill. Mr. Clarke says the old worship of Rome was free from idolatry; to which we can hardly assent. Why they should escape from being called idolators we do not see; though Mr. Clarke says that it was because Jupiter, Juno, Janus, Ops, and Vesta were not represented by idols. Roman worship, until about 300 B.C., was administered by certain patrician families; after that, plebeians were allowed to enter the sacred colleges.

Flamens were the priests of particular deities. There were fifteen in all, who held office for life. The Flamen Dialis, or priests of Jupiter, were obliged to conform to much that seems like ridiculous folly. Augury was particularly attended to in Rome. The name came from an old Aryan word, meaning "sight," or "eye," or from the German *auge*. Augurs were really Roman seers. Their business was to look, at midnight, into the starry heavens, and observe the most trifling thing, thereby to gather a correct knowledge of the future. Most of these stories about signs and wonders are being laid aside by well-informed people, even in Rome, where they originated. They were always unsuited to any but the simple and weak-minded. Yet, strange as it may seem, there is a tendency to believe in all kinds of wonder-working, witchcraft, and jugglery. When at prayer, the Romans covered their heads, so that no sound of evil augury might be heard. Many other practices during devotion might be mentioned to show what strange vagaries haunt the human mind.

Funeral solemnities were held with great care and pomp. Festivals to the dead were also celebrated.

The Romans had no exuberance of thought like the Greeks. Therefore Roman thought became Hellenized.

Mr. Clarke well observes: As the old faith died, more ceremonies were added; for, as life goes out, forms come in. As the winter of unbelief lowers the stream of piety, the ice of ritualism accumulates along its banks. About two centuries before Christ, three colleges had been established for the education of pontiffs.. At length the gods were changed by the Greek statuaries into ornaments suited to adorn a rich man's house. Greek myths are connected with the story of Roman deities. Much that has come to us as history about the Romans before Christ, in regard to their religion and practices, their habits of thought and strangeness of taste, is unreasonable and unreliable.

At the time of Cataline's conspiracy, according to Mr. Merrivale, a remarkable debate took place in the Roman Senate. Cæsar held the highest religious office in the state—that of chief pontiff—and opposed putting the conspirators to death, as death ended all suffering; that after death there could be no pain or pleasure. Cato remarked that Cæsar had spoken well, and said he took it that Cæsar regarded as false all that was told about the sufferings hereafter. Sallust reported these speeches and Cicero confirmed them.

The best-informed, the educated, seemed to think it highly proper to keep the common people in order by the use of superstitions. It is easily seen that the masses in Rome, and in some other countries, were in the habit of imbibing all that was offered them. Nothing was so contrary to reason, so absurd or ridiculous, that they would reject it from those in religious authority. To believe what the priests told them was then, as now, a part of religious duty, a saving grace.

Men like Lucretius, who saw the evil tendency of the miserable superstitions of his time, naturally cried out that all religion was priestcraft and an unmitigated evil. Hence he falls into another extreme and denies the gods and the human soul. The Stoics sought a faith based on reason. Philosophy, for those who had minds to grasp it, was much preferable to wild imaginings. Seneca was right when he declared that there was a sacred spirit in every heart. God and matter, he says, are the two principles of all being: God is the active, matter the passive. God is spirit, and all souls are part of this spirit. Reason is the bond which unites God and all other souls—so God dwells in all souls.

Epictetus declared that the wise man would not rely on tradition and hearsay for the belief that Jupiter is the father of gods and men, unless otherwise inwardly convinced in his soul. He also said the philosopher could have no will but that of the deity. The life of Epictetus was characterized by nobleness and purity. Marcus Aurelius Antoninus, according to Niebuhr, was among the most virtuous of mankind; mild and humble. His time was eighty-six years before the birth of Christ. He had really the soul and heart of a Christian.

Seneca believed in a sacred spirit which was in us all, though, like other Stoics, he was a pantheist. He says: "Will you call God the world? You may do so without mistake. For he is all that you see around you." "What is God? The mind of the universe What is God? All that you see, and all that you do not see." Philosophy did not destroy the Christian religion, for the time of which we are now especially speaking was about one century before the birth of Jesus. But it weakened faith in the national gods. The tendency of the old state religion was downward. The old Roman simplicity and purity was lost. Cæsarism, in destroying things generally, destroyed the life of religion. In speaking of religion, the elder Pliny said: It was "the offspring of necessity, weakness, and fear. What God is, if in truth he be anything distinct from the world, is beyond the compass of man's understanding to know. But it is a foolish delusion, which has sprung from human weakness and human pride, to imagine that such an infinite spirit would concern himself with the petty affairs of man."

CHAPTER X.

TEUTONIC AND SCANDINAVIAN RELIGION.

The great Teutonic, or German, division of the Indo-European family entered Europe subsequently to the Keltic tribes, and béfore the Slavic immigration. They occupied a large portion of Northern and Central Europe, from which the Romans were not able to drive them. Of their early history little is known. Their Runic inscriptions show a desire for making records. Cæsar describes them as of great stature, and warlike; worshiping the Sun, Moon, and Fire; having no regard for priests or sacrifices; devoting themselves to hunting and severe labor; chaste, if only for the promotion of health. They were a pastoral rather than an agricultural people. They fought with cavalry, supported by infantry. Their wealth was largely in flocks and herds. Their language was the old Norse, from which are derived the languages of Ireland, the Faroe Isles, Norway, Sweden, and Denmark. Scandinavia was the place where the Teutonic race developed its civilization and religion. It is there we must go to study the German religion, and to find the influence exercised on modern civilization and the present character of Europe.

We do not know how much those old Northern ideas may be still mingled with our ways of thought. The names of their gods are retained in those of our week-days—Tuesday, Wednesday, Thursday, and Friday. From their assemblies came the idea of a Parliament, Congress, and general assemblies. From the North came respect for women, from the South the admiration for them.

Scandinavia proper consists of those regions now occupied by the kingdoms of Denmark, Sweden, and Norway. The great peninsula of Sweden and Norway has the Northern ocean on its west, the Baltic and gulf of Bothnia on its east, and is penetrated everywhere by creeks, friths, and arms of the sea; surrounded with innumerable islands; studded with lakes, and cleft with rivers. It is unrivaled, except by Switzerland, in the sublime and picturesque beauty of its mountains. The peninsula of Denmark is quite free from mountains.

These Scandinavian people, destined to play so conspicuous a part in the world's history, were, as before stated, a branch of the great Indo-European variety. As modern ethnology shows, all the races that inhabit Europe, with a few exceptions, belong to one family, which originated in Central Asia. The closest resemblance may be noticed between the seven linguistic families of Hindustan, Persia, Greece, Rome, Germany, the Kelts, and the Slavi.

Before our era the peninsula of Denmark was called Cimbric Chersonesus, or the Cimbric Peninsula. This name came from the Cimbri, a people who, about one hundred years B.C., almost overthrew the Roman republic. Incredible as it may seem, more than three hundred thousand men, issuing from the peninsula of Denmark and the contiguous regions, poured like a torrent over Gaul and southern Germany. They overthrew in succession four Roman armies, but were finally conquered by the military skill of Marius. After this the Goths, Vandals, and Huns combined and overthrew the Roman empire. In time the Scandinavians appeared again under the name of Northmen, invading and conquering England in the fifth century as Saxons; in the sixth century as Danes; and in the eleventh as Normans, again overrunning England and France. The Scandinavians were formidable on the water; daring and skillful navigators from having been obliged to encounter the rough sea and tempests of the Northern ocean. Their vessels, though able to withstand the roughest sea, were small and slight, and found their way up the rivers of France and England without check from the shallows or rocks. In these apparently fragile craft they discovered Iceland, which was settled by them A.D. 860. They discovered and settled Greenland A.D. 982. In A.D. 1000 they discovered Labrador, Nova Scotia, and Massachusetts Bay. Five hundred years before the discovery of Columbus they built houses on the southern side of Cape Cod. These facts have for some time been established to the satisfaction of European scholars and historians. This remarkable people have furnished a large part of the population of England, by means of the successive conquests of Saxons, Danes, and Normans, driving the Keltic races into the mountainous regions of Wales and North Scotland, where their descendants still remain. They settled also in various parts of Northern Europe, and in Italy and Greece, and have left the familiar stamp of their ideas and habits in all our modern civilization.

The Scandinavian religion has for its central idea a belief in the free struggle of the soul against material obstacles, the freedom of the Divine will in its conflict with the opposing forces of nature. The gods of the Scandinavians were always at war. It was a system of dualism, in which sunshine, summer, and growth were waging perpetual conflict with storm, snow, winter, ocean, and terrestrial fire. So with the people, war was their business, courage their duty, fortitude their virtue. The light and heat gods were their friends; those of darkness and cold their enemies.

For the same reason that the burning heat of summer, Typhon, was the Egyptian Satan, so, in the North, the Jotuns, ice-giants, were the Scandinavian devils.

In the Teutonic race the chief virtue of man was courage; his unpardonable sin, cowardice. "To fight a good fight"—this was the way to Valhalla. Odin sent his choosers to every battle-field to select the brave dead to become his companions in the joys of heaven.

As Iceland was settled from Norway in the ninth century, the ideas and manners of the Teutonic people were preserved there for many hundred years. The Eddas and Sagas are the chief source of our knowledge of this race. In this barren region, where volcanoes with terrible eruptions destroy large portions of the inhabited country in a few days, we find the purest form of Scandinavian life. Their religion is contained in the two Eddas: the poetic, or elder Edda, consisting of thirty-seven poems, first collected and published at the end of the eleventh century; and the younger, or prose Edda, ascribed to the celebrated Snorro Sturleson, born of a distinguished Icelandic family in the twelfth century, who, after leading a turbulent and ambitious life and being twice chosen supreme magistrate, was killed A.D. 1241.

The elder Edda is the fountain of the mythology. It consists of old songs and ballads which have come down from an immemorial past in the mouths of the people, and first collected and committed to writing by Sæmund, a Christian priest of Iceland, in the eleventh century. He was a bard, or Scald, as well as a priest, and one of his own poems, "The Sun-Song," is in his Edda. This word "Edda" means "Great-Grand-Mother," the ancient Mother of Scandinavian knowledge. Or perhaps this name was given to the legends repeated by grandmothers to their grandchildren at the vast firesides of the old farm-houses in Iceland.

The cosmogony of the Scandinavians is simply development, or evolution, combined with a creation. The Hindu, Gnostic, and Platonic theories suppose the visible world to have emanated from God, by a succession of fallings from the most abstract spirit to the most concrete matter. The resemblance between the Greek account of the origin of gods and men and that of the Scandinavians is striking.

Of the creation of the world the Eddas say: "In the dayspring of the ages there was neither seas, nor shore, nor refreshing breeze. There was neither earth below nor heaven above. The whole was only one vast abyss, without herb and without seas. The sun had no palace, the stars no place, the moon no power. After this there was a bright-shining world of flame to the South, and another, a cloudy and dark one, toward the North. Torrents of venom flowed from the last into the abyss, and froze, and filled it full of ice. But the air oozed up through it in icy vapors, which were melted into living drops by a warm breath from the South; and from these came the giant Ymir. From him came a race of wicked giants.... Then arose also, in a mysterious manner, Bor, the father of three sons, Odin, Vili, and Ve, who, after several adventures—having killed the giant Ymir, and made out of his body Heaven and Earth—proceeded to form a man and woman, named Ask and Embla. Chaos having thus disappeared, Odin became the All-Father, creator of gods and men, with Earth for his wife, and the powerful Thor for his eldest son."

As the Scandinavian gods are numerous, no attempt will be made to give all their names or to explain their duties and powers. There are twelve gods in particular in whom they are bound to believe, and to whom divine honors, according to their faith, ought to be rendered. The oldest is Odin, who governs all things; and, although other deities are powerful, they all serve and obey him, as children do their father. Frigga is his wife. She foresees the destinies of men, but never reveals what is to come. For thus, it is said, Odin himself told Loki: "Senseless Loki, why wilt thou pry into futurity? Frigga alone knoweth the destinies of all, though she telleth them never." Again, it is said, in their sacred books, that Thor is the mightiest of all the other gods. He is called Asa-Thor and Auku-Thor, and is the strongest of all gods and men. His realm is Thordvang, and his mansion Bilskirnir, in which are five hundred and forty halls. It is the largest house ever built. Thor has a car drawn by two goats. From his driving about in this car he is called Auku-Thor (Charioteer-Thor). He likewise has three very precious things. The first is a mallet called Mjölnir, which both the Frost and the Mountain giants know to their cost when they see it hurled against them in the air; and no wonder, for it has split many a skull of their fathers and kindred. The second rare thing he possesses is called the belt of strength or prowess (Megingjardir). When he girds this about him, his divine might is doubly augmented. The third, also, is very precious, being his iron gauntlets, which he is obliged to put on whenever he would lay hold of the handle of his mallet. There is no one so wise as to be able to relate all of Thor's marvelous exploits.

The second son of Odin is called Baldur, who is loudly praised by all mankind, as the Scandinavian books say. He is not only fair, but dazzling. Baldur is called the mildest, the wisest, and the most eloquent of all the Æsir, yet his nature is such that the judgment he has pronounced can never be altered. He dwells in the heavenly mansion called Breidablik.

The third god is Njörd, who dwells in the heavenly region called Noatun. His rule is over the winds. He checks the fury of the sea and of fire. He is so wealthy that he can give possessions and treasures to those who call on him for them. Yet Njörd is not of the lineage of the Æsir, for he was born and bred in Vanaheim. But the Vanir gave him as hostage to the Æsir, receiving from them, in his stead, Hœnir, by which means peace was re-established between the Æsir and Vanir. Njörd took to wife Skadi, daughter of the giant Thjassi. She preferred dwelling in the abode formerly belonging to her father, which is situated among the rocky mountains, in the region called Thrymheim, but Njörd loved to reside near the sea. They at last agreed that they should pass together nine nights in Thrymheim, and then three in Noatun. After that, Skadi returned to the rocky mountains and abode in Thrymheim. There, fastening her snow-skates, and taking her bow, she passed her time in the chase of savage beasts, and is called the Ondu goddess, or Ondurdis. Njörd afterward, at his residence at Noatun, had two children, a son named Frey, and a daughter called Freyja, both of them beauteous and mighty. Frey is one of the most celebrated of the gods. He presides over rain, and sunshine, and all the fruits of the earth, and should be invoked in order to obtain good harvests, and also for peace. He dispenses wealth among men. Freyja is the most propitious of the goddesses. Her abode in heaven is called Folkvang. To whatever field of battle she rides, she asserts her right to one-half of the slain; the other half belong to Odin.

Tyr is the most daring and intrepid of all the gods. He dispenses valor in war. Another god is named Bragi, who is celebrated for his wisdom, eloquence, and correct forms of speech. He is skilled in poetry, and the art itself is called, from his name, *Bragi*. His wife is named Iduna. She keeps, in a box, the apples which the gods, when they feel old age approaching, have only to taste to become young again. It is in this way they will be kept in renovated growth until Ragnarök.

One of the gods is Heimdall, called also the White God. He is the son of nine virgins who were sisters, and is a very sacred and powerful deity. He also bears the name of the Gold-toothed, on account of his teeth being of pure gold. His horse is called Gulltopp, and he dwells in Himinbjörg, at the end of Bifröst. He is the warder of the gods, and is therefore placed on the borders of heaven, to prevent the giants from forcing their way over the bridge.

Another god is named Hodur, who is blind, but very strong.

The foregoing are a few of the main points of the Scandinavian mythology, resembling in many respects that of Zoroaster. Each is in reality a dualism, with its good and evil gods, its worlds, or places, of light and of darkness, in opposition to each other. And each has, behind this dualism, a shadow of monotheism, a supreme God, infinite and eternal. In each the evil powers are now held in partial subjection, but are ultimately to be overthrown. Each system speaks of a great conflagration, when all things shall be destroyed, to be followed by the creation of a new earth, more beautiful than the old, to be the abode of purity, peace, and joy. The duty of man in each system is war in the cause of good to put down evil. The religion of Zoroaster shows a higher tone of morality than the Scandinavian. It is more refined, more spiritual. And still the latter has a powerful influence for good over the people who believe in it.

The religious ceremonies of the Scandinavians were simple, and, during their early days, held in the open air. In later times they had temples, some of which were splendid. Besides their priests, the Northern nations had their soothsayers, wonder-workers, magicians. They also believed that by the power of runes the dead could be made to speak. These runes were called Galder. Another kind of magic, mostly practiced by women, was called Seid. It was thought that these were women who possessed the power of raising and allaying storms, and of hardening the body so that a sword would not cut it. Numerous other wonderful powers were said to be possessed by both male and female magicians.

Not many temple remains are found in the far North. In Norway there are permanent remains of the religion of Odin, in the shape of usages and language.

In Sweden, every ninth year, sacrifices were made in the great Temple at Upsal. The king and all the principal citizens were obliged to attend. Nine human beings were sacrificed annually—generally either captives or slaves; but in times of great calamity a king was sometimes taken. Erl Hakon, of Norway, offered to sacrifice his son to obtain the victory over a band of pirates. If this history be true, we see what degrading superstitions were practiced.

As has been before observed, these Northmen were the most formidable among the nations of their time. The sea-kings of Norway, as they were called, appeared before Constantinople in 866, and soon after a body-guard of the emperors of the East was composed of these pirates, who were called the Varangians. After the death of Charlemagne they pillaged and burned the principal cities of France. In 844 a band of these depredators sailed up the Gaudalquiver and attacked Seville, then in possession of the Moors, and took it, after which they fought a battle with Abderahman II.

Mr. Clarke tells us at length the history of this people, who for many centuries were known by the general designation of Northmen. He says the German races endeavored to establish everywhere the feudal system, the essential character of which was this, that it was an army living on a subject people. About the year A.D 1000 these Northern people began to embrace Christianity.

CHAPTER XI.

THE JEWISH RELIGION.

HAVING in a former volume given our views at length in regard to the Old Testament scriptures, we shall here be very brief on the Jewish religion.

Of the geographical features of Palestine we shall speak in a subsequent chapter.

The Jews belonged to what is known as the Semitic race, the only historic rival of the Japhetic (or Aryan) race. It is ethnologically composed of the Assyrians and Babylonians, the Phœnicians, the Hebrews and other Syrian tribes, the Arabs, and the Carthaginians. It is a race which has been famous on land and sea. In the valleys of the Euphrates and Tigris its sons carried all the arts of social life to the highest perfection, and became mighty conquerors and warlike soldiers. This Semitic race is traceable back to Shem, the son of Noah.

Though the Hebrew religion differed widely from

that of the other nations of the same family, they all believed in a supreme God, yet called him by the different names of Ilu, Bel, Set, Hadad, Moloch, Chemosh, Jaoh, El, Adon, Asshur. All believed in subordinate and secondary beings, emanations from the supreme.

Taking the book of Genesis, with the aid of other history, as a guide, we find Abraham standing forth as the leader and father of a great branch of the Semitic race. We ascertain that the belief in monotheism, though general, was not universal. The tendency of the Hebrews was at least occasionally toward idolatry, which at times became strongly marked, during their whole history.

We learn from Adam Smith's Dictionary that the word Hebrew first occurs as given to Abraham by the Canaanites, because he had crossed the Euphrates. The word is also derived from *eber*, "beyond, on the other side." But this is essentially the same as the preceding explanation, since both imply that Abraham and his posterity were called Hebrews by the races east and west of the Euphrates. It would therefore follow that Hebrew was a cis-Euphratian word applied to trans-Euphratian immigrants. The term Israelite was used by the Jews of themselves, and among themselves, and by it they were known to foreigners. The latter name was accepted by the Jews in their external relations, and, even after the general substitution of the word Jew, it still found a place in that marked and special feature of national contradistinction, the language.

All the books of the Old Testament, with the exception of small portions of Daniel, Ezekiel, and Jeremiah, were written in the Hebrew language. The Hebrew and Chaldaic are sisters of the great family of languages to which the name Semitic is usually given, from the real or supposed descent of the people speaking them from the patriarch Shem.

The Jews not only believed in monotheism, but in theophany. The latter faith they carried to a greater extent than any other nation. So much was said about it, and so many cases were cited, that we do not wonder that it became so thoroughly interwoven with their religion. And it was so very handy to have a God of their own, to care for and protect them from all harm; and not only this, but to be with them as well as over them, to direct them when to act and how to act. In his care and protection they had a constant, unwavering faith. More than all, he was *their* God. Not the least intimation is given in their early history that *their* God had any inclination to aid any other people than the Jews, whose enemies he was at all times ready to punish for opposing his people.

The early Hebrews were measurably like those their ancestors left behind them in Chaldea, with about the same faint conceptions of God. At the time they were being freed from their bondage in Egypt they had a strong faith that their particular God appeared to Moses in the burning bush, conversing with him and giving him minute directions in regard to the most trifling thing, no less than in the working of miracles; and was with him in every performance, every movement. This belief had the tendency to make them think they were his only especial favorites on the earth. The outside world were gentiles, heathens.

The first we hear of Abraham (or Abram), so far as Bible history is concerned, is in Genesis, chapters xi and xii:

27. "Now these are the generations of Terah: Terah begat Abram, Nahor, and Haran; and Haran begat Lot.

28. "And Haran died before his father Terah in the land of his nativity, in Ur of the Chaldees.

29. "And Abram and Nahor took them wives: the name of Abram's wife was Sarai; and the name of Nahor's wife, Milcah, the daughter of Haran, the father of Milcah, and the father of Iscah.

30. "But Sarai was barren; she had no child.

31. "And Terah took Abram his son, and Lot the son of Haran his son's son, and Sarai his daughter-in-law, his son Abram's wife; and they went forth with them from Ur of the Chaldees, to go into the land of Canaan; and they came unto Haran, and dwelt there.

32. "And the days of Terah were two hundred and five years: and Terah died in Haran.

1. "Now the Lord had said unto Abram, Get thee out of thy country, and from thy kindred, and from thy father's house, unto a land that I will shew thee:

2. "And I will make of thee a great nation, and I will bless thee, and make thy name great; and thou shalt be a blessing:

3. "And I will bless them that bless thee, and curse him that curseth thee: and in thee shall all families of the earth be blessed."

This promise was remembered, not at particular times and seasons, but was constantly kept in mind. The Hebrews understood that God would do great things for them; and, more than that, that all who refused them aid he would curse. No such promise of care and guardianship was ever given before. God would bless them only, for that is the plain import. Why should they hesitate to butcher the heathens?

4. "So Abram departed, as the Lord had spoken unto him; and Lot went with him: and Abram was seventy and five years old when he departed out of Haran.

5. "And Abram took Sarai his wife, and Lot his brother's son, and all their substance that they had gathered, and the souls that they had gotten in Haran; and they went forth to go into the land of Canaan; and into the land of Canaan they came.

6. "And Abram passed through the land unto the place of Sichem, unto the plain of Moreh. And the Canaanite was then in the land.

9. "And Abram journeyed, going on still toward the south.

10. "And there was a famine in the land: and Abram went down to Egypt to sojourn there; for the famine was grievous in the land."

Canaan did not then seem to be a land flowing with milk and honey, or any good thing to eat; although that was the story Moses told the Israelites some time after.

Abraham's ideas of theology were very crude, or his integrity and sense of moral obligation were of no great account, for he went to Egypt in a state of starvation, and returned in due time wealthy. Chapter xiii:

1. "And Abram went up out of Egypt, he, and his wife, and all that he had, and Lot with him, into the south.

2. "And Abram was very rich in cattle, in silver, and in gold.

3. "And he went on his journeys from the south even to Beth-el, unto the place where his tent had been at the beginning, between Beth-el and Hai;

4. "Unto the place of the altar, which he had made there at the first; and there Abram called on the name of the Lord."

This may be called the beginning of Hebrew worship, for it is the first of which we read. What Abraham said we do not know. He might have asked the Lord to help him, but it is quite certain that he did not entreat him to aid any one beside his party. In Genesis (xiv, 18) mention is made of one who was called Melchizedek, and designated as a priest of the Most High God, but we do not know that this meant the infinite Jehovah, nor do we know from whom this priest derived his authority, or that he was not an idolatrous priest, or of what value his blessing was to Abraham.

In time Abraham began to have visions as well as promises, and to converse with his Lord, or directing spirit, and to doubt the truth of his possessing the whole land, as he had no children, and Sarah, his wife, was barren. In Genesis xv we have the first detailed conversation, in which Abraham is represented as asking questions and the Lord as answering with increased promises, which all who are acquainted with Hebrew history know were never fulfilled. After this interview, the account of which is probably mere legend, Sarah is represented as advising Abraham: "Behold, now, the Lord hath restrained me from bearing; I pray thee, go in unto my maid; it may be that I may obtain children by her."

In looking over the Abrahamic history, we can but conclude that Abraham had many low as well as high traits of character. His moral and religious training was not such as to deter him from doing what the weakest minds must have known to be wrong. Of an infinite spiritual God he had, we may reasonably infer, no clear and distinct ideas, nor of his government of the world. Now, it happens that all the prominent men of whom history speaks had their faults, and it has been said that the more elevated the man, the more glaring his infirmities. It is to the preponderance of good or bad acts that we must look. David and Solomon were great and good men with great faults. For all of them we ought to have charity. Abraham really believed God was making promises to him and to his posterity, and hence he reasoned that if he had no posterity the great and precious promises, of which we hear so much even at this late day, would be of no avail. These promises came to him by the utterance of God. Should any of us in this age hear what we were able to believe was God's voice, the communication could not fail to impress us deeply. Therefore we do not wonder that Abraham "hearkened to the voice of Sarai." To censure him for taking the course he did would be entirely wrong. When a man cannot be influenced by considerations of his own best interest, he is very likely to be reached by including with them those of his posterity, and coupling all with the belief that this posterity will be so numerous that to estimate or number them would be like counting the particles of sand on a vast sea-beach. Thus this precious pair concluded an arrangement by which the great progenitor (that was to be) was to gain a family addition by cohabiting with the bondwoman of his wife.

And so, if the record be true, this good man Abraham—the only one who was at that time considered worthy to converse with God—was led to commit the detestable crime of fornication. Sarah consented to and connived at the commission of this sin of Abraham with Hagar, and encouraged him in it, believing, no doubt, that Abraham had really held all the conversation with the Lord that he pretended to have done, and that by the course she advised aid was given to the Lord (or God) in furtherance of his plans, in the consummation of his purposes.

Genesis xvii tells us that Abraham, believing his race not only to be perpetual, but that they were forever to constitute God's peculiar people, entertained the idea of adopting some outward mark of distinction, by which they might be known in all time to come. Having doubtless learned from some source that older nations had practiced the rite of circumcision, he determined to adopt it to commemorate the covenant with God, by which, according to this and concurrent promises, he was to bless all the families of the earth. At that time this blessing was thought to be partial; but time, enlarged views, and sober reflection have convinced a large portion of the Christian world that God is impartial.

Abraham hears the voice of the Lord again,

commanding that he make a sacrificial offering of his son Isaac. And on account of his preparing to obey the command, he received the name of "faithful." This story, however, has no other foundation than the assertion of Abraham, who was a deeply-interested party. While we do not say that his story is not true, we are not obliged to believe it.

In due time a famine came upon the people of Canaan, and a detailed history is given of its effect on Jacob and his posterity in connection with and on account of it. Some allowance might be made for the direfulness of the story, from the straits to which Jacob and his party were reduced, or else the land must be taken as very poor and the cultivation slovenly. However that may have been, corn was brought from Egypt and their hunger satisfied. The first installment of corn being consumed, the religious feelings of these Israelites, that seemed for a while to be dormant, were aroused, and, before starting his sons for more corn, Jacob asked the blessing, not of the Lord, but of "God Almighty." Whether this invocation was made standing or kneeling made no difference to the Almighty: the prayer came from the innermost soul; was heard and answered. Soon these Israelites—about seventy souls in all—find their way to Egypt, with their flocks and herds, and such other movable things as could be taken along with them. Nothing is said about their being religiously inclined when they started on their journey, or while they were in Egypt; but we may presume they retained some of the ancestral ideas on that subject common to the people of Chaldea, which naturally became mixed with Egyptian ceremonies and modes of worship.

We have all along seen that emigrants take with them and develop in their new homes many of the customs and usages common in their old abode. We have also seen that parts of the great family of nations became detached, and went abroad to form new and younger families, thus continuing to spread over the face of the earth. Mr. Clarke says the different nations inhabiting the region around the Euphrates and Tigris, Syria and Arabia, belonged to one great race, which the Bible genealogies trace back to Shem, the son of Noah. Mr. Ewald believes this region was inhabited by an aboriginal people long before the days of Abraham—a people who were driven out by the Canaanites—but that they were a Semitic people. This view is strengthened by the fact that the languages of all these nations are closely related—almost dialects of a single tongue; the differences between them being but little greater than between the subdivisions of the German group of languages. What has more than anything else contributed to preserve this homogeneity among these tongues is, that they possess little power of growth or development; and, as M. Renan says, they have less lived than lasted.

The Phœnicians are said to have used a language almost identical with that of the Hebrews. This theory has received additional favor within the last few years by the finding of a sarcophagus of Ezmunazar, king of Sidon, dating from the fifth century before Christ. This interesting relic, which is now in the Louvre in Paris, contains thirty sentences of pure Hebrew. Yet, notwithstanding this similarity of languages, the religion of the Hebrews differed widely from that of other nations of the same family; the religion of the Assyrians, Babylonians, Phœnicians, and Carthaginians being quite similar.

The question may be asked, Why did the Hebrews, under Moses and the prophets who came after him, originate a system so widely different? We answer, Because they believed in a God who was above and over nature; who formed no part of a triad; whose worship required purity, whose aim was holiness, its spirit humane.

With some propriety Judaism has been considered a stepping-stone to Christianity. Many of us have even been taught from our childhood to look upon the Old Testament as inspired, and therefore infallible — its every statement and teaching the literal word of God. Mohammed, as much as Moses or Abraham, was a monotheist. He declared for no new God, but for the same only living and true God whom the Hebrews more distinctly saw in the advanced stage of their civilization and progress.

The Old Testament may properly enough be regarded by candid and religious people as truthful Hebrew and Jewish history, and as fairly entitled to be considered sacred as any of the other books we have previously spoken of, and in some respects more; but in few cases is it regarded as infallible; for we do not think the doctrine of plenary inspiration can justly attach to the Old Testament, if it can to the New, by any possible straining. Mr. Clarke says: "If by a special revelation is meant a grand, profound insight, an inspired vision of truth, so deep and so living as to make it a reality like that of the outward world, then we see no better explanation of the monotheism of the Hebrews than this conviction, transmitted from Abraham through father and son, from generation to generation. For the most curious fact about this Jewish people is that every one of them claims to be a child of Abraham."

We have previously shown that, among all the Semitic nations, behind the numerous beings esteemed divine, there was dimly, though distinctly, seen one great infinite God above all. The existence of this superior being was more distinctly revealed to the minds of some than to others, and this difference of perception constituted their distinctive religious characters.

Abraham, like many others, was a faithful, though not an entirely truthful, man; he had his good and bad qualities. That Abraham's immediate ancestors were idolators has never been disputed. Ur of the Chaldees, where his father lived, was in the region now occupied by Kurds, or bands of robbers, in the mountainous region of Armenia, near the mouth of the Tigris. They were a brave, warlike people; skillful archers, fierce in battle. The Chaldeans were noted in these respects in olden times, as they are now, for physical powers and endurance.

Somewhere in the region referred to, the personage designated as Melchizedek is supposed to have resided, exercising the functions of both king and priest, which was quite a common thing then; but, more than this, he was a kind of judge or arbiter among the surrounding tribes, who submitted to his decision as final. Although the Old Testament says nothing of this, the facts are well authenticated. The name given him denotes his official title only: "Melchizedek, king of Salem," signifies the name and residence of the officer, but was not the real name of the person.

The Jewish traveler Wolff states that a custom similar to the above prevails in Mesopotamia at the present day. One sheik is selected on account of his superior probity and piety, and becomes their "king of peace and righteousness." A like custom is also said to prevail among some of the American native tribes.

The God of Abraham was called the Most High, though he was only the family God of Abraham, of his tribe and descendants. Those who belonged to this tribe could not worship any God but their own without becoming outlaws and false to their tribe.

While we may consider it every man's duty to criticise the conduct of his fellow-men, there is a right spirit and a wrong one in which to do this; the motive is what we must take into account. We were placed here to be progressive, as learners; to be seekers after knowledge; to reason, examine, and deduce; to look after causes and mark the effects that follow; and, as our sweetest American poet says, "Be not like dumb, driven cattle." Some are by nature stupid; others have in them latent fires easily set burning. Trying to show that God has attributes which we would think unbecoming in a human being, has a direct tendency to corrupt our own nature. The moment we abate in the least his perfection of character, our great example is, in part at least, lost. No perfect being can be filled with wrath and fury, but rather with feelings of compassion, as he looks upon us frail, erring mortals as we are.

There is a wide difference between examining to find what is right and what is wrong, and looking for weak points, in a pretended anxiety to ease our minds of disagreeable doubts, but in reality to find some excuse for sin, some chance to avoid doing what we feel we ought to do. Let every one, then, examine with proper intent, praying that light may come to him from the one great and only Source of light. The prime object should be to know how to act, how to think. Let this be our earnest study, and let all else be subservient to it.

Now, there are certain portions of our general belief which we gain nothing by trying to question. There is so much more reason in the belief in a governing power, a directing force, which is included in the general term God—if not always known by the same name, in all cases understood as the great, supreme, eternal—that to deny such a being is, in a measure, like denying our own existence. The formation of matter, though going on through countless ages, had its conception, had its beginning. There were inherent laws, which we are not able to explain, so we take the most rational theory. The world has advanced in a knowledge of laws governing matter, and will continue to do so. We find the earth, at a later period, peopled with human beings. There is an attempt in the book of Genesis to explain the manner of the first appearance of mankind; and although this is in a sacred book—probably taken from an old legend, possibly from an older book—we do not consider that this ancient theory is as much to be relied upon as that advanced by Darwin. The latter has some reason in it, the former none. To say that there was no such person as Abraham is to deny a portion of history not alone dependent upon the book of Genesis. And so of various other things that are fully established by concurrent testimony: as the Noachian deluge (or a deluge of some kind); the advent of Moses as a great leader and deliverer, his ability as a wonder-worker and law-giver.

There is no fiction about the existence of such men as Moses and Joshua. Exaggerated stories may have been told of them, as to what they did and said; there has been a tendency of this kind in every age. In cases where the truth would not excite wonder enough, sufficient coloring was added to constitute a marvel. During the whole period of Jewish history, not only that nation, but many other nations, were on the constant watch to see strange sights. Getting up an appetite for wondrous things is not a hard matter. Legerdemain, thaumaturgy, necromancy, and like arts were studied then as a branch of learning, as they are now. To understand the tricks and deceptions these performers practice is not in the power of the unlearned. Moses had one advantage over the Egyptian performers: his people were ready to believe that God helped him in all things; for, believing Moses saw God in the burning bush and talked with him, when Moses essayed to speak for God, who had sent him to be their deliverer, how could they deny his acts or discredit his story? Amid all their seasons of doubt and despondency, the Israelites kept up a faith in God, such as it was; and, notwithstanding their idolatry, they continued to advance from a lower to a higher state.

During what is chronologically denominated the prophetic period in Jewish history, and from four to ten or eleven centuries before the birth of Christ, was a season of great development. The prophets were great lights in the Jewish path. Their magnificent temple at Jerusalem made them conspicuous among other nations. In short, on various accounts, they were the most fitting to become the foster-mother of Christianity. Let us, who, through Jewish descendants, have been blessed with signal displays of God's goodness and mercy, not despise those from whom we sprang. They had light; we have more light: let us glorify God for it. Moses had very marked and contradictory peculiarities. His heart yearned toward his brethren—we might say he loved them; but it was that stern love of the hard, rather than the soft and tender, kind. His impetuous nature often broke out against them on account of improper acts and sins of no small account, but sound discretion soon came to his aid. This was especially noticeable when the golden calf was made by Aaron—an act of profanation which so incensed Moses that his temper assumed such entire control of him that he broke the sacred tables of stone. Had it been impossible to make an exact copy of this divinely-prepared record, his sin would have fully equaled that of forming a golden calf to worship; for there is no reason to think that the people looked upon such an idol as being anything more than a representation of God, without possessing a single attribute of his character, which they so little understood.

Monotheism was the foundation upon which the laws instituted by Moses rested. There are, however, different grades of that belief; some much purer and more consistent than others. Moses was far in advance of the great body of the Hebrew nation. With a mind more susceptible to cultivation and the highest attainments that could be reached, with all the advantage derivable from the sources open to him, Moses was one of the few really great men who have shed a bright luster on the world's historic page. In giving him full credit for all he deserves, we do not think he was the originator of all the laws and ordinances that were given by his sanction. That they were compiled by him, or by some person or persons by his authority, however, there is no doubt.

Moses was not only a man of genius; he was a man of profound learning. The Egyptian sacred books taught the spirituality of God, the immortality of the soul, and a judgment in the future world, beside teaching the arts and sciences. Moses knew all these books could teach, and made good use of his knowledge. Concerning the future life of which the Egyptians had much to say, Moses said nothing. His retribution, individual and national, took place here; though we infer he had an idea that actions would be examined and a balance taken, and this was what most of the nations in early times believed. If he did not believe in immortality, as we now term it, the reason might have been that he could not comprehend it; and it has been the practice of the wisest men that have lived on the earth not to advocate any theory, doctrine, or principle which they did not understand; hence, it was remarked by a most profound scholar, that, while he believed in a God, he could not utter him, could not describe him.

We have before alluded to a previous work, entitled "Scripture Speculations," to which the reader is referred for many additional particulars respecting the Jews and their religion.

PART II.

CHRISTIANITY.

CHAPTER I.

HISTORY AND GEOGRAPHY OF PALESTINE.

In the time of Jesus, called the Christ, the country of Palestine was known under three separate divisions—Judea, Samaria, and Galilee—with boundaries then well defined and established. Judea included the territory of the tribes of Judah, Simeon, Benjamin, and Dan; Samaria, that of Ephraim and the half tribe of Manasseh; and Galilee, the remaining tribes of Issachar, Zebulon, Asher, and Naphtali. Samaria is smaller in extent, but more fertile, than Judea, while Galilee surpasses both in fertility of soil and grandeur of scenery. The whole were under the Romans, and were ruled over by Herod, with nearly the authority of an independent sovereign.

The death of Herod occurred soon after the birth

of Jesus; and his empire was divided by will between his three sons, though not equally. To Archelaus was allotted Judea, with the provinces south and east of Judea, known then as Idumea; to Herod Antipas, Galilee and the southern portion of Peræa, in the region beyond Jordan. That portion of Peræa which Antipas inherited comprised the ancient territories of the children of Ammon and Moab. To Herod Philip was allotted the northern part of Peræa, including all the country east of Jordan which belonged to the half tribe of Manasseh, from Bashan, below the sea of Galilee, to the northern boundary of the country, toward Mount Hermon and Damascus.

Prof. Lyman Coleman, in his Bible Geography, from which we make copious extracts, says this territory comprised the provinces of Gaulonitis, Iturea, and Trachonitis. The first extended from the east side of the sea of Galilee northward nearly or quite to Cæsarea Philippi. East of Gaulonitis was Iturea, which extended further north toward Damascus, but not so far south as the former province.

TRACHONITIS extended from the plain south of Damascus to Bozrah, including the volcanic region of the Lejah, forbidding in appearance, and rent by enormous fissures in the midst of plains extremely fertile. This tetrarchy of Philip was mostly a high tableland, about two thousand five hundred feet above the sealevel, with a mild and salubrious climate; though once populous, it is now a deserted waste, overrun in the summer season with numerous herds of goats and camels, which come up from the great Arabian desert for pasturage.

Archelaus was soon dethroned and banished to Gaul, and in his stead Pontius Pilate was acting as governor at the time of Jesus' ministry and death. The great festivals at Jerusalem were usually attended by Pilate, that order might be better preserved; hence his presence at the time of Christ's trial and crucifixion. Pilate is represented as weak, timid, crafty, and voluptuous.

GALILEE, after the Captivity, was settled by a mixed race of both foreigners and Jews. Two great caravan routes passed through this country: one from the Euphrates, through Damascus to Egypt; the other from the same region to the Mediterranean coast. It was also near the great marts of trade and commerce, Tyre and Zidon. By this admixture of foreigners the Galileans had acquired a strong provincial character and dialect, which made them particularly obnoxious to the Jews. The native language was so corrupted by foreign idioms that a Galilean was easily detected, as in the speech of Peter on the night of Jesus' arrest. For the same reasons, however, the Galileans were less characterized by Jewish bigotry, and were more tolerant toward the new religion, although it was a decided innovation of their own. On this account the greater part of Jesus' public ministry, as well as that of his private life, was passed in Galilee, where he chose his disciples. His working of miracles excited less hostility there than in Jerusalem.

The extreme fertility of Galilee is spoken of by Josephus and many others, who say that within the space of thirty square miles there were fifteen thousand inhabitants in each of the two hundred towns and villages which it contained. Josephus asserts that he raised one hundred thousand volunteers in a short time for the war against the Romans. They were noted for bravery in their country's defense.

SAMARIA was the smallest of the four provinces before mentioned, comprising only the principal part of the territory of the tribes of Ephraim and Manasseh. The people of this province were very bitter toward the Galileans, being composed of the remnants of the revolted tribes. They strenuously opposed the rebuilding of the temple, and erected an altar at Mount Gerizim. The sacred books of the Jews were rejected by them. Their religion was a mixture of Judaism and Paganism. To the Jews the term Samaritan was suggestive of reproach. They accused Jesus of being a Samaritan and having a devil.

JUDEA.—This division included the tribe of Benjamin on the north, and extended south to the boundaries of ancient Palestine; it was larger than either of the preceding divisions, having for a long time been the particular land of the Jews. This hilly region was less fertile than Galilee, though some portions were highly productive. It was the place for holding the great yearly festivals; the seat of their religion; here was the temple. Here the Jew felt most emphatically that he was the seed of Abraham, the favorite of Heaven; he blindly observed the rites of his religion without regard to the purity of its principles, looking down with proud contempt upon all foreigners. These remarks are made with particular reference to the times of Jesus' public ministry and death, when Pontius Pilate was governor of Judea, and reluctantly allowed the Jews to crucify the good man—the same whom Christians now say the Jewish prophets foretold and expected.

NAZARETH.—Considerable portions of the time, for nearly thirty years, Nazareth was the residence of Jesus, and many contend that it was his birthplace. It lies about sixty-five miles north of Jerusalem, between which and Nazareth are Bethel, Shiloh, and Samaria. The plain of Esdraelon stretches from Jordan on the east, thirty miles westward to the Mediterranean, and from the mountains of Samaria to lower Galilee. No mention is made of such a place in the Old Testament, and but little is said of it in the New in connection with Jesus' life and ministry. The people of that city had no faith in him, and gave no credit to the miracles he was said to have performed. Jesus himself tacitly acknowledged that he was born there by saying, when referring to their want of faith, that "a prophet was not without honor save in his own country and among his own kinsfolk."

The valley in which the town of Nazareth is situated is deeply embosomed in the hills of lower Galilee, and is about eight hundred feet above the sea-level. Its entire length is stated to be not more than seven hundred yards, with a breadth of three hundred. On the east, north, and west are abrupt elevations; these are higher on the north than on the west, some of the mountains being five hundred feet in height. The houses are built of stone, which is the material principally used in Palestine. They are generally two stories high, with very thick walls, which are intended to guard, in a measure, against injury from earthquakes. The roofs are flat; hence the mention so often made of going up to and coming down from the housetop. But few buildings in the town are imposing. Living fountains and unfailing wells were not so plenty as to prevent the necessity of carrying water a considerable distance by many families. We find much to corroborate this in both the Old and New Testaments, as in the carrying of water in pitchers and pots by the maidens.

Mr. Brown, in his Encyclopedia, says that Nazareth was the usual residence of Jesus for nearly thirty years, where he lived subject to the commands of Joseph and Mary, and therefore was entitled to be called a Nazarene. Occasionally he preached there. But the meanness of his origin caused him to be looked upon with disfavor by the people. On account of their lack of faith in his power to perform miracles, even after his work in that direction had begun, he left Nazareth, and fixed his abode at Capernaum, where he lived most of the time during the latter part of his life. Nazareth is described by Mr. Brown as situated upon an eminence, on one side of which was a precipice, from whence the people sought to cast Jesus down because he upbraided them for their incredulity. A modern traveler says it is one of the principal towns in the Pashalic of Acre, containing about three thousand inhabitants, about five hundred of whom are Turks, the remainder Christians.

THE WILDERNESS.—This was a desolate region lying between the Mount of Olives, east of Jerusalem, and the plains of Jordan, extending along the river Jordan and the Dead Sea, and is believed to have been the place where John the Baptist began his ministry and the administration of his particular rite; where Jesus was baptized by him, and where he continued for forty days and nights, fasting and praying. The region is bare, bleak, and dreary, covered with yellow rocks and gray sand. No trees are to be seen. A few shrubs are found in the slopes and dells. It is mentioned in Scripture as the wilderness of Judea. Mr. Coleman says the country was not entirely destitute of the means of subsistence, and that the food of John, and doubtless of Jesus, also, was what the desert is known to have afforded — locusts, and wild honey from the rocks. Josephus informs us that he himself subsisted in a similar manner for three years in this wilderness, having had no other food than what grew of its own accord. Against this direct and reliable authority we are asked to believe that Jesus lived in this same locality for the space of forty days without any food, fasting and praying. Tradition, Mr. Coleman says, assigns the place where this long period of fasting was spent, but he does not intimate that it was the place; so we are invited by him to infer that the story, like many others, is only mythical.

MACHÆRUS.—This was the place where the palace of Herod was located. It is to the east of the Dead sea, above the hot springs of Callirrohoe, eight or nine miles from the sea, and about fifteen from the outlet of the Jordan. About fifty years since, its ruins were discovered, still imposing and extensive, on the summit of a lofty rock with precipitous sides, and surrounded by a deep chasm, making it inaccessible, except at one point by a high bridge. Josephus says it could not be easily ascended, ditched about as it was on all sides with valleys, the bottoms of which the eye could hardly reach, and which it was not possible to fill up with earth or pass over; for the valley that cuts it off on the west extends threescore furlongs, and does not end till it reaches the lake Asphaltis. Lieut. Lynch found the walls of this chasm near the hot springs still standing, over one hundred feet apart, lofty and perpendicular; they were composed of red and yellow sandstone, and presented a majestic and imposing appearance. Through this chasm rushes with great velocity a stream of hot water twelve feet wide and ten inches deep. This stream is supplied by many springs, gushing out their heated waters along the line of the chasm for three or four miles. The existence of these hot springs and the volcanic rocks which abound in this region give unmistakable evidence of its volcanic character. John the Baptist was imprisoned and executed at this place.

JACOB'S WELL.—This well was situated a short distance from the foot of Mount Gerizim. It was here that Jesus stopped to rest on his journey from Jerusalem to Shechem, and where he met the Samaritan woman who came there to draw water. This well, which is supposed to have been a work of the patriarch Jacob, was a perpendicular shaft extending into the ground over one hundred feet. It has recently been filled up by the envious Arabs.

CAPERNAUM.—This place was on the northwest shore of Genesareth, fifteen miles northeast of Cana. For a time it was the residence of Jesus. The inhabitants are represented as having been slow to credit the substantial nature of his miracles, on which account he denounced them, and predicted their moral ruin. Its length is thirty stadi, with a breadth of twenty stadi. Dr. Robinson found on the coast, near the northern limits of Gennesar, by a large fountain, the remains of an ancient city, which he supposes to have been Capernaum. Ruins of an ancient city were also discovered by a later traveler, who supposed them to have been the site of Capernaum and Bethsaida. The exact locality, relatively to other places, could not be ascertained. The city is now in ruins, and the place is recognized with difficulty. North of Tiberias, and about midway of the coast, the hills form a kind of triangular plain, of great beauty and fertility, four miles in length and two in breadth, which constitutes the ancient land of Gennesaret. The country now known as Gennesar extends along the lake. It is remarkable both for its fertility and beauty. Trees of all kinds not indigenous to the soil are planted with success; the climate appearing congenial to trees and shrubs of all kinds. Walnut trees, which require a cold climate, and the native palm, olive, and fig trees, requiring heat, are all seen growing, alike thrifty, near each other. Fruits of almost every variety are not only produced in great abundance, but they are, for a comparatively long time, kept from decay. Grapes and figs, and fruits generally, are in plentiful supply for ten months in the year without intermission; some kinds during the entire year.

CHORAZIN is assumed to have been the place now known by the name of Tel-hun; it is about four miles north of Capernaum, at the northwest angle of the lake, at which point are found extensive mines. Several reasons are assigned for assuming this to be the site of Chorazin. Bethsaida was probably north of Capernaum.

SEA OF GALILEE, or TIBERIAS.—This sea is really a wide expanse of the Jordan, running through a deep valley surrounded by mountains rising on the east, near the water's edge, by a steep ascent, to the height of ten or twelve hundred feet. On the west the elevations are broken hills merely. In some places small but very fertile plains extend along the shores of this lake, or sea, which is about twelve miles long and five broad. The waters are pure, and abound with fish. Navigation on this lake is by no means of the safest kind, on account of the strong and sudden gusts of wind which prevail. But few boats are at present found upon it. The rocks are mostly limestone, with a volcanic appearance. On the southwest and southeast shores are several hot springs. This lake is supposed by some to occupy the crater of an extinct volcano. The surface of the lake is calculated to be from six hundred to seven hundred feet below the level of the Mediterranean. Tiberias is the only town on the lake, and is renowned from having been built by Herod. It is now mostly in ruins. In summer the heat is oppressive and the climate unhealthy. Early grapes and vegetables are cultivated with profit for the Damascus market. The landscape has much attractive beauty. To the approaching traveler the view from several points is beautiful in the extreme. Cultivation extends some distance up the mountain sides from the plains along the shore. Few, if any, places made memorable for being the scene of events recorded in the New Testament are regarded with more veneration by devout Christians than this, from its having been hallowed by the presence and ministry of the great author of our salvation.

Around the sea of Galilee is the coast of Magdala, the land of Gennesaret, upon the site of Chorazin, Bethsaida, and Capernaum, where most of Jesus' mighty works were done. Jerusalem and its environs are alone richer in interesting associations than this region.

DECAPOLIS.—This place was the designation of several cities south of the sea of Galilee and easterly of the Jordan, inhabited mostly by pagans. Some of these cities were separated by a considerable distance, yet they all had certain common rights and privileges and mutual affinities. Although under neither the jurisdiction of Herod nor Philip, they were yet subject to the Roman power; hence the security Jesus and his followers enjoyed in this region, and the reason why they so loved to linger in this beautiful retreat, away from the persecuting power which the Jews, with the aid of Herod, were anxious to exercise. Gardara, Scythopolis, Pella, Gerasa, Abila, Capitolias, Canatha and Philadelphia are included in the cities of the Decapolis. The miraculous feeding of the four thousand was near the sea of Galilee.

MAGDALA, the native place of Mary Magdalene, was situated about four miles above Tiberias, at the southern extremity of the fertile plain of Gennesaret.

HERMON.—Mount Hermon is computed to be ten thousand feet in height. The view from its summit, while gazing on the extensive panorama and looking down on the deeply-depressed waters of the sea of Galilee, is grand in the extreme. A narrow valley, plainly traceable, marks the course of the Jordan, on the left of which are the hills of Gilead. Extending far eastward is the land of Bashan; on the north, the parallel ridges of Lebanon. At the eastern base of Anti-Lebanon is a broad plain, through which flow the rivers Abana and Pharpar, near the city of Damascus. The ruins of what are thought to have been a temple and an altar, consisting of huge stones hewn and beveled, apparently of great antiquity, have been discovered on the summit of Mount Hermon.

BETHANY is now a poor village of not more than

twenty families. It is on the southeastern declivity of the Mount of Olives, in a little valley about one mile southeast of Jerusalem.

CALVARY.—Mr. Coleman says that the exact location of this place has never been fixed, and is not likely to be in time to come. Some have thought that it was near the eastern gate of the city, above the road leading to Gethsemane, where the martyr Stephen yielded up his life, and who, like his Divine Master, asked that his executioners might be forgiven.

CÆSAREA.—Frequent mention is made of this place in the Acts of the Apostles. Its location is about thirty-five miles north of Joppa, twenty-five miles south of Mount Carmel, and fifty-five miles northwest of Jerusalem. Herod the Great was the founder. In the building of this city an immense sum was expended. By the aid of a breakwater the harbor was so constructed as to contain and protect a small fleet against the storms that rage on that coast. The work was done with great thoroughness by sinking large stones, which had been brought from a great distance, to the depth of a hundred and twenty feet. In addition to this, Herod added a temple, a theater, and an amphitheater, with many splendid buildings, constituting it the capital of Judea, and adopting it as his own place of residence. After him it became the residence of the Roman governors, under whom it was a large and thriving metropolis, though now in ruins. Extensive foundations, arches, pillars and other building materials cover a large space, all showing plainly that they are the ruins of a city more ancient than that of Herod or Strabo, of which the name and age are alike unknown. These ruins are now the abodes of wild beasts.

JOPPA.—This constitutes the seaport of Jerusalem, and is about thirty miles northwesterly from the city. From the beach the land rises somewhat abruptly, but to no great height, and is supported by successive terraces. Buildings extend quite up to these elevations. The roofs are flat. Late travelers inform us that no inns are to be found there, and that those who visit the place are obliged to seek shelter under their own tents without the city, where they make their meals from fruits, with other ordinary articles of food, of which there are an abundance.

The present Joppa, or some other occupying about the same site, tradition says, existed long before the flood; the devastation of which it is said to have survived, and to have been peopled again by Japhet, the son of Noah, and his posterity. Certain it is that it dates back beyond the remotest period of recorded history. In the long lapse of ages gone by, countless generations of men have lived and passed away, to be seen no more until the great day of accounts when all the dead shall come forth. Thus sweeps on the relentless tide of life. One generation passes, and another succeeds it, like the ocean waves that roll on and on without a stop. The morning dawns, noonday splendor appears, then the storms come, the evening approaches, darkness and death succeed, and our bodies return to the dust from whence they came.

Joppa was a city of the Philistines, and a place of note, more than fifteen hundred years before the birth of Jesus. Materials for constructing both the first and second temples at Jerusalem were obtained through the port of Joppa. Jonah repaired to this port, from near Nazareth, to take ship that he might "flee from the presence of the Lord unto Tarshish," as the Bible account says, though it sounds strangely enough when we stop to consider it. It was in this city that Peter fell into a trance and was induced to yield his belief that the Gospel was for the Jews only, and to begin at once to preach to the Gentiles. Some of the people in Joppa pretend to point out the place where Peter was when he saw the vision.

PHŒNICIA.—This region of country, sometimes called Phenice, extends from the neighborhood of Mount Carmel about one hundred miles to the northward, partly along the Mediterranean coast, and the base or western slope of Mount Lebanon, to near the summit of Lebanon, some distance in the interior. Tyre and Zidon form the central and most populous portion of Phœnicia. Mr. Coleman says: "The mountains towering to the regions of perpetual snow and ice, with the graceful sweep of their waving summits, sloping sides; and mountain dells covered with the deepest verdure adapted to every climate, from Alpine forests to tropical suns; and the ocean, sleeping at its base or lashed into fury by the tempest—form a succession of goodly prospects so grand, so beautiful, so endlessly diversified as to charm the dullest eye, and kindle into poetic fervor the coldest heart. Numberless streams flow down to fertilize the narrow plain of the coast, and open harbors for a boundless commerce." "Phœnicia was settled soon after the Deluge, and became the earliest and most renowned commercial region of antiquity. When the Israelites conquered this country, the coast was occupied by powerful maritime towns, which, though given to the Jews for an inheritance, maintained their independence through all the vicissitudes and aggressions of the Jewish nation."

Paul, the Persecutor.—This man, among others who have figured conspicuously in the world's history by participating, in one way or another, in important events, deserves some mention here. His birth took place about the same time as that of Jesus, in the city of Tarsus, a city of Cilicia. Like other bigoted Pharisees, he was entirely destitute of charity, as well as of all the finer feelings that shine forth with so much beauty to relieve the dark shades found in the life of every human being. He was known extensively as Saul of Tarsus, an unrelenting persecutor of the early

Christians. No cruelty was too great for him to practice, no affliction too severe for him to put upon the humble followers of Jesus. Saul's rage knew no bounds, his vengeance had no limit. As a pattern of religious intolerance he stands out in bold relief. But for his conduct and that of some other persecutors, the world would never have known to what extremes the blindness of fanaticism could lead men. Those meek Christians who suffered from his persecutions were, of all men that ever lived, the most inoffensive. Theirs was the young and early love, pure and trustful. Jewish bigotry could not brook such simple, unostentatious devotion. Saul, therefore, urged on by command and inclination, went forward scattering misery in his path.

Paul, the Apostle of Jesus of Nazareth, is quite another man, shining out in a different character. Like many others who contain under a rough outside covering the really brilliant diamond, Paul in due time shed forth an effulgence that astonished the world. With a banner on which was inscribed "Jesus," Paul was dauntless. His purer nature was brave, in the highest sense of that term: that is, he was brave in a moral sense. Men trained to war are brave in another way. They have no higher conception of human life than its uses: to maintain power, to conquer, to cast down, or to build up. Paul valued his life in so far as it gave him power to do, to act, to accomplish, to shed light, to foster and guard the most estimable of all things—truth. Of all the bright stars of Christianity, Jesus only excepted, Paul stands forth preeminent. As he says, among all the apostles he was not a whit behind the best.

CORINTH.—In wealth and commerce, as well as in luxury and licentiousness, Corinth rivaled Athens; nor was she much inferior in the fine arts. Her situation was on the isthmus of the Peloponnesus, about fifty miles west of Athens, guarded and defended by the lofty Auopolis, which is elevated two thousand feet above the main part of the city. Only a few miserable dwellings now remain where stood the famous city of Corinth. Deep interest is felt by all travelers in its ruins.

ANTIOCH was situated on the Orontes, three hundred miles north of Jerusalem, and twenty miles from the Mediterranean. It was there the disciples of Jesus were first called Christians. Next after Rome and Alexandria, this was the largest city of the Roman empire; and in luxury, licentiousness, and every vice, including idolatry, was not surpassed. The inhabitants numbered from 150,000 to 200,000. The city had four wards, each ward being inclosed by a separate wall, and all within the inclosure of a common wall. For a suburb it had Daphne, celebrated for its forest of laurels and cypress, embracing a circumference of ten miles, forming an impenetrable shade in the heat of summer, and being rendered still more delightful by fountains and numerous streams of pure water. Antioch was celebrated for its refinement in the arts and the cultivation of literature, and for its learned men. Paul was a frequent visitor to this luxurious, dissolute and idolatrous city, and made it for many years the center of his missionary labors. This city suffered greatly in former times by war, pestilence, and earthquakes. History tells us that in the sixth century not less than two hundred and fifty thousand persons were destroyed by an earthquake. Portions of an old Roman wall, from thirty to fifty feet in height, and fifteen feet in thickness, with towers at short intervals, for the occupancy of soldiers, are still standing.

CILICIA formed the port of Antioch; it was sixteen and a half miles distant from it by land, and five miles north of the mouth of the Orontes. The distance from Antioch to this port by water, owing to the winding course of the river, was forty miles. The town was situated on a rocky eminence overlooking the harbor and a large extent of country toward the west. Remains of an inner and outer harbor are easily traced by the large stones by which it is indicated; some of these are twenty feet in length and five or six feet in breadth. The work was in such a state of preservation, says a late traveler, as to admit of being put in order without a very large outlay.

CYPRUS.—This island lies at a distance of about one hundred miles from the Syrian coast, and fifty miles from Cilicia. It is one hundred and forty miles in length, with a breadth of not more than fifty miles at any point. Portions of the surface are remarkably fertile; the northerly part is mountainous, yielding abundant supplies of timber and mineral productions.

SALAMIS is a large city by the seashore, spreading over considerable surface, but thinly populated.

ICONIUM lies ninety miles south of Antioch, in an extended plain in the interior of Asia Minor, surrounded by lofty mountains, some of which are covered with perpetual snow.

In a large portion of this chapter we have followed the plan of that able writer, Mr. Coleman; taking the places in the same order he has given them, and, in a measure, adopting his ideas. As a reason for this, we have only to say that this part of his work, entitled "Text-Book and Atlas of Biblical Geography," is of he most interesting character, ably and truthfully gotten up.

Many other places in the country known as Palestine that are mentioned in the New Testament writings as being in some way connected with the life and mission of Jesus and his apostles might be spoken of, did the limits of this work permit.

CHAPTER II.

INTRODUCTORY TO CHRISTIANITY.

We believe the New Testament to be, in its general scope, correct and truthful; but still we think that, in passing through the hands of incompetent and fallible men, mistakes have, by ignorance or design, been made. The Old Testament, or Jewish history, we intend to regard with that degree of favor to which it is entitled. Through it we can understand the religious views of the people from whom the Christian nations are, in part, at least, descended. It cannot be denied that, with all their faults and bitter opposition to Jesus, the Jews opened the way to Christianity.

Our highest estimate of the New Testament will not come up to its real merits. On the other hand, nothing is gained by claiming for that or anything else more than it deserves. Collectively, it may well be called a priceless gift from God to man, through his partially inspired servants. Only in the voice of nature and providence do we hear God's real utterances. What we learn from man is communicated through earthly mediums, and is liable in passing to be corrupted. Therefore it would be improper to claim that the New Testament Scriptures are all the inspired word of God.

The learned scholar Edward Clodd says: Christians believe that the Bible is the work of men especially helped by God to reveal truths needful for us to know, and which none of us could ever have found out for himself, and that it is free from the errors and defects which every other book contains; which is precisely the case with the Brahmans concerning the Veda, and with the Mussulmans concerning the Koran. He says it is well to inquire whether we have any surer proof of the truth of our book than the Brahman has of his. By neglecting to make this inquiry we obviously shrink from comparing one with the other, lest the truths which our own contains become less dear to us.

Mr. Clodd continues: There are certain facts in regard to the Bible, which are more or less known, but are much overlooked, upon which all proof as to its value must forever rest. The first is, that the Bible was produced like any other book: *men wrote it*. It is made up of a number of works of the most varied kind: history, poem, proverb, prophecy, epistle; written by both learned and unlearned men, many of them unknown to one another, since they lived in different lands, and centuries apart. Each, as he wrote his history or poured forth his song, little thought it would form part of a book destined to be precious to millions of people in future ages; which would be found alike in the cottage of the peasant and in the palace of the king; which would be woven into the literature of the scholar and the talk of the street; which would mingle in all the griefs and cheerfulness of life; blessing us when we are born, rejoicing with us in our prosperity, sympathizing with our mourning, and giving names to half of Christendom—a book, in fine, every portion of which would be regarded as of equal value, whether it be the book of Esther or the Epistle to the Romans. Not only did men write, but men also collected and arranged, its separate books together. The books of the Old Testament were compiled by the Jews; when, or by whom among them, is not known. That ancient people guarded them with jealous care.

The books of the New Testament were chosen from many others, and assumed their present form about the end of the second century after Christ; but men and churches have differed much, and still differ, as to which books should be left out and which admitted. Not only did men write the several books of the Bible and collect them into one volume: *men also translated them* into our own and other tongues, doing in the case of our translation a great and noble work, filled with the richness, simplicity and power of our sweet mother-tongue before cramped and stilted words of Latin origin were introduced into it. Words printed in italics are not in the original manuscripts, but were added by our translators to complete the sense, although they in some cases obscure it.

Now, no one pretends that the men who collected the books together were inspired by God to do it, as in that case they could not leave out the right books and put in the wrong ones; nor is it pretended that the men who translated the Bible were inspired, for then they could not give a wrong meaning to the Greek or Hebrew language in changing it into our own or any other tongue. We must, therefore, pass to the men who wrote the books, and who, it is commonly believed, were inspired by God to write them, and were preserved by him from all error in their work.

Some few believe that every word, every syllable and every letter in the Bible is the direct utterance of God; others, that the writers were kept from error while revealing his will, but not when speaking upon matters of history, science, etc. If any manuscripts ever existed which were the work of men thus helped, we have no true copies of them, since the oldest manuscripts differ in important details. It is said the Bible writers claim to speak the very words of God, and for that reason we should listen to them with obedient hearts and trustful souls.

The Scriptures bear traces of the long years through which they were slowly growing, book by book. In the earlier pages we find legends like those of the nations with whom the Jews were connected by race, or with whom they came in contact. We find there ideas about God that are coarse and degrading. Inspiration dwelt in those earnest ones whose yearnings after the unseen found utterance in Bible, Rig-Veda, Zend-Avesta, Tripataka, King, and Koran; and it dwells in earnest souls to-day wherever the love of truth abides. In whatever written or spoken word or sound of many-voiced nature we find that which speaks to our hearts as true, there is "an inspired truth."

True and vital piety is not confined to any single class of religionists. Faith in God is not only universal with all who claim to be Christians, but is so with nearly every human being. There are many varieties of this faith, growing out of true and false ideas of God's character. Some contend that God sent his son into the world to redeem, purify and save every soul in it, and reconcile all to himself; free them from Adam's sin and all other sin that has been, may or can be committed. Such as these say God is able to save *all*, desires to save *all*, and therefore will save and bring *all* to a higher and holier state, ever to sing praises forever at his right hand. This is called God's impartial grace, or the Abrahamic faith. What a glorious faith, what a sublime contemplation! Think of a whole world saved, redeemed, regenerated, and made happy in God's presence forever! Not a soul lost, and the old Adversary himself destroyed; God conquering the Devil, instead of the Devil's getting the better of God, and holding through all eternity a large portion of the human race in the most awful torments.

There are others who exult in the faith of a vicarious atonement; assuming, first, that Adam and Eve, after being put in the Garden of Eden, with nothing to do but enjoy themselves, pick and eat berries, and other fruit, were foolish enough to eat an apple from a tree which the Lord told them not to touch; by which act they laid themselves and all their posterity liable to the pains of hell forever; from which there was no possible way of escape but for God to reconcile himself to himself, on account of this sin of Adam, by begetting a son and sending him into the world, who, after preaching awhile, must suffer death on the cross at the hands of his own people. By this means, and this only, could God manage to save a single soul. And then those he would save were saved, and all the rest were reprobated, according to John Calvin. Was there ever anything so strange and shocking? And what makes it all the more wonderful is that God should put Adam and Eve into this dangerous garden while he himself conceived and executed this plan of salvation for all men, not for a part.

The more earnestly we inquire, the more our thoughts are centered on the one important fact that there is an Omnipotent Power; that we have a Heaven-Father, a directing force; a great fountain of goodness, of love and purity—the more certain it will appear that there is a a river of God flowing constantly, watering the soul of every one who is athirst and will drink. The sense of gratitude every one should feel for a gift so precious cannot be expressed by words. Scarcely can the most lively emotions of the heart compass it. This broad river is not a fitful stream, rising high at one time and at another dried-up and gone. From it we can draw a full supply every hour, every day. What a cheering thought, what a pleasing theme, upon which we can dwell forever, and which alone should inspire us to press on in the path of duty, in the way of holiness and peace! Following it we shall be led into all truth; but reason is needed as a guide. Without that we are ever unsafe.

The doctrine we contend for, if doctrine it can be called, is the universal brotherhood of man; the doctrine of God's impartial grace, of his sole government and power; that he is the eternal, invisible, incomprehensible, unknown God, full of mercy and kindness, but who will by no means clear the guilty, and yet will not inflict, on any, eternal punishment, which could in no possible way redound to his glory or be productive of the least good to any part of the creatures he has made. If God sent his only son for the benefit of the whole world, to save the whole world, and if he loses one half or more, does he accomplish what he aimed to do? The plan of salvation, as it is called, was for the whole; if it takes any, it must take all. To say that some are not willing to be saved is no argument against the theory we set up—that no one is or can be condemned for the apple-eating transaction. The sins we ourselves commit are what will trouble us; it is from them we want absolution. Adam's sin will never be laid to our charge, if sin he committed when he did not know good from evil. Adam had no information about the vile thing called a snake.

This taking away of sin by propitiatory sacrifice was an old dogma thousands of years before Adam came upon the earth; and though the Bible has much to say about it, there is no way to reconcile it with human jurisprudence; there is neither justice nor reason in one man's suffering for another; and especially is there no sense in the suffering of an infinite God that he might forgive his creatures for the sins they had committed against him. The idea of the advent of Jesus, the theory of his life and teaching, were not that all were condemned for the sin of Adam or any one else, but for sinning against that high and holy law written on every one's heart and conscience. The law of Moses was very important at the time he gave it to the Jews, and is now, and will so remain forever. The same, in substance, was given long before Moses, but it is not the less valuable on that account. All may thank God that they can read his perfect law without a printed book. One edition of it can be read in the heavens above, and one in our hearts. If the Bible, and every other book, were burned, we could easily tell what our duty was. With a desire to do right there would be little danger of going astray.

Religion is homage paid to some being, person, or thing; a reverence for a God or gods; the recognition of God as an object of worship, love, and obedience; any system of faith and worship; piety, sanctity. Religion is a high sense of moral obligation, a spirit of reverence or worship which affects the heart of man with regard to Deity. Piety is shown in the feelings of a child toward a parent, and is the first outcropping of religion in the human soul. Veneration and love come under the head of religion, but more especially when bestowed on the great Father of us all—God. In the truest sense it is the worship of God in such form as seems to each individual most fitting and proper.

With the hope that we shall hereafter be gathered together in a region of peace, of rest, of joy, we should strive to walk uprightly, and every possible effort should be made to live while here such a life that the remembrance of it may be sweet. There can be no comfort in reflecting on a life of sin and folly. We have a battle to fight that begins with our earliest capacity to discriminate between good and evil; and it lasts as long as life lasts. Blessed indeed is he who conquers: he shall eat the hidden manna of the heart. It is wrong to cavil at unimportant things, or object to words and terms which on their face appear inconsistent. While here we see only in part—cannot discern how we can bear the image of God, or how he can be considered a person—and yet it is quite natural we should so speak, when we know as well as we can know anything that God is a spirit, and, though he may be able at times to assume a temporal form, the spirit is what we mean. The Hebrews were strong believers in theophany, and seem to have adhered to that belief partially, if not fully. And this idea helped confirm the Christians in the belief that Jesus as a God could show himself in bodily form after his temporal death.

We are apt to forget how recently in our era was the invention of the printing-press—viz., toward the middle of the fifteenth century—or how much care and labor had to be bestowed on the manuscripts in use twenty centuries ago. And still more difficult is it to realize the great liability to errors in manuscripts. Now, with all the rewriting and careful revising of written pages, they are seldom free from errors. It is not till printing is carefully done, with the most painstaking reading and correction of first and second proofs, that errors are entirely eradicated, if indeed such be the case even then. The vocation of scribe was a responsible and difficult one. Having a perfect copy to work from gave no certainty that the new copy would be an exact transcript of the old.

Labor of all kinds was cheap two thousand years ago, the average compensation being only about a penny a day. But for this cheapness libraries as large as that at Alexandria could not have been so fully supplied. It may be fairly inferred that, from the time of Alexander's conquests, knowledge was more eagerly sought in what was then designated the whole world than it had been for many centuries before. This desire to know all that was valuable rendered the promulgation of new ideas and the spread of new thoughts, as mind became developed, much easier than they would otherwise have been. The liberality displayed by Alexander the Great in his new city, more famous in some respects than Jerusalem itself, opened a wide door for progress.

In order to obtain a proper conception of the value of the writings concerning the life of Jesus, and of the scriptures or books deemed sacred, as we have them now in the New Testament, we must take the foregoing remarks into account.

The term of Jesus' ministry is variously estimated by different writers, but all agree that it was brief; and on that account what he did say could be more easily remembered, though at most imperfectly. Such teachings and conversations were spoken of by those present to others who were not hearers, and by them in turn to others still. In this way the new, and, to most of the people, strange, doctrine became the main topic of conversation. All was treasured up in faithful and honest hearts, and the narrators intended at all times to relate truthfully the different stories that came to them; but if they were not more careful eighteen hundred years ago than people are now in carrying information correctly from mouth to mouth, there might have been great unintentional changes made. Statements are given to us as to what was said by parties interested, when no one else could have been present, which, however improbable they may appear, we are asked to believe not only as true, but as a part of what we must at all times consider to be the express word of God, an infallible record.

The Epistles come to us in a much more authentic shape; they were to be sent abroad, and therefore were written out in full, and the copy was examined by the author. They were written in a language generally conceded to have been Hebraistic Greek, which was chiefly used by the Jews during the first century; and biblical scholars mostly agree that a large part, if not all, of the New Testament, in its earliest and imperfect form, was written during the first and second centuries. Prof. Stowe does not contend for the inspiration of these writings, but for the credibility of the writers as men, and their competency as far as testimony is concerned. This is especially asked for Matthew, Mark, and John, and for Luke as a compiler (for that is all he is claimed to be). Certainly they gave proof of simplicity as well as of honesty, inasmuch as their own faults, as well as those of their brethren, are spoken of without reserve.

CHAPTER III.

CHRONOLOGY, BIRTH OF JESUS, AND OUR ERA.

Before entering upon a general consideration of the New Testament and of the Christian religion, something in relation to the birth of Jesus seems to be in order. A few dates are given, though it is not at all certain that they are correct. And this fact should create no surprise Many events in our age of observation, notwithstanding the aid afforded by printing and stenography, will be fixed with difficulty a thousand years hence. That, not very long after the birth of Jesus, the time of that event should have been fixed from four to six years later than it ought to have been, is not, indeed, strange. If the date which was accepted is so far from the truth, as we are now sure it is, what can we think of other dates of much less importance ? The conclusion, therefore, is that they are mostly unreliable.

The general Christian belief tnat the God of heaven

and earth caused a sudden appearance of a star to guide a few travelers to see what they had no interest in seeing, except to gratify a mere idle curiosity, is of all things the most improbable. What interest could the Persians have had in the rising Jewish king? Latterly, the best astronomers favor the idea that the wonderful star of Bethlehem was none other than a conjunction of the planets Jupiter and Saturn. If this is admitted, it will relieve the passage in Scripture referring to this phenomenon of some of the obscurity which surrounds it. We learn from the great prince of astronomers, Kepler, that a conjunction of Jupiter, Saturn and Mars took place in 1604, by which he was led to think that the true year of Jesus' birth was discovered. Making his calculations with great care and accuracy, he found that Jupiter and Saturn were in conjunction, in the constellation of the Fishes (a fish was the astronomical symbol of Judea), in the latter half of the year of Rome 747, and were joined by Mars in 748. Here, then, he fixed the first figure in the date of our era, and here he found the appearance in the heavens which induced the Magi to undertake their journey.

Others have adopted this view, freed it from astrological impurities, and shown its trustworthiness and applicability to the case under consideration. Jupiter and Saturn, it appears, came together for the first time May 10th, in the twentieth degree of the constellation of the Fishes. They then stood, before sunrise, in the eastern part of the heavens, and were so seen by the Magi. Jupiter then passed by Saturn, toward the north. About the middle of September they were, near midnight, both in opposition to the sun; Saturn in the thirteenth degree, Jupiter in the fifteenth, being distant from each other about a degree and a half. They then drew nearer. On October 27th there was a second conjunction, in the sixteenth degree, and on November 12th a third conjunction took place, in the fifteenth degree of the same constellation. In the last two conjunctions the planets were not more than a degree apart, so that to the unassisted eye the rays of one planet were mingled with those of the other. The two planets passed each other three times, came very near together, and showed themselves all night long, for months, in conjunction with each other, as if they would never separate again. Their first union in the east awakened the interest of the Magi (as we may readily imagine), who started without delay for Judea (the fish-land). When they reached Jerusalem, the two planets were once more blended together. Then, in the evening, they stood in the southern part of the sky, pointing with their united rays to Bethlehem. Judging from this, the conclusion is that Jesus was born in the latter part of the year of Rome 747, or six years before the common era.

Thus we see, if Kepler be correct (and the position

has never been challenged), that out of a natural phenomenon in the heavens, as natural as the sun rising, a marvelous story has been told for these eighteen hundred years, and a notable miracle vouched for. What is the use of contending for this as a miracle? If it were such, no aid would be afforded in fixing a date in which the whole Christian world have an interest.

Whether Jesus was born two years earlier or later, whether the Magi traveled one or two hundred miles to solve an astronomical phenomenon, adds nothing to, and takes away nothing from, the importance of his advent—does not prove that he was a God, or the son of a God—and in reality is of no consequence. Nor did his being born in a manger add to or diminish his real characteristics. This story, as we find it in the New Testament, gained credit early in the history of the Church, and helped to push the best of all religions forward. The great body of the people required something to startle them. Allowing this position to be correct, at the end of the year A.D. 1, as we now reckon it, Jesus must have been six years old, and, in all cases of the ordinary date, before or at the time of Jesus' death, six years must be added to show his age.

To introduce something at this point in relation to the calendar will not, we trust, be thought out of place.

The scheme of three years of 365 days each and a fourth of 366 was invented for Julius Cæsar by Sosigenes of Alexandria, B.C. 45, and lasted without alteration until the time of Pope Gregory XIII. It was then found that the real equinox fell ten days before the nominal one of March 21, and that Easter was four days wrong, from the error in the Metonic cycle. Ten days were accordingly struck out of the calendar—between the 4th and 15th of October, 1572—and, to prevent a like error in the future, it was decreed that every 100th year should lose its leap-day, except those divisible by 400.

This is the Gregorian, or new style, which was invented by Clavius, a Jesuit, and adopted in all the Roman Catholic countries before the end of 1572, and by the Protestant German states in 1700, but not by England till 1752, in Sweden the year after, and not yet by Russia, nor by the Greek Church. In 1751 the English Parliament enacted that the day after September 2, 1752, should be September 14; thus dropping eleven days, as we were one day further wrong by allowing 1700 to be a leap-year. Before this change of style the year legally began March 25.

A year of the average length of $365\frac{1}{4}$ days is called a Julian year; but the years of the Julian era were reckoned from the first of January, 4713 B.C.; so 1872 was 6585 of the Julian era. Our present era begins four to six years after the birth of Jesus, usually called Christ.

Clavius suggested that it would be better to make Easter always the Sunday after march 21, rather than to let all the great festivals and holidays, except Christmas, wander over five weeks of the calendar in the vain attempt to follow the moon.

Archbishop Usher, a man of profound learning and great application, who flourished during the first half of the seventeenth century, published his work on Chronology, which was at the time thought to be quite reliable, and has therefore been adopted by many biblical writers up to this nineteenth century. He fixes the time of Jesus' birth at four years before the beginning of our era.

Alvan Bond's edition of Kitto's "Bible History" has much in it of correct information, and fixes the date of the most important events of the first century of our era—a few of which will be given here.

To get the true date, four to six years must in each case be added to what we call A.D.

	B.C.
Augustus declared Emperor by the Roman Senate....	27
The Septuagint in general use among the Jews......	27
Birth of John the Baptist............................	5
Birth of Jesus. Arrival of the Magi. Flight to Egypt	4
Murder of the male infants at Bethlehem by Herod.	3
Archelaus succeeds his father in Judea...............	2
	A.D.
Jesus accompanies Joseph and Mary to Jerusalem....	8
Herod Antipas founds the city of Tiberias..........	10

The Temple polluted by Samaritans	14
John the Baptist begins to preach	26
Jesus baptized	27
Jesus' first appearance in the Temple	27
Imprisonment of John the Baptist	27
Jesus' second visit to Jerusalem	27
Commencement of Jesus' public ministry	27
Second Passover. Third Passover	28
Transfiguration of Jesus. Feast of Dedication	29
Last Supper. Fourth Passover. Crucifixion	30
Ascension. Conversion of five thousand	30
The effort to suppress Christianity	30
Community of goods. Death of Ananias and Sapphira.	30
Second attempt to suppress Christianity	33
Martyrdom of Stephen. Death of Tiberius	37
Saul converted. Josephus born at Jerusalem	37
Saul retires to Arabia, and returns to Damascus	38
Saul visits Jerusalem and Tarsus	40
Herod Agrippa king of all Palestine	41 to 44
Disciples first called Christians, at Antioch	42
Britain invaded by the Romans	43
Death of Herod Agrippa	43
Judea a distinct Roman province	44
Epistle of James	44
Epistle of Peter	48
London founded	49
Council of Apostles and Elders	50
Paul arrives at Troas	51
Edict of Claudius against the Jews	51
Paul at Athens; at Corinth also	52
Paul's first Epistle to the Thessalonians	53
Second Epistle to the Thessalonians	53
Paul's Epistle to the Gallatians	53
First Epistle to the Corinthians	56
Epistle to Titus. Paul's visit to Crete	56

First Epistle to Timothy	56
Second Epistle to the Corinthians	57
Paul's Epistle to the Romans	58
Epistle to the Ephesians and Colossians	61
Second Epistle to Timothy. Epistle to Philemon	61
Mark martyred. Epistle to the Philippians	62
London burned, and sixty thousand perished	62
Rome burned by order of Nero	64
Second Epistle of Peter	65
St. Paul beheaded at Rome	67
Jerusalem destroyed by Titus	70
Titus demolishes the Temple to its foundation	74
Vespasian dies, and is succeeded by Titus	79
Coliseum of Vespasian completed	80
John exiled to Patmos	95
John writes the Apocalypse	96
Death of John, about	100

CHAPTER IV.

THE NEW TESTAMENT.

OF all the histories that have come down to us, none equals in interest the New Testament account of Christianity, commencing with the Synoptical Gospels, giving us an account of Jesus of Nazareth, confessedly the most wonderful personage that ever appeared among the children of men. Therefore, a careful study of this book becomes an imperative duty. In attending to this duty let us endeavor to do it honestly, thoughtfully, and prayerfully, with no effort to make more or less of it than we ought, using the best of our reason and judgment, considering well the time in which it was written, and all the attendant circumstances.

As Prof. Stowe remarks, we must take the Bible as it is, just as we would any other book, with minds free from all bias or prejudice for or against it; with a view, not to disparage, carp at, or find fault with it, but with an endeavor to benefit our own souls, to warm our hearts, enliven our understanding, and help us to press on heavenward. We must not pass judgment hastily, but examine patiently, remembering that what we read concerns life and death, our well-being in this world and in the world to come.

Prof. Stowe says that it was about two hundred years from the death of the apostle John to the collation of the first full manuscripts we have of the whole New Testament, though we have fragments dating back nearly to the time of John. The exact date of most, if not of all, old manuscripts is fixed with difficulty. The letters used in the most ancient are called *uncial*, from the Latin, meaning inch; as if the letters were originally an inch long: but this letter fell into disuse before the tenth century, and the cursive was generally adopted, which resembles the type in which Greek books have generally been printed. The manuscripts of the Greek Testament are all in book form; none of them in the Oriental form of rolls. Very few of them contain the whole of the New Testament. The total number of these manuscripts is estimated at one thousand. Those referring to the Gospels are at least four hundred, of which twenty-seven are uncial, and at least one thousand years old. Of Paul's Epistles, nine of the two hundred and fifty-five manuscripts are uncial; of the Acts, eight of the two hundred are uncial; of the Apocalypse, three of the ninety-one are uncial. In all, we have nine hundred and seventy-two entire manuscripts of the different volumes of the New Testament, of which forty-seven are more than one thousand years old. Several books of the New Testament are oftener in manuscripts entirely independent of the other books. Some books were more generally copied and more frequently used than others.

The Latin term generally used to designate manuscript books is the word *codex*. The Codex Alexandrinus is so called from the place of its origin, the city of Alexandria, in Egypt. In the year 1628, Cyril Lucan, Patriarch of Constantinople, who for some time held the same office at Alexandria, sent, by Sir Thomas Roe, the English embassador, a magnificent Greek manuscript of the whole Bible, as a present, to King Charles I of England. This book, which is now carefully preserved in the British Museum, is said to have been written by a noble Egyptian lady and martyr, by the name of Thula, about 325 to 350 A.D.

Mr. Stowe says the Codex Vaticanus is highly valued, and takes its name from the library in which it was kept—the Vatican, at Rome, which was established by Pope Nicholas V, about 1450 A.D. It is probably somewhat older than the Alexandrian, and originally contained the whole of the Greek Bible, though many of its leaves are lost.

This New Testament is now a quarto volume, bound in red morocco, ten and a half inches long, ten inches broad, and four inches thick, written on very fine vellum, in a small, elegant, square letter, three columns on a page; so that, on opening the volume anywhere, six columns of well-formed letters are presented to the eye. For the most part, each column contains forty-two lines, and each line sixteen or eighteen letters. Its value as an authority is very high, and before the beginning of the present century it had been three times collated for printed editions of the Greek Testament. In the Vatican it is kept with great care and childish reverence. In 1843 the great scholar Tischendorf went to Rome expressly to examine it. He found it carefully locked up in a drawer of the library and no easy matter to obtain even a sight of it. After considerable delay he was allowed to examine it two separate days, for three hours each day, after being carefully searched, to prevent the possibility of his having about him pen, ink, or paper, for fear that he might take notes. During every moment of the time, also, he was carefully watched. In 1844 Edward de Muralt was allowed to examine it on three different days, three hours each day, but with the same precautions and under the same jealous watchfulness. In 1855 Dr. Tregelles went from England to Rome, with a letter of recommendation from Cardinal Wiseman, for the express purpose of examining the manuscript; but, though he was allowed to see it, he was effectually hindered from transcribing a syllable. In the year 1828 an edition of it was undertaken by Angelo Mai, afterward Cardinal, a learned and able man, at the instance of Pope Leo XII. The work was published three years after the Cardinal's death, which happened in 1857, but in so slovenly a manner that the Papists were ashamed of it; and in 1859 Charles Vircellone, a monk of St. Barnabas, and a friend of the Cardinal, published a revised edition, which was a little better, but still below the scholarship of the age; and, worst of all, it was not an exact reprint of the Vatican manuscript. It was very inaccurate, containing hundreds of errors, very many of which Tischendorf corrected in a work published by him in 1867, entitled the Novum Testamentum Vaticanum. Numerous further corrections were made in the two following years by others.

In time we shall doubtless get a perfectly correct reprint of the original; as, since the above attempts were made for a careful examination, the restrictions have been greatly modified, and may be still further. Great efforts are being made to produce a more perfect edition of the New Testament from all the materials now obtainable; and as there has been in time past, so there is now, among the highly educated who are not warped by prejudice, swayed by dogmatism, or blinded by creeds, a desire for a faithful and complete version of every word and sentence.

The Sinaitic Codex was discovered in 1844, by

Dr. Tischendorf, while he was traveling, under the patronage of the king of Saxony, for research in biblical science. And at the convent of St. Catherine, on Mount Sinai, from a basket of rubbish which was intended for the purpose of kindling fires, he picked out forty-three beautiful parchment leaves, belonging to the manuscript of the Septuagint, hitherto unknown. On his return to Europe they were published. On the 4th of February, 1859, he visited the convent a third time, when he obtained from a monk the other leaves, loosely tied in a napkin. To his great delight he found here not only the remaining portions of the Septuagint, but also the entire New Testament, with the Epistle of Barnabas and portions of the Shepherd of Hermas: the most complete, the most ancient, the best manuscript copy of the entire New Testament that has yet been discovered. After much persuasion, he was allowed to take the manuscript with him to Cairo in Egypt, and finally to St. Petersburg in Europe, as a present to the Russian emperor Alexander II, the great patron of the Greek Church throughout the world.

Various other old manuscripts which are entitled to consideration, and of which Prof. Stowe speaks somewhat at length, might be mentioned.

Constantine Tischendorf, a world-renowned Christian divine and biblical scholar, in his introduction to a work of great labor—comparing the authorized version of the New Testament with the three most celebrated manuscripts of the Greek text—says: "To place the glorious works which adorn the literature of England and America within reach of the readers of other countries was the aim of the noble originator of the 'Tauchnitz Collection.'" And in selecting the word of God, as recorded by the apostles, for the thousandth volume of the series, he has chosen the most appropriate crown for such a structure of human genius.

The English nation, as early as the reign of Queen Elizabeth, had an authorized translation, under the guidance of Archbishop Parker, which, half a century later, in the year 1611, was revised, at the command of James I, by a body of learned divines, and became the present "Authorized Version." It is the New Testament portion of this version which forms the thousandth volume of the "Tauchnitz Collection." Founded as it was on the Greek text at that time, accepted by Protestant theologians, and translated with scholarship and conscientious care, this version of the New Testament has deservedly become an object of great reverence, and a valuable treasure to the English Church. The German Church alone possesses, in Luther's New Testament, a treasure of similar value.

But the Greek text of the apostolic writings has, since its origin, suffered many a mischance at the hands of those who have used and studied it; the mere process of constant copying and recopying alone having given rise to many alterations. The authorized version, like Luther's, was made from Greek text, which Erasmus in 1516, and Robert Stephens in 1550, had formed from manuscripts of later date than the tenth century. Whether these manuscripts were thoroughly trustworthy—in other words, whether they exhibited the apostolic original as perfectly as possible—has long been a matter of diligent and learned investigation. Since the sixteenth century Greek manuscripts have been discovered of far greater antiquity than those of Erasmus and Stephens, as well as others in Latin, Syriac, Coptic, and Gothic, into which languages the sacred text was translated between the second and fourth centuries, while in the works of the Fathers, from the second century downward, many quotations from the New Testament have been found and compared. The result has been that, while, on the one hand, scholars have become aware that the text of Erasmus and Stephens was in use in the Byzantine Church long before the tenth century, on the other hand, they have discovered thousands of readings which had escaped the notice of those editors. The question then arose, Which reading in each case most correctly represented what the apostles had written? By no means an easy question, since the variations in the documents are very ancient. Scholars are divided as to the readings which most exactly convey the word of God. But one thing is agreed upon by the majority of those who understand the subject, namely: that the older copies approach the original text more nearly than the later ones.

The Alexandrinus, the Vaticanus, and the Sinaitic manuscripts undoubtedly stand at the head of all the ancient copies of the New Testament now known, and it is by their standard that both the early editions of the Greek text and the modern versions are to be compared and corrected. The effect of comparing the common English text with the most ancient authorities will as often disclose agreement as disagreement. The three great manuscripts differ from each other both in age and authority, and no one of them can be said to stand so high that its sole verdict is sufficient to silence all contradiction. But to treat such ancient authorities with neglect would be sheer arrogance. It may be urged that all criticism is opposed to true reverence, and that, by thus exposing the inaccuracies of the English version, we shall bring discredit upon a work which has been for centuries the object of love and veneration, both in public and private. "But those who stigmatize the process of scientific criticism and test, which we propose," says Tischendorf, "are greatly mistaken. To us," he continues, "the most reverential course appears to be to accept nothing as the word of God which is not proved to be so by the evidence of the oldest, and therefore the most certain, witness that he has put into our hands." He says that, with this view and this intention, his time has been occupied for thirty years in searching the libraries of Europe, the obscurest convents of the East, both in Africa and Asia, for the most ancient manuscripts of the Bible, and in correcting and arranging such documents for the use of the present age and for posterity. In agreement with other biblical writers, he says that the first manuscript which came into the possession of Europe was the Vatican Codex. Whence it was acquired by the Vatican library is not known, but it appears in the first catalogue of that collection, which dates from the year 1475. Of the New Testament it contains the four Gospels, the Acts, the seven Catholic Epistles, nine of the Pauline Epistles, and the Epistle to the Hebrews as far as chap. ix, 14, from which verse to the end of the New Testament it is deficient, so that not only the last chapters of the Hebrews, but the Epistles to Timothy, Titus, and Philemon, as well as the Revelations, are missing. The peculiarities of the writing, the arrangement of the manuscript, and the character of the text—especially very remarkable readings—all combine to place the execution of this Codex at about the middle of the fourth century.

In the Alexandrian Codex the following passages of the New Testament are wanting: Matt. i, 1, to xxv, 6; John vi, 50, to viii, 52; II Cor. iv, 13, to xii, 6. It contains the Epistles of Clemens and Romanus (the only known copy), a letter of Athanasius, and a treatise of Eusebius upon the Psalms. Probably written about the middle of the fifth century.

For age and extent the Sinaitic Codex stands first, the Vaticanic second, the Alexandrian third.

Tischendorf deems it remarkable that the ordinary conclusion of the Gospel of St. Mark (xvi, 9–20) is found in more than five hundred Greek manuscripts, in the whole of the Syriac and Coptic, and most of the Latin, manuscripts, and even in the Gothic version. But by Eusebius and Jerome (the former of whom died in 340) it is stated expressly that these verses were not in the trustworthy copies used by either Marcion (A. D. 130–140) or Origen (185–254). Basil the Great, who died in 379, also states that they were wanting in the old manuscripts of his time; and the omission agrees well with the encyclical character of the epistle. At the present day the words are found in many ancient Greek manuscripts; and in all the ancient versions, even to Jerome, no copy was known that did not contain them. Now, however, the Sinaitic and Vaticanic manuscripts alone agree with Basil, Origen, and Marcion.

Origen states, and his statement is confirmed by various quotations before his time, that in John i, 4, some copies contained: " In him *is* life," instead of " In him *was* life"; whereas that reading is only found in the Sinaitic manuscript, and in the famous Cambridge copy of the Gospels known as the Codex Berzæ, although it is shown in most copies of the Italic version, and in the old Syriac and Coptic versions.

Jerome says, in reference to Matt. xiii, 35, that Porphyry, the opponent of Christianity in the third century, accused the evangelist of having said, "which was spoken by the prophet Isaiah"—a reading which is also exhibited by an authority of the second century. To which Jerome adds that well-informed people had long before removed the name of Isaiah from the passage. Now, of all our manuscripts of a thousand years old, not one exhibits the name of Isaiah except the Sinaitic. The passage, John xiii, 10, is cited six times by Origen; but the Sinaitic manuscript and a few copies of the old Italic version alone give it as Origen does, namely: "He that is washed needeth not to wash, but is clean every whit." John vi, 51: the Sinaitic alone, among all the Greek manuscripts, has no doubt the right reading, namely: "If any man eat of my bread, he shall live forever. The bread which I will give for the life of the world is my flesh" —which is confirmed by Tertullian, at the end of the second century.

We could cite hundreds of instances in regard to disputed texts, and might with some propriety say that there is not a scholar in the world who can unequivocally claim to understand and can give exactly the meaning and wording of the New Testament. All enthusiastic believers do not care whether they have the correct reading or not. If they read life where it ought to be death, what concern is it to them? They think they know enough, whether that be much or little. Not one layman in a thousand would stop to look at what is known as the Scholar's Edition of the New Testament. And it may be that when the new edition of the Bible appears there will be many to doubt it, and think it a trap to endanger their souls. They enjoyed religion under the old book—that blessed book! Suppose, in dropping the old for the new, their souls should be lost, how sad it would be! God pity all those whose only ideal, perchance, is a creed! The class of readers is large who think they have all the light they need; who are not only in darkness, but in gross darkness. I beg of such not to touch Tischendorf's book. Why should they? Is not the Bible the word of God—an infallible boon? How is it possible that the God of all things, or any of his agents, has written anything wrong? If they were inspired by God, why speak about mistakes!

Tischendorf says that many obvious blunders which are found in the manuscripts are passed over in silence. Others are so glaringly wrong that every honest man must feel it an imperative duty to point them out—a duty he owes to the cause of truth and the God of truth.

Very shortly after the books of the New Testament were written, and before they were protected by Church authority, there is great probability that alterations and additions were made to them. Many of the variations are obviously only matters of pronunciation; others arise from the Greek idiom, and are not noticed.

However reluctantly, we must come to the conclusion, in justice to our own souls and to the cause of truth, that it is not a perfect book, in any fair sense of that term; neither is all of it "the word of God," an infallible record, in strict agreement with the three great manuscripts; and, taking them and the English Bible, no two of them agree in the essential parts, to say nothing of the non-essential. Notwithstanding all this, there is enough about which there is no doubt expressed by the severest critics to lead us into all truth when honestly considered. In conclusion, Tischendorf says: "No single work of ancient Greek classical literature can command three such original witnesses, as the Sinaitic, Vaticanic and Alexandrian manuscripts, to the integrity and accuracy of its text. That they are available in the case of a book which is at once the most sacred and the most important in the world is surely matter of deep thankfulness to God."

CHAPTER V.

EVANGELICAL AND APOSTOLICAL AUTHORITY.

In the present, King James', edition of the New Testament we have the writings ascribed to Matthew set before us as first of the Synoptical Gospels. This evangelist, who was a Galilean Jew, by the Hebrew name of Levi, when called to an apostleship filled the office of tax-gatherer by authority of the Roman government. Like all other provincial subjects, the Jews were required to aid in supporting the government of Rome by the payment of whatever tax was imposed upon them. The Jews did not dare to resist the collection of these taxes, although, as the descendants of Abraham, they were naturally reluctant to submit to the Roman yoke, and were especially averse to burdensome taxation. Matthew, as one of the instruments in the collection of these taxes, was, of course, exceedingly unpopular. We infer that he had authority to collect in a somewhat extended district; such rights were sometimes sold for considerable portions of country, and were resold in smaller parcels, at a profit. However this may have been, Matthew left his official duties and enlisted in the service of the young reformer, Jesus of Nazareth.

We shall speak of Matthew's writings, and those of the other evangelists, with that freedom and honesty of purpose which we feel that our duty demands. For these Synoptical Gospels we have all the respect and veneration due to records of such great antiquity.

That we have now a perfect idea of all that took place during the early history of Christianity is not presumable. Looking back nineteen centuries, and comprehending as best we may the important occurrences of that time—the taking root and spreading of a new religion, under the lead of a young man of very limited education, and of poor and illiterate parentage, who had spent his time working at the carpenter's trade—it is hardly possible that the results achieved by such a person, with the aid of a few humble fishermen, could have anything more than a limited history, and that at first unavoidably fragmentary and incorrect. Something in the shape of records was kept, and, in a measure, preserved, but without the slightest expectation, as we boldly assert, that the then infant sect was destined to develop into its present extent and importance.

Everything must wait for its growth, which requires time. The Christian religion, as we have it to-day, is anything but what it was during the early centuries. Hebrew history did not attain to its present orderly arrangement until it was revised and arranged by that able writer Ezra. How much of the early purity and true faith of Christianity have been lost by constant additions, alterations and omissions of the original records, no one can tell. People of the second and third centuries would hardly recognize in our present the Christianity of their time.

As with Matthew's gospel so it may have been with the other Synoptical writings, and with the Acts, whoever their author may have been. They grew up from the crudest state. Many writers have labored to find the particular dates at which the books of the New Testament were written. By some the date of the first rude fragments of Matthew's gospel is fixed as early as A.D. 40 to 45; by others, 60 to 65. Of late, many of the best biblical scholars bring the time down some centuries later. The order in which the books are found in our present popular version is not considered to be in accordance with the time in which the books were written—beginning with Matthew, and so on. Matthew, being a conspicuous actor and a man of business, would naturally keep a crude record of events. As early as A.D. 40 many of these had been brought into something like a formal shape, and were rewritten by him some twenty years after. From

A.D. 70 to 100 other writings were collected and put in a better state for preservation. This collecting and revising, we have good reason to believe, was continued up to about the close of the tenth century, or later.

Matthew's gospel, in its early, imperfect form, was written for the Jewish Christians in Palestine. Such arguments were advanced as its author thought would have the most weight with the Jews in proof of Jesus' Messiahship. It is quite certain that this early writing of Matthew's was in the Hebrew language—that is, the Syro-Chaldaic, which was then spoken by the Jews in their own land. This in the New Testament is called Hebrew, though it is not the pure Hebrew. It is the language in which Jesus usually conversed, and was adhered to by the Jews as their national tongue.

Josephus was contemporary with Matthew, and, although a Jew by birth, was well versed in Greek, and educated in the most thorough manner. The question may be asked how it happened that a Greek gospel of Matthew was preserved, and none in Hebrew. The time or times when Matthew's gospel was promulgated, at first in Greek and afterward in Hebrew, cannot be fixed at this time with certainty.

Among the manuscripts brought to the British Museum in 1842 there is a very ancient "Syrian Matthew," which Dr. Cureton has published, and which he supposes to be the original book of Matthew. From it we give the following variations between the Greek and the Syrian, as translated by Prof. Stowe:

Greek.	Syrian.
I, 20.—He shall save his people from their sins.	I, 20.—He shall save the world from its sins.
I, 23.—God with us.	I, 23.—Our God with us.
I, 25.—Knew her not.	I, 25.—Dwelt with her in purity.
VII, 5.—Hypocrite.	VII, 5.—Acceptor of persons.
XV, 22.—Grievously demoralized.	XV, 22.—Badly conducted by a devil's hand.
XVI, 19.—The keys of the kingdom.	XVI, 19.—The keys of the gates of the kingdom.

Our present Greek is no translation, Prof. Stowe says, but the original from Matthew's own hand; but this is too improbable to gain credit. Eusebius says the Hebrew gospel was found among the Christians in India in the latter part of the second century, by Pantaenus, a missionary and philosopher, who afterward presided over the Catechetical school at Alexandria. He contends that the book was carried thither by the apostle Bartholomew, who first preached the gospel in those regions.

This gospel of Matthew is written in a plain, matter-of-fact style, more like that of a man of business, as he was, than of a scholar. By him Jesus is exhibited in his earthly character, and on this account his gospel was called by the ancients *somatikon*, or the "bodily" gospel. In his narrative he is brief, and regardless, generally, of the order of time. In many cases only enough of the narrative is given to introduce the discourse. In this respect, as well as in several other particulars, he resembles Zenophon.

Some writers have taken great pains to prove that there was such a gospel as Matthew's, which we consider as unnecessary as it would be to demonstrate that there is a sun in the firmament. It may not have come down to us exactly as Matthew wrote it; and, again, we are as sure as we can be of any negative that he did not confine his writing to actual and personal knowledge, though he honestly believed that all he said was true. He did not pretend to be inspired, and writes more as a historian than as an enthusiast.

Tertullian tells us that Matthew, in his endeavor to make us acquainted with the carnal origin of Jesus, begins by saying, "Jesus Christ, the son of David, the son of Abraham." Matthew gives in detail the origin of the Lord from Abraham, and says, "Jacob begat Joseph, the husband of Mary, of whom was born Jesus, who is called Christ." Prof. Stowe informs us that the genuineness of the first two chapters of Matthew have been questioned by many; and, as portions of them are in conflict with other gospels, we have good reason to doubt their accuracy. It is certain that many learned men, at a time not long subsequent to the first century, criticised a considerable portion of this book, and, we think, justly. Matthew had far less means of knowing the genealogy of Jesus than have the great biblical scholars of our age. The men who lived seventeen centuries ago were undoubtedly less qualified to speak correctly of things which happened then than we are, for, in addition to the knowledge they had, we have what has been gained since. Matthew felt it his duty (and we thank God that he did) to write, according to his faith and ability, an account of the birth and ministry of Jesus of Nazareth, usually called the Christ, who may be justly regarded as the world's great redeemer.

Judaism was worn out; although it had served a good purpose, it had accomplished its mission, and had had its day. Something better was wanted—something to touch the heart. In all the Jewish rites and ceremonials God was dimly discerned, but not really felt. Jesus appeared in the form of a man, as one of the people, with all the outward peculiarities of a man. In commencing his record Matthew saw no other way than to give the genealogy of Jesus, using the best materials he had. Up to the advent of Jesus no remarkable character had appeared on the earth whose birth was in the common order. Something unusually extraordinary must be connected with it, as it was no uncommon thing for men to be begotten of the gods. Hence we can see the necessity of associating his name and birth with the genealogy of King David, and of attributing his conception to the Jewish God; for Joseph and Mary were both Jews.

It is not possible that the present gospel of Matthew was written as early as A.D. 68. Let us look at chap. xxviii, 15 : "So they took the money, and did as they were taught; and this saying is commonly reported among the Jews until this day." Meaning, of course, that the book, or at least some part of it, had been written a long time, several generations, after the occurrence: many say as late as the third century. Some of the German critics are decided in their opinion that the first two chapters of Matthew are not genuine. Portions of these two chapters are noticed in another part of this work. The first part of Matthew is taken by some to be merely legend. There is difficulty in reconciling the stories of Jesus' paternity. If he was the son of God and was with the Father before the worlds were made, he was a part, at least, of infinity; and to establish the theory that infinity can suffer, a new logic, of which we have no knowledge, would have to be invented. If Jesus was born a human being, he could not make an infinite atonement: so in trying to avoid one difficulty we encounter another.

The Jewish prophet and the angel that appeared to Joseph did not agree as to what the child, when born, should be called. The former said his name should be called Immanuel; the latter, Jesus. The wise men from the East did not ask for one who was born to be a Savior, but for one born "King of the Jews." So much had been said by the Jews about a king who would in time appear, that Herod thought it possible that an infant prince was really born to be king of the Jewish nation. From the coming of the so-called wise men from the East (probably Persia) we might infer that they had heard the wondrous story; but Prof. Coleman puts this supposed object of their visit at rest by showing that they came solely on account of an astronomical phenomenon, as we have explained in another chapter.

Chap. iii says: "In those days came John the Baptist, preaching in the wilderness of Judea." John was about two years older than Jesus. In connecting the beginning of John's ministry with Jesus' birth so closely by the words "in those days," the writer shows pretty plainly that he was not much of a historian, or else the writing was done a long time after the occurrences of which he is speaking. The record is sadly mixed up, for in almost the same sentence we are told of the birth of the infant Jesus, and then of John's baptizing, and the coming of Jesus, infant as he was, to John for baptism. Immediately after this (chap. iv), Jesus is delivered over to the Devil to be tempted, but for what reason we are not told. If he was not only born a God, but was a God before all worlds, we cannot see why he was thus given up to be tormented. The story is, in and of itself, incredible. The thought that Jesus was thus in the hands of the Evil One, and by him placed upon the highest pinnacle of the temple, is too absurd to entertain. Who took note of the conversation when Jesus and the Devil were up that dizzy height? It seems the Devil understood Scripture, for he and his captive had quite a talk together, the former seeming to be perfectly at home on sacred topics.

The whole idea of a devil was borrowed from older religions, and is interwoven with Christianity just as it was with other previous systems. Evidently no story could have been gotten up about the apple-eating matter without a devil. And but for this act of Adam and Eve, by the aid and instigation of the Devil, they and all their posterity might possibly have remained in a state of sinlessness and purity, not knowing good from evil. Jesus would have had no tempter to try his virtue. In short, without a devil all would have been sadly out of joint. With the Devil as an adversary, an opposing force, matters seemed to work satisfactorily all around! There was something to contend with, somebody to fight!

Matt. iv, 23, 24, says: "And Jesus went about all Galilee, teaching in their synagogues, and preaching the gospel of the kingdom, and healing all manner of sickness and all manner of disease among the people." "And his fame went throughout all Syria." The Jews, it must be admitted, were remarkably tolerant to allow Jesus to teach the new religion. Many sects nowadays would turn any one out of doors who attempted such a thing. Jesus was a Jewish citizen, and as such, of course, had privileges, but he had not the right to innovate the Jewish religion; and the great wonder is that he escaped death as long as he did.

In chap. x the twelve apostles are named:

1. "And when he had called unto him his twelve disciples, he gave them power against unclean spirits, to cast them out, and to heal all manner of sickness and all manner of disease.

2. "Now the names of the twelve apostles are these: the first, Simon, who is called Peter, and Andrew his brother; James the son of Zebedee, and John his brother;

3. "Philip, and Bartholomew; Thomas, and Matthew the publican; James the son of Alphæus, and Lebbæus, whose surname was Thaddeus;

4. "Simon the Canaanite, and Judas Iscariot, who also betrayed him.

5. "These twelve Jesus sent forth, and commanded them, saying, Go not into the way of the Gentiles, and into any city of the Samaritans enter ye not:

6. "But go rather to the lost sheep of the house of Israel.

7. "And as ye go, preach, saying, The kingdom of heaven is at hand.

8. "Heal the sick, cleanse the lepers, raise the dead, cast out devils: freely ye have received, freely give.

9. "Provide neither gold, nor silver, nor brass in your purses,

10. "Nor scrip for your journey, neither two coats, neither shoes, nor yet staves; for the workman is worthy of his meat."

In chap. ii, 12, we read:

12. "And from the days of John the Baptist until now the kingdom of heaven suffereth violence, and the violent take it by force.

13. "For all the prophets and the law prophesied until John.

14. "And if ye will receive it, this is Elias, which was for to come."

What are we to understand by this? John was not dead. Does it not look as if this writing was done a long time after Jesus' death? And what safety can there be in a place that can be stormed by the wicked and violent? And what of the writers who penned, or rather dictated, such things? for we are told by the most learned scholars that very little, if any portion, of the Gospels or Epistles was written by those whose names appear as the authors. Admitting that the authors were inspired, it does not follow that the scribes were inspired likewise. The latter had no interest in what they wrote, and could easily have interpolated and altered the record had they been so disposed; or it could have been done by other hands a long time after. The most important of these old manuscripts, dating back to the fore part of the third century, were of course compiled from other and still older manuscripts; so that the entire authenticity of the New Testament does not rest on the most solid ground. Do not start at this assertion, Christian friend and brother. While we admit that there is enough in the Bible about which there is no dispute, that we do fully understand, to guide us into all truth, there is too much that we cannot believe, or do not understand, to allow of our worshiping it. Our duty is to worship God and serve him.

As to the genealogy back from Joseph to David, the noted writer Julius Africanus considered it very imperfect. He gives an elaborate statement of the different genealogies of Jesus as they stand in Matthew and Luke, and endeavors to reconcile them, but without success.

THE EVANGELICAL WRITERS.—*Mark* was the son of a pious woman in Jerusalem, and the intimate friend of the apostle Peter. A misunderstanding growing up between Paul and Barnabas respecting Mark, produced a separation from him for a time. Paul afterward became reconciled, and speaks of Mark in several of his epistles with confidence and affection. With great unanimity his gospel is believed to have been written at Rome, under the superintendence of Peter. Prof. Stowe says he has many pure Latin words written in Greek letters, where the other evangelists use the appropriate Greek words.

Luke was a Gentile by birth, and a physician, and, according to the most reliable testimony, was a citizen of Antioch, where the followers of Christ were first called Christians. He was familiar with Greek literature, as appears evident from his style of writing. His gospel and the book of Acts were written by him. His introductory verses are elegantly pure Greek, and the same is true of the Acts. He became a zealous Christian, and took great pains to gain correct information, applying himself to the study of the Hebrew Scriptures and the circumstances attending the origin of Christianity.

Of Theophilus, the friend to whom Luke addresses his two works, nothing is known that is reliable. He is thought to have been a Greek, who lived out of Palestine, or at Antioch, Luke's native city. Luke's gospel may have been written about the same time as Mark's, and was probably intended for the use of the Greeks.

Luke represents Christ as the Savior of the world, without distinction of nations, and traces his genealogy, through his mother, Mary, to Adam, the progenitor of the whole human family, in bold contrast to the obviously Jewish feature of the first chapter of Matthew.

He is circumstantial in narrative, and gives many details, and is the only one of the evangelists from whom we have a detailed account of what preceded the birth of John the Baptist and of Jesus. In this part of his gospel the style is strongly Hebraistic—more so than in any other part of the New Testament, if we except the Apocalypse. Luke was often the companion of Paul in his journeys, and it is reported that after Paul's martyrdom Luke preached in Italy.

John was the son of Zebedee and Salome, and the brother of James. He was born in Bethsaida of Galilee, where also Andrew and Peter were born. John's father owned vessels or sailing craft on the sea of Galilee, and kept servants; his mother was one of those who provided for the support of Jesus, and procured costly spices for his embalming. Zebedee had a house in Jerusalem, and knew the high priest personally. This superiority in circumstances might have emboldened the mother of James and John to make for them the request for precedence over the other disciples. John's mother was a devout follower of Jesus, though we are not informed as to the religious character of his father. John was originally a disciple of John the Baptist, and was one of the first whom Jesus called to the apostleship. He is supposed to have written the Apocalypse during his banishment to Patmos. Returning to Ephesus, he established a theological school for the supply of competent pastors, the season of miracles having ended for some reason which we will not undertake to give. While superintending this school he wrote his gospel and epistles.

There was much in John to admire, and some things to condemn. His temper was bad, which, with his irritable turn of mind and his impetuosity, marred his character. Some historians say that he overcame these defects in his advanced age. The dreamily dull and sluggishly even-tempered seldom attain to anything above mediocrity. The ardent, high-toned, and of youthful temper, are those who do most for the world. So, on the whole, John is entitled to our grateful remembrance. All his qualities combined in the end in softness, mildness, richness of feeling, and love.

In speaking of the Gospels, Origen says that, as they are the chief of all writings, so the gospel of John is the chief of all the Gospels. Matthias Claudius, an eccentric German writer, says: "It delights me most of all to read in St. John. There is in him something so entirely wonderful; twilight and night, and through it the swift, darting lightning; twilight and cloud, and behind the cloud the full moon, bodily; something so deeply, sadly pensive, so high, so full of anticipation, that one cannot have enough of it. With me, reading John is as though I saw him leaning on the bosom of his Master at the Last Supper. I am far from understanding everything I read, but it often seems to me as if what John meant was floating before me in the distance; and even here I look into a passage altogether dark: I have a foretaste of some great, glorious meaning which I shall one day understand; and for this reason I grasp so eagerly after every new interpretation of the gospel of John." According to Prof. Stowe, John was the youngest of the apostles, and four or five years younger than Jesus.

Mark writes for the grave, severe, matter-of-fact Romans; Luke for the versatile and learned Greek, whose eager curiosity could never sleep; and John for the deep, reflecting spirit, which feels the want of that which earth cannot afford. Matthew exhibited the human and subordinate; John, the spiritual and divine; Mark, his official character; and Luke, his personal history of Jesus.

The common belief among High-Church people—who intend, at all events, to believe enough and perform ceremony enough to carry them to heaven, if such a place is to be gained in that way—is, that all the writings which now comprise the New Testament were prepared under the direct guidance of the Maker and Governor of all things, so that no important error could be committed, and that, therefore, they constitute a perfect and harmonious whole. Careful examination will show how groundless such an opinion is. We have a right to ask for the evidence that all the writers of the New Testament had imbibed the spirit of Jesus, and were all faithful and infallible expounders of his doctrine. To presume that such was the case is not enough. In a matter of such transcendent importance presumption will not do.. The important fact remains, and will not be ignored by the unprejudiced reader, that these evangelists and apostles do not agree in their statements.

We make copious extracts from a carefully and ably written work, "The Creed of Christendom," by W. R. Greg. He says:

"The apostles did disagree among themselves in their exposition of the nature and constituents of their Master's system—and this, too, in matters of no small significance: they are not, therefore, infallible or certain guides.

"Putting aside personal and angry contentions, such as those recorded in Acts xv, 39, which, however undignified, are, we fear, natural even to holy men, the first recorded dispute among the apostles we find to have related to a matter of the most essential importance to the character of Christianity, viz., whether or not the Gospel should be preached to any but Jews—whether the Gentiles were to be admitted into the fold of Christ. We find (chap. xi) that when the apostles and brethren in Judea heard that Peter had ventured to visit Gentiles, to eat with them, to preach to them, and even to baptize them, they were astonished and scandalized by the innovation, and 'contended with him.' The account of the discussion which ensued throws light upon two very interesting questions: upon the views entertained by Jesus himself (or at least as to those conveyed by him to his disciples) as to the range and limit of his mission; and upon the manner in which, and the grounds on which, controversies were decided in the early Church.

"We have been taught to regard Jesus as a prophet who announced himself as sent from God on a mission to preach repentance, and to teach the way of life to all mankind, and who left behind him the apostles to complete the work which he was compelled to leave unfinished. The mission of Moses was to separate and educate a peculiar people, apart from the rest of the world, for the knowledge and worship of the one true God; the mission of Christ was to bring all nations to that knowledge and worship—to extend to all mankind that salvation which, in his time, was considered to belong to the Jews alone, as well as to point to a better and wider way of life. Such is the popular and established notion. But when we look into the New Testament we find little to confirm this view, and much to negative it. Putting aside our own prepossessions, and inferences drawn from the character of Christ, and the comprehensive grandeur of his doctrine, nothing can well be clearer, from the evidence presented to us in the Scriptures, than that Jesus considered himself sent not so much to the world at large as to the Jews exclusively—to bring back his countrymen to the true essence and spirit of that religion whose purity had in his days been so grievously corrupted, and to elevate and enlarge their views from the stores of his own rich and comprehensive mind.

"It will be allowed by all that the apostles, at the commencement of their ministry after the crucifixion of their Lord, had not the least idea that their mission extended to any but the Jews, or that their Master was anything but a Jewish Messiah and Deliverer. Their first impatient question to him when assembled together after the resurrection is said to have been, 'Lord, wilt thou at this time restore the kingdom to Israel?' (Acts i, 6). The whole of the account we are now considering brings out in strong relief their notions as to the narrow limits of their ministry. When Peter is sent for by Cornelius, and hears the relation of his vision, he exclaims, as if a perfectly new idea had struck him, 'Of a truth I perceive that God is no respecter of persons; but in every nation he that feareth him and worketh righteousness is accepted of him' (Acts x, 34); and he goes on to expound 'the word which God sent to *the children of Israel*' (36), and which the apostles were commanded to 'preach to the people' (42); 'the people,' as the context (41) shows, meaning simply the Jews. The Jewish believers, we are told (45), 'as many as came with

Peter, were astonished, *because that on the Gentiles also* was poured out the gift of the Holy Ghost.' When Peter was called to account by the other apostles for having preached to and baptized Gentiles (xi, 1)—a proceeding which evidently (xi, 2, 3) shocked and surprised them all—he justified himself, not by reference to any commands of Jesus, not by quoting precept or example of his Master, but simply by relating a vision or dream which he supposed to proceed from a divine suggestion. The defense appeared valid to the brethren, and they inferred from it, in a manner which shows what a new and unexpected light had broken in upon them, '*Then* hath God also to the Gentiles granted repentance unto life' (xi, 18). Now, could this have been the case had Christ given his disciples any commission to preach the gospel to the Gentiles, or given them the slightest reason to suppose that other nations besides the Jews were included in that commission? (See also, for confirmation, xi, 19, and xiii, 46.) It is to be observed, also, that throughout the elaborate arguments contained in the Epistle to the Romans to show that the gospel *ought* to be preached to the Gentiles—that there is no difference between Greek and Jew, etc.—Paul, though he quotes largely from the Hebrew prophets, *never appeals to any sayings of Jesus* in confirmation of his view; and in the Acts, in two instances, his mission to the Gentiles is represented as arising out of a direct subsequent revelation (in a vision) to himself (Acts xxii, 21; xxvi, 17; ix, 15).

"As, therefore, none of the apostles, either in their writings or in their discussions, appeal to the sayings or deeds of Jesus during his lifetime as their warrant for preaching the gospel to the Gentiles, but, on the contrary, one and all manifest a total ignorance of any such deeds or sayings, we think it must be concluded that the various texts extant conveying his commands to 'preach the Gospel to all nations' could never have proceeded from him, but are to be ranked among the many *ascribed* sayings, embodying the ideas of a later period, which we find both in the Acts and the Evangelists. None of these are quoted or referred to by the apostles in their justification, and therefore could not have been known to them, and, since unknown, could not be authentic.

"On the other hand, there are several passages in the Gospels which, if genuine (as they appear to be), clearly indicate that it was not from any neglect or misunderstanding of the instructions of their Lord that the apostles regarded their mission as confined to the Jews. 'Go not into the way of the Gentiles, and into any city of the Samaritans enter ye not: but go rather to the lost sheep of the house of Israel' (Matt. x, 5, 6). 'I am not sent but to the lost sheep of the house of Israel' (Matt. xv, 24). 'Verily I say unto you, that ye which have followed me, in the regeneration when the Son of Man shall sit on the throne of his glory, ye also shall sit upon twelve thrones, judging the twelve tribes of Israel' (Matt. xix, 28). 'It is easier for heaven and earth to pass than one tittle of the law to fail' (Luke xvi, 17). 'Think not I am come to destroy the law and the prophets: I am not come to destroy, but to fulfill' (Matt. v, 17). 'This day is salvation come to this house, forasmuch as he also is a son of Abraham' (Luke xix, 9). 'Salvation is of the Jews' (John iv, 22).

"It would appear, then, that neither the historical nor the epistolary Scriptures give us any reason for surmising that Jesus directed, or contemplated, the spread of his gospel beyond the pale of the Jewish nation; that the apostles at least had no cognizance of any such views on his part; that when the question of the admission of the Gentiles to the knowledge of the gospel came before them, in the natural progress of events, it created considerable difference of opinion among them, and at first the majority were decidedly hostile to any such liberality of view, or such extension of their missionary labors. The mode in which the controversy was conducted, and the grounds on which it was decided, are strongly characteristic of the moral and intellectual condition of the struggling Church at that early period. The objectors bring no argument to show why the Gentiles should *not* be admitted to the gospel light, but they put Peter at once on his defense, as having, in preaching to others than Jews, done a thing which, *prima facie*, was out of rule, and required justification. And Peter replies to them, not by appeals to the paramount authority of Jesus; not by reference to the tenor of his life and teaching; not by citing the case of the centurion's servant, or the Canaanitish woman, or the parables of the vineyard and the supper; not by showing, from the nature and fitness of things, that so splendid a plan of moral elevation, of instruction—such a comprehensive scheme of redemption, according to the orthodox view—ought to be as widely preached as possible; not by arguing that Jesus had come into the world to spread the healing knowledge of Jehovah, of our God and Father, to all nations, to save all sinners and all believers; but simply by relating a vision, or rather a dream— the most natural one possible to a man as hungry as Peter is represented to have been—the interpretation of which, *at first a puzzle to him*, is suggested by the simultaneous appearance of the messengers of Cornelius, who also pleads a heavenly vision as a reason for the summons. This justification would scarcely by itself have been sufficient, for the dream might have meant nothing at all, or Peter's interpretation of it— evidently a doubtful and *tentative* one—might have been erroneous; so he goes on to argue that the event showed him to have been right, inasmuch as, after his preaching, the Holy Ghost fell upon all the household of Cornelius: 'And as I began to speak, the Holy Ghost fell on them, as on us at the beginning.... Forasmuch, then, as God gave them the like gift as unto us who believed on the Lord Jesus Christ, what was I, that I could withstand God?' (Acts xi, 15, 17). This argument clenched the matter, satisfied the brethren, and settled, once for all, the question as to the admission of the Gentiles into the Church of Christ.

"It becomes necessary, therefore, to inquire more closely into the nature of this argument which appeared to the apostles so conclusive and irrefragable. What was this Holy Spirit? and in what way did it manifest its presence, so that the apostles recognized it at once as the special and most peculiar gift vouchsafed to believers?

"The case, as far as the Acts and the Epistles enable us to learn it, appears clearly to have been this: The indication—or at least the most common, specific, and indubitable indication—of the Holy Spirit having fallen upon any one, was his beginning to 'speak with tongues,' to utter strange exclamations, unknown words, or words in an unknown tongue. Thus, in the case of the apostles on the day of Pentecost, we are told, 'They were all filled with the Holy Ghost, and *began to speak with other tongues*, as the Spirit gave them utterance' (Acts ii, 4). Again, in the case of the household of Cornelius: 'And they .... were astonished.... because that on the Gentiles also was poured out the gift of the Holy Ghost. *For they heard them speak with tongues*, and magnify God' (x, 45, 46). The same indication appeared also in the case of the disciples of the Baptist whom Paul found at Ephesus: 'And when Paul had laid his hands on them, the Holy Ghost came upon them; *and they spake with tongues*, and prophesied' (xix, 6). The 'speaking with tongues' (to which in the last instance is added 'prophesying,' or preaching) is the only specified external manifestation, cognizable by the senses, by which it was known that such and such individuals had received the Holy Ghost. What, then, was this 'speaking with tongues'?

"The popular idea is, that it was the power of speaking foreign languages without having learned them—supernaturally, in fact. This interpretation derives countenance, and probably its foundation, from the statement of Luke (Acts ii, 2–8), which is considered to intimate that the apostles preached to each man of their vast and motley audience in his own native language. But there are many difficulties in the way of this interpretation, and much reason to suspect in the whole narrative a large admixture of the mythic element.

"We have already seen that Luke is not to be implicitly trusted as an historian.

"It appears from Matthew (x, 1, 8, 20) that the Holy Spirit had been already imparted to the apostles during the lifetime of Jesus, and a second outpouring, therefore, could not be required. John, however, tells us (xx, 20) that Jesus expressly and *personally* conferred this gift after his resurrection, but *before his ascension:* 'And when he had said this, he *breathed* on them, and saith unto them, *Receive ye the Holy Ghost.*' But in the Acts, the 'breathing' had become 'a rushing mighty wind,' and the outpouring of the Spirit is placed some days *after the ascension*, and the personal interposition is dispensed with. These discrepant accounts cannot all be faithful, and for obvious reasons we think that of Luke least authentic.

"We have no evidence anywhere that the apostles knew, or employed, any language except Hebrew and Greek—Greek being (as Haug has clearly proved) the common language in use throughout the eastern provinces of the Roman empire. Nay, we have *some* reason to believe that they were *not* acquainted with other languages; for, by the general tradition of the early Church, Mark is called the 'interpreter' of Peter. Now, if Peter had been gifted as we imagine on the day of Pentecost, he would have needed no interpreter.

"If the knowledge of foreign languages possessed by the apostles was the work of the Holy Spirit, the work was most imperfectly done (a monstrous conception), for, by universal consent, their Greek was a bald, barbarous, and incorrect idiom.

"The language in which the occurrence is related would seem to imply that the miracle was wrought upon the hearers, rather than on the speakers—that whatever the language in which the apostles *spoke*, the audience *heard* them each man in his own. 'When the multitude came together they were confounded, because that *every man heard them speak in his own language.*'.... 'Behold, are not all these which speak Galileans? And how *hear we every man in our own tongue,* wherein we were born?' The supposition that the different apostles addressed different audiences in different languages, successively, is inconsistent with the text, which clearly indicates that the whole was one transaction, and took place at one time. 'Peter, standing up,.... said,.... These are not drunken, as ye suppose, seeing *it is but the third hour of the day.*'

"The people, we are told, 'were in doubt' at the strange and incomprehensible phenomenon, and said, 'What meaneth this?' while others thought the apostles must be drunk—a natural perplexity and surmise, if the utterances were incoherent and unintelligible ejaculations; but not so, if they were discourses addressed to each set of foreigners in their respective languages. Moreover, Peter's defense is not what it would have been in the latter case. He does not say, 'We have been endowed from on high with the power of speaking foreign languages which we have never learned. We are, as you say, ignorant Galileans, but

God has given us this faculty that we might tell you of his Son'; but he assures them that those utterances which led them to suppose him and his fellow-disciples to be drunk were the consequences of that outpouring of spiritual emotion which had been prophesied as one of the concomitants of the millennium. 'This is that which was spoken by the prophet Joel: And it shall come to pass in the last days, saith Jehovah, I will pour out of my spirit upon all flesh; and your sons and daughters shall prophesy, and your young men shall see visions, and your old men shall dream dreams.'

"Luke indicates in several passages that in the other cases mentioned the Holy Spirit fell upon the recipients *in the same manner, and with the same results*, as on the apostles on the day of Pentecost (Acts x, 47; xi, 15–17; xv, 8, 9). Now, in these cases there is no reason whatever to believe that the 'gift of tongues' meant the power of speaking foreign languages. In the first case (that of Cornelius) it could not have been this; for as all the recipients began to 'speak with tongues,' and yet were members of one household, such an unnecessary display of newly-acquired knowledge or powers would have been in the highest degree impertinent and ostentatious.

"There can, we think, be no doubt—indeed, we are not aware that any doubt has ever been expressed— —that the remarks of Paul in the twelfth, thirteenth and fourteenth chapters of the first epistle to the Corinthians, respecting the 'speaking with tongues,' the 'gift of tongues,' 'the unknown tongue,' etc., refer to the same faculty, or supposed spiritual endowment, spoken of in the Acts, which fell on the apostles at the day of Pentecost, and on the household of Cornelius and the disciples of Apollos, as already cited. The identity of the gift referred to in all the cases is, we believe, unquestioned. Now, the language of Paul clearly shows that this 'speaking with tongues' was not preaching in a *foreign* language, but in an *unknown* language—that it consisted of unintelligible, and, probably, incoherent, utterances. He repeatedly distinguishes the gift of tongues from that of preaching (or, as it is there called, prophecy), and the gift of speaking the unknown tongues from the gift of interpreting the same. 'To one is given by the Spirit.... the working of miracles; to another, prophecy; to another, *divers kinds of tongues;* to another, *the interpretation of tongues.*'....'Have all the gifts of healing? do all speak with tongues? do all interpret?' (I Cor. xii, 10–30; see also xiii, 1, 2, 8). 'Let him that speaketh in an unknown tongue pray that he may interpret' (xiv, 13). Again, he classes this power or tongues (so invaluable to missionaries, had it been really a capacity of speaking foreign languages) very low among spiritual endowments. 'First apostles, secondarily prophets, thirdly teachers, *after that* miracles, *then* gifts of healing, helps, governments, *diversities of tongues*' (xii, 28). 'Greater is he that prophesieth than he that speaketh with tongues' (xiv, 5). He further expressly explains this gift to consist in unintelligible utterances, which were useless to, and lost upon, the audience. 'He that speaketh in an unknown tongue speaketh not unto man, but unto God, *for no man understandeth him*' (xiv, 2; see also 6-9, 16). Finally he intimates pretty plainly that the practice of speaking these unknown tongues was becoming vexatious, and bringing discredit on the Church; and he labors hard to discourage it. 'I thank my God that I speak with tongues more than ye all: yet in the Church I had rather speak five words with my understanding, that I might teach others also, than ten thousand words in an unknown tongue' (xiv, 18, 19). 'If the whole Church be come together into one place, and all speak with tongues, and there come in unlearned men or unbelievers, will they not say ye are mad?' (23). 'If any man speak in an unknown tongue, let it be by two, or at most by three, and that by course; and let one interpret......For God is not the author of confusion, but of peace' (27-33; see also 39, 40).

"It is, we think, almost impossible to read the whole of the three chapters from which the above citations were made, without coming to the conclusion that in the early Church there were a number of weak, mobile, imaginative minds, who, over-excited by the sublimity of the new doctrine expounded to them, and by the stirring eloquence of its preachers, passed the faint and undefinable line which separates enthusiasm from delirium, and gave vent to their exaltation in incoherent or inarticulate utterances, which the compassionate sympathy, or the consanguineous fancies, of those around them dignified with the description of speaking, or prophesying, in an unknown tongue. No one familiar with physiology, or medical or religious history, can be ignorant how contagious delusions of this nature always prove; and when once these incoherences became the recognized sign of the descent of the Spirit, every one would, of course, be anxious to experience and to propagate them.

"The language of Paul in reference to the 'unknown tongues' appears to us clearly that of an honest and a puzzled man, whose life in an age of miracles, and whose belief in so many grand religious marvels, has prepared him to have faith in more; whose religious humility will not allow him to prescribe in what manner the Spirit of God may, or may not, operate; but, at the same time, whose strong, good sense makes him feel that these incomprehensible utterances must be useless, and were most probably nonsensical, unworthy, and grotesque. He seems to have been anxious to repress the unknown tongue, yet unwilling harshly to condemn it as a vain delusion.

"That there was a vast amount of delusion and unsound enthusiasm in the Christian Church at the time of the apostles not only seems certain, but it could not possibly have been otherwise without such an interference with the ordinary operations of natural causes as would have amounted to an incessant miracle. Wonders, real or supposed, were of daily occurrence. The subjects habitually brought before the contemplation of believers were of such exciting and sublime magnificence that even the strongest minds cannot too long dwell upon them without some degree of perilous emotion. The recent events which closed the life of the founder of their faith, and, above all, the glorious truth, or the splendid fiction, of his resurrection and ascension, were depicted with all the exaggerating grandeur of Oriental imagination. The expectation of an almost immediate end of the world, and the reception into glory and power of the living believer, the hope which each one entertained of being 'caught up' to meet his Redeemer in the clouds, was of itself sufficient to overthrow all but the coldest tempers; while the constant state of mental tension in which they were kept by the antagonism and persecution of the world without could not fail to maintain a degree of exaltation very unfavorable to sobriety either of thought or feeling. All these influences, too, were brought to bear upon minds the most ignorant and unprepared, upon the poor and the oppressed, upon women and children; and, to crown the whole, the most prominent doctrine of their faith was that of the immediate, special, and hourly influence of the Holy Spirit—a doctrine of all others the most liable to utter and gross misconception, and the most apt to lead to perilous mental excitement. Hence they were constantly on the lookout for miracles. Their creed did not supply, and indeed scarcely admitted, any criterion of what was of divine origin—for who could venture to pronounce or define how the Spirit might or should manifest itself?—and thus ignorance and folly too often became the arbiters of wisdom, and the ravings of delirium were listened to as the words of inspiration and of God. If Jesus could have returned to earth thirty years after his death, and sat in the midst of an assembly of his followers who were listening in hushed and wondering prostration of mind to a speaker in the 'unknown tongue,' how would he have wept over the humiliating and disappointing spectacle! How would he have grieved to think that the incoherent jargon of delirium or hysteria should be mistaken for the promptings of his Father's Spirit!

. "We are driven, then, to the painful, but unavoidable, conclusion that those mysterious and unintelligible utterances which the apostles and the early Christians generally looked upon as the effects of the Holy Spirit, the manifestation of its presence, the signs of its operation, the especial indication and criterion of its having fallen upon any one, were in fact simply the physiologically natural results of morbid and perilous cerebral exaltation, induced by strong religious excitement acting on uncultivated and susceptible minds—results which, in all ages and nations, have followed in similar circumstances and from similar stimuli; and that these 'signs' to which Peter appealed, and to which the other brethren succumbed, as proving that God intended the gospel to be preached to Gentiles as well as to Jews, showed only that Gentiles were susceptible to the same excitements, and manifested that susceptibility in the same manner, as the Jews.

"Shortly after the question as to the admission of the Gentiles into the Christian Church had been decided in the singular and inconclusive manner above related, a second subject of dispute arose among the brethren—a corollary, almost, of the first—the nature of which strongly confirms some of the views we have just put forth. The dispute was this: whether it was necessary for those Gentiles who had been baptized and admitted into the Christian community to observe the ritual portion of the Jewish law?—whether, in fact, by becoming Christians, they had, *ipso facto*, become Jews, and liable to Judaic observances? The mere broaching of such a question, and the serious schism it threatened in the infant sect, show how little the idea had yet taken root among the disciples of *the distinctness of the essence,* the superiority of the spirit, the newness of the dispensation, taught by Jesus, and how commonly Christianity was regarded as simply a purification and renewal of Judaism.

"It appears from the fifteenth chapter of the Acts that when Paul and Barnabas were at Antioch, teaching and baptizing the Gentiles, certain Jewish Christians (Pharisees, we are told in verse 5) caused considerable trouble and dissension by asserting that it was necessary for the new converts 'to be circumcised, and to keep the law of Moses'—a doctrine which Paul and Barnabas vehemently opposed. The question was so important, and the dissension became so serious, that a council of the apostles and elders was summoned at Jerusalem to discuss and decide the matter.

"The apostles not only differed from each other, but their respective views varied materially on important subjects in the course of their ministry.

"The apostles held some opinions which we know to be erroneous. They unanimously and unquestioningly believed and taught that the end of the world was at hand, and would arrive in the lifetime of the then-existing generation. The following are the passages of the apostolic writings which most strongly express, or most clearly imply, this conviction:

"*Paul:* 'This *we say unto you by the word of the Lord,* that *we which are alive and remain unto the coming of the Lord* shall not prevent them which are asleep. For.... the dead in Christ shall rise first; then *we which are alive and remain* shall be caught up together with them in the clouds to meet the Lord in the air: and so shall we ever be with the Lord' (I Thess. iv, 15, 16, 17). 'But this I say, brethren, *the time is short:* it remaineth that both they that have wives be as though they had none; and they that weep, as though they wept not; and they that rejoice, as though they rejoiced not; and they that buy, as though they possessed not; and they that use this world, as not abusing it; *for the fashion of this world passeth away*' (I Cor. vii, 29). 'Behold, I show you a mystery; *we shall not all sleep*, but we shall all be changed' (I Cor. xv, 51; see also I Tim. ix, 1; II Tim. iii, 1).

"*Peter:* 'An inheritance incorruptible, and undefiled, and that fadeth not away, reserved in heaven for you, who are kept by the power of God through faith unto salvation, *ready to be revealed in the last time*' (I Ep. i, 4, 5). 'Christ,.....who verily was foreordained before the foundation of the world, but was manifest *in these last times* for you' (19, 20). '*The end of all things is at hand*' (iv, 7).

"*John:* 'Little children, *it is the last time:* and as ye have heard that antichrist shall come, even now there are many antichrists; whereby *we know that it is the last time*' (I Ep. ii, 18).

"*James:* 'Be ye also patient;....*for the coming of the Lord draweth nigh*' (v, 8).

"We may well conceive that this strong conviction must, in men like the apostles, have been something far beyond a mere abstract or speculative opinion. In fact, it modified their whole tone of thought and feeling, and could not fail to do so. The firm and living faith that a few years would bring the second coming of their Lord in his glory, and the fearful termination of all earthly things, when 'the heavens should be gathered together as a scroll, and the elements should melt with fervent heat'; and that many among them should be still alive, and should witness these awful occurrences with human eyes, and should join their glorified Master without passing through the portals of the grave, could not exist in their minds without producing a profound contempt for all the pomps and distinctions of the world.

"The death and resurrection of Christ must have worked, and evidently did work, a very great modification in many of the notions of the twelve apostles, and materially changed their point of view of their Lord's mission. But there are many indications that this change was not a radical one: it affected rather the *accessories* than the *essence* of their Messianic notions; for though they relinquished their expectation of an *immediate* restoration of the kingdom, they still, as we have seen, retained the conviction that

that restoration would take place, in their own day, in a far more signal and glorious manner. Their views were spiritualized up to a certain point, *but no further*, even as to this great subject; and on other points the change seems to have been even less complete. The Epistle of James, indeed, is a worthy relic of one who had drunk in the spirit and appreciated the lessons of the meek, practical, and spiritual Jesus. But in the case of the other two apostles, Peter is Peter still, and John is the John of the Gospel. Peter is the same fine, simple, affectionate, impetuous, daring, energetic, *impulsive* character who asked to walk on the water, and was over-confident in his attachment to his Master, but who has now derived new strength and dignity from his new position, and, from the sad experience of the past, has learned to look with a steady eye on suffering and death. And John, in the Epistles, is precisely the same mixture of warm affectionateness to his friends and uncharitableness to his enemies which the few glimpses we have of him in the Gospels would lead us to specify as his characteristics. We meet with several passages in his writings which indicate that the gentle, forbearing and forgiving spirit of the Master had not yet thoroughly penetrated and chastened the mind of the disciple, several passages which Jesus, had he read them, would have rebuked as before, by reminding his zealous follower that he knew not what manner of spirit he was of.

"The case of Paul is peculiar, and must be considered by itself. His writings are more voluminous than those of the other apostles, in a tenfold proportion, and have a distinctive character of their own; yet he never saw Christ in the flesh, and was a bitter persecutor of his followers till suddenly converted by a vision. What, then, were his means of becoming acquainted with the spirit and doctrines of his Lord?

"And, first, as to the vision which converted him. We have *four* narratives of this remarkable occurrence: one given by Luke as an historian in the ninth chapter of the Acts; a second, *reported* by Luke (xxii) as having been given by Paul himself in his speech to the people at Jerusalem; a third, reported also by Luke (xxvi) as having been given by Paul to King Agrippa; and a fourth, more cursory, from Paul himself, in the first chapter of his Epistle to the Galatians, which omits entirely the external and marvelous part of the conversion, and speaks only of an internal revelation.

"Now, there are certain discrepancies in these accounts, which, while they seem to show that the occurrence — either from carelessness, confusion, or defect of memory — has not been related with perfect accuracy, leave us also in doubt as to the precise nature of this vision: as to whether, in fact, it was mental or external. Luke, in his narrative, omits to state whether the supernatural light was visible to the companions of Paul as well as to himself. Paul, in his speech to the Jews, declares that it was. Paul is said to have heard a voice speaking to him, saying, 'Saul, Saul, why persecutest thou me?' Luke affirms that Paul's companions heard this voice as well as himself; but this assertion Paul afterward, in his speech at Jerusalem (Acts xxii, 9), expressly contradicts; and we are, therefore, left with the impression that the supernatural voice fell rather upon Paul's mental than on his outward ear—was, in fact, a spiritual suggestion, not an objective fact. Again, in his speech at Jerusalem, Paul represents the heavenly voice as referring him to future conferences, at Damascus (xxii, 10), for particulars of his commission; in his address to Agrippa (xxvi, 16–18), he represents the same voice as giving him his commission on the spot.

"Thus, in the three versions of the story which come, entirely or proximately, from the pen of Luke, we have positive and not reconcilable contradictions; while in that reference to it which alone we are *certain* proceeded from Paul, the supernatural and external is wholly ignored.

"But the important practical question for our consideration is this: In what manner, and from what source, did Paul receive instruction in the doctrines of Christianity? Was it from the other apostles, like an ordinary convert, or by special and private revelation from heaven? Here, again, we find a discrepancy between the statements of Luke and Paul. In Acts ix, 19, 20; xxii, 10; and xxvi, 20, it is expressly stated that immediately after his conversion, and during his abode with the disciples at Damascus, he was instructed in the peculiar doctrines of his new faith, and commenced his missionary career accordingly, *there and then*. If this statement be correct, his teaching will have the authority due to that of an intelligent and able man *well instructed at second hand*, but no more. Paul, however, entirely contradicts this supposition, and on several occasions distinctly and emphatically declares that he did not receive his religious teaching from any of the disciples or apostles (whom he rather avoided than otherwise), but by direct supernatural communications from the Lord Jesus Christ."

CHAPTER VI.

CORRECTNESS OF GOSPEL HISTORY

It is not our intention in this chapter to assail the truth of the Christian Gospel in regard to what may really be called Gospel, or to express any sentiment which may justly be considered irreverent. If there be anything that we ought to love and revere, it is what we call the Gospel of Jesus; but what is mere history of the times in which he lived, or a record of the life and conduct of those associated with him during his brief ministry, or a recital of the fabulous stories put forth in connection with what was said and done, we are disposed to accept with such allowance as sound sense dictates. All that fell from the lips of Jesus which may be called instruction and direction for holy living, we support and maintain against all doubt or cavil as the truth of God and God's truth. Anything that cannot be sustained on the basis of sound reason ought not to be contended for by us or by any one else.

We continue, at some length, our quotations from "The Creed of Christendom." Mr. Greg observes:

"According to the universal expectation, the Messiah was to be born of the seed of Abraham and the lineage and tribe of David. Accordingly, the Gospel opens with an elaborate genealogy of Jesus, tracing him through David to Abraham. Now, in the *first* place, this genealogy is not correct; *secondly*, if the remainder of the chapter is to be received as true, it is in no sense the genealogy of Jesus; and, *thirdly*, it is wholly and irreconcilably at variance with that given by Luke."

Matthew says there were fourteen generations from Abraham to David; from David to the carrying away into Babylon, fourteen; and from the carrying away into Babylon to Christ, fourteen generations. This cannot be made out in the last series without disturbing the count of the others. The number fourteen in the second series is only obtained by the omission of four generations, viz.: three between Joram and Ozias, and one between Josiah and Jeconiah. Only four generations are reckoned between Nahshon, who lived in the time of Moses, and David—a period of four hundred years. (Compare Numbers i, 7, with Ruth, iv, 20.)

Mr. Greg goes on to say:

"The genealogy here given, correct or incorrect, is the genealogy of *Joseph*, who was in no sense whatever the father (or any relation at all) of Jesus, since this last, we are assured (verses 18 and 25), was in his mother's womb before she and her husband came together. The story of the Incarnation and the genealogy are obviously at variance; and no ingenuity, unscrupulously as it has been applied, can produce even the shadow of an agreement; and when the flat contradiction given to each other by the 1st and the 18th verses is considered, it is difficult for an unprejudiced mind not to feel convinced that the author of the genealogy both in the first and third gospels was ignorant of the story of the Incarnation. The relation in Matthew is simple, natural, and probable: the surprise of Joseph at the pregnancy of his *betrothed*, his anxiety to avoid scandal and exposure, his satisfaction through the means of a dream, present precisely the line of conduct we should expect from a simple, pious, and confiding Jew.

"'All these things were done,' says Matthew, 'that it might be fulfilled which was spoken of the Lord by the prophet, saying, Behold, a virgin shall be with child, and shall bring forth a son,' etc., etc. Now, this is one of the many instances which we shall have to notice in which this evangelist quotes prophecies as intended for Jesus, and as fulfilled in him, which have not the slightest relation to him or his career.

The adduced prophecy is simply an assurance sent to the unbelieving Ahaz that before the child which the wife of Isaiah would shortly conceive (see Isa. viii, 2–4) was old enough to speak, or to know good from evil, the conspiracy of Syria and Ephraim against the king of Judea should be dissolved, and had manifestly no reference to Jesus.

"We shall find many instances in which this tendency of Matthew to find in Jesus the fulfillment of prophecies, which he *erroneously* conceived to refer to him, has led him to narrate circumstances respecting which the other evangelists are silent. Thus, in ii, 13–15, we are told that, immediately after the visit of the Magi, Joseph took Mary and the child, and fled into Egypt, remaining there till the death of Herod, 'that it might be fulfilled which was spoken of the Lord by the prophet, saying, Out of Egypt have I called my son.' The passage in question occurs in Hosea xi, 1, and has not the slightest reference to Christ. It is as follows: 'When Israel was a child, then I loved him, and called my son out of Egypt.' Here is an event related, very improbable in itself, flatly contradicted by Luke's history, and which occurred, we are told, that a prophecy might be fulfilled to which it had no reference, of which it was no fulfillment, and which, in fact, was no prophecy at all.

"A similar instance occurs immediately afterward in the same chapter. We are told that Herod, when he found 'that he was mocked of the wise men, was exceeding wroth, and sent forth and slew all the children that were in Bethlehem, and in all the coasts thereof, from two years old and under'—an act which is not suitable to the known character of Herod, who was cruel and tyrannical, but at the same time crafty and politic, not silly nor insane; which, if it had occurred, must have created a prodigious sensation, and made one of the most prominent points in Herod's history: yet of which none of the other evangelists, nor any historian of the day, nor Josephus, makes any mention. But this also, according to Matthew's notion, was the fulfillment of a prophecy. 'Then was fulfilled that which was spoken by Jeremy the prophet, saying, In Rama there was a voice heard, lamentation, and weeping, and great mourning, Rachel weeping for her children, and would not be comforted, because they are not.' Here, again, the adduced prophecy was quite irrelevant, being simply a description of the grief of Judea for the captivity of her children, accompanied by a promise of their return.

"A still more unfortunate instance is found at the 23d verse, where we are told that Joseph abandoned his intention of returning into Judea, and turned aside into Galilee, and came and dwelt at Nazareth, 'that it might be fulfilled which was spoken by the prophets, He shall be called a Nazarene.' Now, in the first place, the name Nazarene was not in use till long afterward; secondly, there is no such prophecy in the Old Testament. The evangelist, perhaps, had in his mind the words that were spoken to the mother of Samson (Judges xiii, 5) respecting her son: 'The child shall be a Nazarite [*i. e.*, one bound by a vow, whose hair was forbidden to be cut—which never was the case with Jesus] unto God from the womb.'

"In this place we must notice the marked discrepancy between Matthew and Luke as to the original residence of the parents of Jesus. Luke speaks of them as living at Nazareth *before* the birth of Jesus; Matthew as having left their former residence, Bethlehem, to go to Nazareth, only after that event, and from peculiar considerations. Critics, however, are disposed to think Matthew right on this occasion.

"The Jews are frequently represented as urging that Jesus could not be the Messiah, because he was *not* born at Bethlehem; and neither Jesus nor his followers ever set them right on this point.

"The three Synoptical evangelists (Matt. xxii, 41; Mark xii, 35; Luke xx, 41) all record an argument of Christ addressed to the Pharisees, the purport of which is to show that the Messiah need not be, and could not be, the son of David. 'While the Pharisees were gathered together, Jesus asked them, saying, What think ye of Christ? whose son is he? They say unto him, The son of David. He saith unto them, How then doth David in spirit call him Lord, saying,

The Lord saith unto my Lord, Sit thou on my right hand, till I make thine enemies thy footstool? If David then call him Lord, how is he his son?' Now, be the argument good or bad, is it conceivable that Jesus should have brought it forward if he were really a descendant of David? Must not the intention of it have been to argue that, though *not* a son of David, he might still be the Christ?

"In xxi, 2–4, 6–7, the entry into Jerusalem is thus described: 'Then sent Jesus two disciples, saying unto them, Go into the village over against you, and straightway ye shall find an ass tied, *and a colt with her:* loose them, and bring them to me.... And the disciples went and did as Jesus commanded them, and brought the ass *and the colt,* and put on *them* their clothes, and set him thereon.' Mark, Luke, and John, who all mention the same occurrence, agree in speaking of one animal only. But the liberty which Matthew has taken with both fact and probability is at once explained when we read in the 4th verse: 'All this was done that it might be fulfilled which was spoken by the prophet, saying, Tell ye the daughter of Zion, Behold, thy king cometh unto thee, meek, and sitting on an ass, and a colt the foal of an ass'; this has no allusion to any times but those in which it was uttered, and which, moreover, is not found in the prophet whom Matthew quotes from, but in another.

"The second chapter opens with an account (peculiar to Matthew) of the visit of the wise men of the East to Bethlehem, whither they were guided by a star which went before them and stood over the house in which the infant Jesus lay. The general legendary character of the narrative, its similarity in style with those contained in the apocryphal gospels, and more especially its conformity with those astrological notions which, though prevalent in the time of Matthew, have been exploded by the sounder scientific knowledge of our days—all unite to stamp upon the story the impress of poetic or mythic fiction.

"In Matt. viii, 28–34, we have an account of the healing of *two* demoniacs, whose disease (or whose devils, according to the evangelist) was communicated to an adjacent herd of swine. Now, putting aside the great improbability of two madmen, as fierce as these are described to be, living together, Mark and Luke, who both relate the same occurrence, state that there was *one* demoniac—obviously a much preferable version of the narrative.

"In the same manner, in xx, 30–34, Matthew relates the cure of *two* blind men near Jericho. Mark and Luke narrate the same occurrence, but speak of only *one* blind man. This story affords, also, an example of the evangelist's carelessness as a compiler, for (in ix, 27) he has already given the same narrative, but has assigned to it a different locality.

"The feeding of the five thousand is related by all

four evangelists; but the repetition of the miracle, with a slight variation in the number of the multitude and of the loaves and fragments, is peculiar to Matthew and to Mark.

"The story contained in xvii, 27, *et seq.*, of Jesus commanding Peter to catch a fish in whose mouth he should find the tribute money, has a most pagan and unworthy character about it, harmonizes admirably with the puerile narratives which abound in the apocryphal gospels, and is ignored by all the other evangelists.

"By Matthew we have crowded into one sermon the teachings and aphorisms which in the other evangelists are spread over the whole of Christ's ministry. In chap. xiii we find collected together no less than six parables of similitudes for the kingdom of heaven. In chap. x Matthew compresses into one occasion a variety of instructions and reflections which must have belonged to a subsequent part of the career of Jesus, where, indeed, they are placed by the other evangelists. In chap. xxiv, in the same manner, all the prophecies relating to the destruction of Jerusalem and the end of the world are grouped together; while, in many instances, remarks of Jesus are introduced in the midst of others with which they have no connection, and where they are obviously out of place.

"In chap. xi, 12, is the following expression: 'And *from the days of John the Baptist until now*, the kingdom of heaven suffereth violence, and the violent take it by storm.' Now, though the meaning of the passage is difficult to ascertain with precision, yet the expression 'from the days of John the Baptist until now' clearly implies that the speaker lived at a considerable distance of time from John; and though appropriate enough in a man who wrote in the year A.D. 65, or thirty years after John, could not have been used by one who spoke in the year A.D. 30 or 33, while John was yet alive. This passage, therefore, is from Matthew, not from Jesus.

"In chap. xvi, 9–10, is another remark which we may say with perfect certainty was put unwarrantably into the mouth of Christ, either by the evangelist or the source from which he copied. We have already seen that there could not have been more than *one* miraculous feeding of the multitude; yet Jesus is here made to refer to *two*.

"The passage at chap. xvi, 18, 19, bears obvious marks of being either an addition to the words of Christ, or a corruption of them. 'He saith unto them, But whom say ye that I am? And Simon Peter answered and said, Thou art the Christ, the son of the living God. And Jesus answered and said unto him, Blessed art thou, Simon Bar-jona: for flesh and blood hath not revealed it unto thee, but my Father which is in Heaven. And I say also unto thee, That thou art Peter, and upon this rock I will build my Church;

and the gates of hell shall not prevail against it. And I will give unto thee the keys of the kingdom of Heaven: and whatsoever thou shalt bind on earth shall be bound in heaven; and whatsoever thou shalt loose on earth shall be loosed in heaven.'

"The confession by Simon Peter of his belief in the Messiahship of Jesus is given by all the four evangelists, and there is no reason to question the accuracy of this part of the narrative. Mark and John, as well as Matthew, relate that Jesus bestowed on Simon the surname of Peter, and this part, therefore, may also be admitted. The remainder of the narrative corresponds almost exactly with the equivalent passages in the other evangelists; but the 18th verse has no parallel in any of them. Moreover, the word 'Church' betrays its later origin. The word was used by the disciples to signify those assemblies and organizations into which they formed themselves after the death of Jesus, and is met with frequently in the Epistles, but nowhere in the Gospels, except in the passage under consideration, and one other, which is equally, or even more, contestable. It was in use when the gospel was written, but not when the discourse of Jesus was delivered. It belongs, therefore, to Matthew, not to Jesus.

"The following verse, conferring spiritual authority, or, as it is commonly called, 'the power of the keys,' upon Peter, is repeated by Matthew in connection with another discourse (in chap. xviii, 18); and a similar passage is found in John (chap. xx, 23), who, however, places the promise after the resurrection, and represents it as made to the apostles generally, subsequent to the descent of the Holy Spirit. But there are considerations which effectually forbid our receiving this promise, at least as given by Matthew, as having really emanated from Christ. In the *first* place, in both passages it occurs in connection with the suspicious word 'Church,' and indicates an ecclesiastical, as opposed to a Christian, origin. *Secondly*, Mark, who narrates the previous conversation, omits this promise, so honorable and distinguishing to Peter, which it is impossible for those who consider him as Peter's mouthpiece, or amanuensis, to believe he would have done, had any such promise been actually made. Luke, the companion and intimate of Paul and other apostles, equally omits all mention of this singular conversation. *Thirdly*, not only do we know Peter's utter unfitness to be the depositary of such a fearful power, from his impetuosity and instability of character, and Christ's thorough perception of this unfitness, but we find that immediately after it is said to have been conferred upon him, his Lord addresses him indignantly by the epithet of Satan, and rebukes him for his presumption and unspirituality; and shortly afterward this very man thrice denied his Master. Can any one maintain it to be conceivable that Jesus should have conferred the awful power of deciding the salvation or damnation of his fellow-men upon one so frail, so faulty, and so fallible?

"In chap. xxviii, 19, there is another passage which we may say with almost certainty never came from the mouth of Christ: 'Go ye therefore and teach all nations, baptizing them in the name of the Father, and of the Son, and of the Holy Ghost.' That this definite form of baptism proceeded from Jesus is opposed by the fact that such an allocation of the Father, Son and Spirit does not elsewhere appear, except as a form of salutation in the epistles; while as a definite form of baptism it is nowhere met with throughout the New Testament. Moreover, it was not the form *used*, and could scarcely, therefore, have been the form *commanded*; for in the apostolic epistles, and even in the Acts, the form always is 'baptizing into Christ Jesus,' or 'into the name of the Lord Jesus'; while the threefold reference to God, Jesus and the Holy Ghost is only found in ecclesiastical writers, as Justin. Indeed, the formula in Matthew sounds so exactly as if it had been borrowed from the ecclesiastical ritual that it is difficult to avoid the supposition that it was transferred thence into the mouth of Jesus. Many critics, in consequence, regard it as a subsequent interpolation.

"There are two other classes of discourses attributed to Jesus both in this and in the other gospels, over the character of which much obscurity hangs:

those in which he is said to have foretold his own death and resurrection, and those in which he is represented as speaking of his second advent.

"Now, we will at once concede that it is extremely probable that Christ might easily have foreseen that a career and conduct like his could, in such a time and country, terminate only in a violent and cruel death; and that indications of such an impending fate thickened fast around him as his ministry drew nearer to a close. It is even possible, though in the highest degree unlikely, that his study of the prophets might have led him to the conclusion that the expected Messiah, whose functions he believed himself sent to fulfill, was to be a suffering and dying Prince. We do not even dispute that he might have been so amply endowed with the spirit of prophecy as distinctly to foresee his approaching crucifixion and resurrection. But we find in the evangelists themselves insuperable difficulties in the way of admitting the belief that he actually did predict these events in the language, or with anything of the precision, which is there ascribed to him.

In the fourth gospel these predictions are three in number, and in all the language is doubtful, mysterious, and obscure, and the interpretation commonly put upon them is not suggested by the words themselves, nor that which suggested itself to those who heard them; but is one affixed to them by the evangelist after the event supposed to be referred to; it is an *interpretatio ex eventu.*

"In the three Synoptical Gospels, however, the predictions are numerous, precise, and conveyed in language which it was impossible to mistake. Thus (in Matt. xx, 18, 19, and parallel passages): 'Behold, we go up to Jerusalem, and the Son of Man shall be betrayed unto the chief priests, and unto the scribes, and they shall condemn him to death, and shall deliver him to the Gentiles to mock, and to scourge, and to crucify him: and the third day he shall rise again.' Language such as this, definite, positive, explicit, and circumstantial, if really uttered, could not have been misunderstood, but must have made a deep and ineradicable impression on all who heard it, especially when repeated, as it is stated to have been, on several distinct occasions. Yet we find ample proof that *no such impression was made;* that the disciples had no conception of their Lord's approaching death—still less of his resurrection; and that, so far from their expecting either of these events, both, when they occurred, took them entirely by surprise: they were utterly confounded by the one, and could not believe the other.

"We find them, shortly after (nay; in one instance instantly after) these predictions were uttered, disputing which among them should be greatest in their coming dominion (Matt. xx, 24; Mark ix, 35; Luke xxii, 25); glorying in the idea of thrones, and asking for seats on his right hand and on his left, in his Messianic kingdom (Matt. xix, 28, xx, 21; Mark x, 37; Luke xxii, 30); which, when he approached Jerusalem, they thought 'would immediately appear' (Luke xix, 11; xxiv, 21). When Jesus was arrested in the garden of Gethsemane, they first attempted resistance, and then 'forsook him and fled'; and so completely were they scattered, that it was left for one of the Sanhedrim, Joseph of Arimathea, to provide even for his decent burial; while the women who had 'watched afar off,' and were still faithful to his memory, brought spices to embalm the body—a sure sign, were any needed, that the idea of his resurrection had never entered into their minds. Further, when the women reported his resurrection to the disciples, 'their words seemed to them as idle tales, and they believed them not' (Luke xxiv, 11). The conversation, moreover, of the two disciples on the road to Emmaus is sufficient proof that the resurrection of their Lord was a conception which had never crossed their thoughts; and, finally, according to John, when Mary found the body gone, her only notion was that it must have been removed by the gardener (xx, 15).

"All this shows, beyond, we think, the possibility of question, that the crucifixion and resurrection of Jesus were wholly unexpected by his disciples. If further proof were wanted, we find it in the words of the evangelists, who repeatedly intimate (as if struck by the incongruity we have pointed out) that they 'knew not,' or 'understood not,' these sayings (Mark ix, 31; Luke ix, 45, xviii, 34; John xx, 9).

"Here, then, we have two distinct statements, which mutually exclude and contradict each other. If Jesus really foretold his death and resurrection in the terms recorded in the Gospels, it is inconceivable that the disciples should have *misunderstood* him; for no words could be more positive, precise or intelligible than those which he is said to have repeatedly addressed to them. Neither could they have *forgotten* what had been so strongly urged upon their memory by their Master, as completely as it is evident from their subsequent conduct they actually did. They might, indeed, have *disbelieved* his prediction (as Peter appears in the first instance to have done), but in that case his crucifixion would have led him to expect his resurrection, or, at all events, to think of it: which it did not. The fulfillment of one prophecy would necessarily have recalled the other to their minds.

"The conclusion, therefore, is inevitable, that the predictions were ascribed to Jesus after the event, not really uttered by him. It is, indeed, very probable that, as gloomy anticipations of his own death pressed upon his mind, and became stronger and more confirmed as the danger came nearer, he endeavored to communicate these apprehensions to his followers, in order to prepare them for an event so fatal to their worldly hopes. That he did so, we think the conversations during, and previous to, the last supper, afford ample proof. These vague intimations of coming evil—*intermingled and relieved, doubtless, by strongly-expressed convictions of a future existence of reunion and reward*, disbelieved or disregarded by the disciples at the time—recurred to their minds after all was over, and, gathering strength and expanding in definiteness and fullness during constant repetition for nearly forty years, had, at the period when the evangelists wrote, become consolidated into the fixed prophetic form in which they have been transmitted to us.

"Lessing and other German writers presume the existence *of a number of fragmentary narratives*, some oral, some written, of the actions and sayings of Christ, such as would naturally be preserved and transmitted by persons who had witnessed those wonderful words and deeds. Sometimes there would be two or more narratives of the same event, proceeding from different witnesses; sometimes the same original narrative in its transmission would receive intentional or accidental variations, and thus come slightly modified into the hands of different evangelists. Sometimes detached sayings would be preserved without the context, and the evangelists would *locate* them where they thought them most appropriate, or provide a context for them, instances of which are numberless in the Gospels. But all these materials would be fragmentary. Each witness would retain and transmit that portion of a discourse which had impressed him most forcibly, and two witnesses would retain the same expressions with varying degrees of accuracy. One witness heard one discourse, or was present at one transaction only, and recorded that one by writing or verbally, as he best might. Of these fragments some fell into the hands of all the evangelists, some only into the hands of one, or of two; and in some cases different narratives of the same event, expression, or discourse would fall into the hands of different evangelists, which would account for their discrepancies—sometimes into the hands of one evangelist, in which case he would select that one which his judgment (or information from other sources) prompted, or would compile an account from them jointly. In any case, the evangelical narratives would be *compilations from a series of fragments of varying accuracy and completeness*. The correctness of this theory of the origin of the gospels seems to be not so much confirmed as distinctly *asserted* by Luke. 'Forasmuch as many have taken in hand to set forth in order a declaration of those things *which are most surely believed among us, even as they delivered them unto us which from the beginning were eye-witnesses and ministers of the word.*'"

Mr. Greg continues at length, and says:

"Having arrived at the conclusion that the Gospels are compilations from a variety of fragmentary narratives, and reports of discourses and conversations, oral or written, which were current in Palestine from thirty to forty years after the death of Jesus, we now come to the very interesting and momentous inquiry, how far these narratives and discourses can be accepted as accurate and faithful records of what was actually said and done? whether they can be regarded as thoroughly and minutely correct? and, if not, in what respects and to what extent do they deviate from that thorough and minute correctness?"

Mr. Greg adds:

"The prophecies of the second coming of Christ (Matt. xxiv; Mark xiii; Luke xvii, 22–37, xxi, 5–36) are mixed up with those of the destruction of Jerusalem by Titus in a manner which has long been the perplexity and despair of orthodox commentators. The obvious meaning of the passages which contain these predictions—the sense in which they were evidently understood by the evangelists who wrote them down, the sense which we know from many sources they conveyed to the minds of the early Christians—clearly is, that the coming of Christ to judge the world should follow *immediately* ('immediately,' 'in those days') the destruction of the Holy City, and should take place during the lifetime of the then-existing generation. 'Verily, I say unto you, This generation shall not pass away till all these things be fulfilled' (Matt. xxiv, 34; Mark xiii, 30; Luke xxi, 32). 'There be some standing here that shall not taste of death till they see the Son of Man coming in his kingdom' (Matt. xvi, 28). 'Verily, I say unto you, ye shall not have gone over the cities of Israel till the Son of Man be come' (Matt. x, 23). 'If I will that he tarry till I come, what is that to thee?' (John xxi, 23).

"The opinions of Christ, as recorded in the Gospels, present remarkable discrepancies, and even contradictions. On the one hand, we read of his saying, 'Think not that I am come to destroy the law or the prophets: I am not come to destroy, but to fulfill. For verily I say unto you, till heaven and earth pass, one jot or one tittle shall in no wise pass from the law, till all be fulfilled.'"

"The writings which compose the volume called by us the New Testament had assumed their present collective form, and were generally received throughout the Christian Churches, about the end of the second century. They were selected out of a number of others; but by whom they were selected, or what principle guided the selection, history leaves in doubt. We find, moreover, that the early Fathers disagreed among themselves in their estimate of the genuineness and authority of many of the books; that some of them received books which we exclude, and excluded others which we admit.

"The Gospels, as professed records of Christ's deeds and words, will be allowed to form the most important portion of the New Testament collection. Now, the idea of God having inspired *four* different men to write a history of the same transactions—or, rather, of many different men having undertaken to write such a history, of whom God inspired *four* only to write correctly, leaving the others to their own unaided resources, and giving us no test by which to distinguish the inspired from the uninspired—certainly appears self-confuting, and anything but 'natural.' If the accounts of the same transactions agree, where was the necessity for more than one? If they differ (as they notoriously do), it is certain that only one can be inspired—and which is that one? In all other religions claiming a divine origin this incongruity is avoided.

"Further, the Gospels nowhere affirm, or even intimate, their own inspiration—a claim to credence which, had they possessed it, they assuredly would not have failed to put forth. Luke, it is clear from his exordium, had no notion of his own inspiration, but founds his title to take his place among the annalists, and to be listened to as at least equally competent with any of his competitors, on his having been from the first cognizant of the transactions he was about to relate. Nor do the apostolic writings bear any such testimony to them; nor could they well do so, having (with the exception of the Epistles of John) been composed previous to them.

"It is true that we find in John much dogmatic assertion of being the sole teacher of truth, and much denunciation of all who did not listen submissively to him; but neither in his epistles nor in those of Peter, James, or Jude, do we find any claim to special knowledge of truth, or guarantee from error by direct spiritual aid.

"But, it will be urged, the Gospels record that Christ promised inspiration to his apostles. In the first place, Paul was not included in this promise. In the next place, we have already seen that the divine origin of these books is a doctrine for which no ground can be shown; and their correctness, as records of Christ's words, is still to be established. The apostles clearly were not altogether inspired, inasmuch as they fell into mistakes, disputed, and disagreed among themselves.

"The only one of the New Testament writings which contains a clear affirmation of its own inspiration is the one which in all ages has been regarded as of the most doubtful authenticity—viz., the Apocalypse. It was rejected by many of the earliest Christian authorities. It is rejected by most of the ablest biblical critics of to-day. Luther, in the preface to his translation, inserted a protest against the inspiration of the Apocalypse, which protest he solemnly charged every one to prefix who chose to publish the translation. In this protest one of his chief grounds for the rejection is the suspicious fact that this writer alone blazons forth his own inspiration.

"We can discover no ground for believing that the Scriptures are *inspired*, taking that word in its ordinary acceptation—viz., that they 'came from God,' were dictated or suggested by him, were supernaturally preserved from error, both as to fact and doctrine, and must therefore be received in all their parts as authoritative and infallible. This conclusion is perfectly compatible with the belief that they *contain* a human record, and, in substance, a faithful record; a human history, and, in the main, a true history—of the dealings of God with man: *records, not revelations;* histories to be investigated like other histories; documents of which the date, the authorship, the genuineness, the accuracy of the text, are to be ascertained by the same principles of investigation as we apply to other documents.

"But when we come to the fourth gospel, especially to those portions of it whose peculiar style betrays that they came from John, and not from Jesus, the case is very different. We find here many passages evidently intended to convey the impression that Jesus was endowed with a superhuman nature, but nearly all expressed in language savoring less of Christian simplicity than of Alexandrian philosophy. The evangelist commences his gospel with a confused statement of the Platonic doctrine as modified in Alexandria, and that the Logos was a partaker of the Divine Nature, and was the Creator of the world; on which he proceeds to ingraft his own notion, that Jesus was this Logos; that the Logos, or the divine wisdom, the second person in Plato's Trinity, became flesh in the person of the prophet of Nazareth. Now, can any one read the epistles, or the first three gospels, or even the whole of the fourth, and not at once repudiate the notion that Jesus was, and knew himself to be, the Creator of the world?—which John affirms him to have been. Throughout this gospel we find constant repetitions of the same endeavor to make out a superhuman nature for Christ; but the ungenuineness of these passages has already been fully considered.

"Once more: the doctrine of the Atonement, of Christ's death having been a sacrifice in expiation of the sins of mankind, is the keystone of modern orthodoxy. It takes its origin from the epistles, but, we believe, can only appeal to *three* texts in the evangelists for even partial confirmation. In Matt. xx, 28, it is said, 'The Son of Man came, not to be ministered unto, but to minister, and to give his life *a ransom for many*'—an expression which may *countenance* the doctrine, but assuredly does not contain it. Again, in Matt. xxvi, 28, we find, 'This is my blood of the New Testament, which is shed for many *for the re-*

mission of sins.' Mark (xiv, 24) and Luke (xxi, 20), however, who give the same sentence, *both omit the significant expression.* In the fourth gospel, John the Baptist is represented as saying of Jesus (i, 29), 'Behold the Lamb of God, which taketh away the sin of the world'—an expression which may be intended to convey the doctrine, but which occurs in what we have already shown to be about the most apocryphal portion of the whole gospel.

"We conclude that nearly all the discourses of Jesus in the fourth gospel are mainly the composition of the evangelist from memory or tradition, rather than the genuine utterances of our great Teacher. It may be satisfactory, as further confirmation, to select a few single passages and expressions, as to the unauthentic character of which there can be no question. Thus, at chap. iii, 11, Jesus is represented as saying to Nicodemus, in the midst of his discourse about regeneration: 'We speak that we do know, and testify that which we have seen; and receive ye not our witness'—expressions wholly unmeaning and out of place in the mouth of Jesus on an occasion where he is testifying nothing at all, but merely propounding a mystical dogma to an auditor dull of comprehension; but expressions which are the evangelist's habitual form of asseveration and complain

"As to Christ's changing water into pure wine, it may well be said to be plain honesty perverted by an originally false assumption. No portion of the gospel history, scarcely any portion of Old Testament, or even of apocryphal, narratives, bears such unmistakable marks of fiction. It is a story which, if found in any other volume, would at once have been dismissed as a clumsy and manifest invention. In the first place, it is a miracle wrought to supply more wine to men who had already drunk much—a deed which has no suitability to the character of Jesus, and no analogy to any other of his miracles. *Secondly*, though it was, as we are told, the first of his miracles, his mother is represented as expecting him to work a miracle, and to commence his public career with so unfit and improbable a one. *Thirdly*, Jesus is said to have spoken harshly to his mother, asking her what they had in common, and telling her that 'his hour [for working miracles] was not yet come,' when he knew that it *was* come. *Fourthly*, in spite of this rebuff, Mary is represented as still expecting a miracle, and *this particular one*, and as making preparation for it: 'She saith to the servants, Whatsoever he saith unto you, do it'; and accordingly Jesus immediately began to give orders to them. *Fifthly*, the superior quality of the wine, and the enormous quantity produced (135 gallons, or, in our language, above 43 dozen) are obviously fabulous. And those who are familiar with the Apocryphal Gospels will have no difficulty in recognizing the close consanguinity between the whole narrative and the stories of miracles with which they abound. It is perfectly hopeless, as well as mischievous, to endeavor to retain it as a portion of authentic history.

"In all the Synoptical Gospels we find instances of the cure of demoniacs by Jesus early in his career, in which the demons promptly, spontaneously and loudly bear testimony to his Messiahship. These statements occur once in Matthew (viii, 29); four times in Mark (i, 24, 34; iii, 11; v, 7); and three times in Luke (iv, 33, 41; viii, 28). Now, two points are evident to common sense, and are fully admitted by honest criticism: *first*, that these demoniacs were lunatic and epileptic patients; and, *secondly*, that Jesus (or the narrators who framed the language of Jesus throughout the Synoptical Gospels) shared the common belief that these maladies were caused by evil spirits inhabiting the bodies of the sufferers. We are then landed in this conclusion (certainly not a probable one, nor the one intended to be conveyed by the narrators): that the idea of Jesus being the Messiah was adopted by madmen before it had found entrance into the public mind, apparently even before it was received by his immediate disciples—was in fact first suggested by madmen; in other words, that it was an idea which originated with insane brains, which presented itself to, and found acceptance with, insane brains more readily than sane ones. The conception of the evangelists clearly was that Jesus derived honor (and his mission confirmation) from this early recognition of his Messianic character by hostile spirits of a superior order of intelligences; but to us, who know that these supposed superior intelligences were really unhappy men whose natural intellect had been perverted or impaired, the effect of the narratives becomes absolutely reversed; and if they are to be accepted as historical, they lead inevitably to the conclusion that the idea of the Messiahship of Jesus was originally formed in disordered brains, and spread thence among the mass of the disciples. The only rescue from this conclusion lies in the admission that these narratives are not historical, but mythic, and belong to that class of additions which early grew up in the Christian Church, out of the desire to honor and aggrandize the memory of its Founder, and which our uncritical evangelists embodied as they found them.

"Passing over a few minor passages of doubtful authenticity or accuracy, we come to one near the close of the gospel which we have no scruple in pronouncing to be an unwarranted interpolation. In chap. xxii, 36–38, Jesus is reported, after the Last Supper, to have said to his disciples, 'He that hath no sword, let him sell his garment and buy one. And they said, Lord, behold, here are two swords. And he said, It is enough.' Christ never could have uttered such a command, nor, we should imagine, anything which could have been mistaken for it. The very idea is contradicted by his whole character, and utterly precluded by the narratives of the other evangelists; for when Peter did use the sword, he met with a severe rebuke from his Master: 'Put up thy sword into the sheath; the cup which my Father hath given me, shall I not drink it?' according to John. 'Put up again thy sword into its place; for all they that take the sword shall perish by the sword,' according to Matthew. The passage we conceive to be a clumsy invention of some early narrator, to account for the remarkable fact of Peter having a sword at the time of Christ's apprehension; and it is inconceivable to us how a sensible compiler like Luke could have admitted into his history such an apocryphal and unharmonizing fragment."

We have quoted from Mr. Greg more largely than was our intention, but the subjects are so ably handled that we could not refrain from giving his remarks to the extent we have. One more extract only will be made:

"The account given by Luke (iii, 21) of the visible and audible signs from heaven at the baptism of Jesus has been very generally felt and allowed to be incompatible with the inquiry subsequently made by John the Baptist (vii, 19) as to whether Jesus were the Messiah or not; and the incongruity is considered to indicate inaccuracy or interpolation in one of the two narratives. It is justly held impossible that if John had seen the Holy Spirit descending upon Jesus, and had heard a heavenly voice declaring him to be the beloved Son of God, he could ever have entertained a doubt that he was the Messiah, whose coming he himself had just announced (16). According to Luke, as he now stands, John expected the Messiah; described himself as his forerunner; saw at the moment of the baptism a supernatural shape, and heard a supernatural voice announcing Jesus to be that Messiah: and yet, shortly after—on hearing, too, of miracles which should have confirmed his belief, had it ever wavered—he sends a message implying doubt (or rather ignorance), and asking the question which Heaven itself had already answered in his hearing. Some commentators have endeavored to escape from the difficulty by pleading that the appearances at baptism might have been perceptible to Jesus alone; and they have adduced the use of the second person by the divine voice ('*Thou art* my beloved Son') in Mark and Luke, and the peculiar language of Matthew, in confirmation of this view. But (not to argue that, if the vision and the voice were imperceptible to the spectators, they could not have given that public and conclusive attestation to the Messiahship of Jesus which was their obvious object and intention) a comparison of the four accounts clearly shows that the evangelists *meant* to state that the dove was visible and the voice audible to John and to all the spectators, who, according to Luke, must have been numerous. In Matthew, the grammatical construction of iii, 16, would intimate that it was Jesus who saw the heavens open and the dove descend, but that the expression 'alighting upon him,' ἐζχομενον ἐπ' αὐτόν, should in this case have been ἐφ' αὐτόν, 'upon himself.' However, it is very possible that Matthew may have written inaccurate, as he certainly wrote unclassical, Greek. But the voice in the next verse, speaking in the third person, 'This is my beloved Son,' must have been addressed to the spectators, not to Jesus. Mark has the same unharmonizing expression, ἐπ' αὐτον. Luke describes the scene as passing before numbers, 'when all the people were baptized, it came to pass that Jesus also being baptized'; and then adds to the account of the other evangelists that the dove descended 'in a bodily shape,' ἐν σωματικῷ εἴδει, as if to contradict the idea that it was a subjective, not an objective, fact—a vision, not a phenomenon; he can only mean that it was an appearance visible to all present. The version given in the fourth evangelist shows still more clearly that such was the meaning generally attached to the tradition current among the Christians at the time it was embodied in the Gospels. The Baptist is there represented as affirming that he himself saw the Spirit descending like a dove upon Jesus, and that it was this appearance which convinced him of the Messiahship of Jesus.

"Considering all this, then, we must admit that, while the naturalness of John's message to Christ, and the exact accordance. of the two accounts given of it, render the historical accuracy of that relation highly probable, the discrepancies in the four narratives of the baptism strongly indicate either that the original tradition came from different sources, or that it has undergone considerable modification in the course of transmission; and also that the narratives themselves are discredited by the subsequent message."

If, as most Christians contend, the New Testament was all written by inspiration, how did it happen that, in matters so simple and plain as the inscription over the cross and the time of Jesus' crucifixion, the accounts should be so different? Mark says he was crucified the third hour (nine in the morning); John says it was the sixth hour (twelve at noon). Matthew gives the inscription, "This is Jesus the King of the Jews"; Mark, "The King of the Jews"; Luke, "This is the King of the Jews"; John, "Jesus of Nazareth, King of the Jews."

These circumstances may be called trivial, and yet if the writers disagree so materially in what was plainly written before them, what gross errors may we not expect in the relation of other matters, much more difficult to remember, that were not written down at all, but told and retold from one to another, and at last recorded by persons who were not present at the time they happened! We are not informed that any of the apostles except Peter were present at the crucifixion, and he, according to Matthew, behaved badly (xxvi, 74): "Then Peter began to curse and to swear, saying, I know not the man." Yet we are now called upon to believe in this same Peter—who, according to this inspired book, is guilty of the vilest perjury—as holding the keys to Paradise!

The circumstances attending the crucifixion are differently related in the four Synoptical books. Matthew says there was darkness over all the land, from the sixth hour to the ninth; that the veil of the temple was rent in twain from the top to the bottom; that there was an earthquake, and the rocks were rent; that the graves opened, and the bodies of many of the saints which slept arose and came out of their graves after the resurrection, and went into the holy city, and appeared unto many. What would our high Christians say if Spiritualists should relate, as truth, a thing of this sort now? Mark makes no mention of an earthquake and the rocks rending, nor of the graves opening and the dead men walking out. Luke is also silent in regard to these occurrences. And though the writer of the book of John, whoever he was, details all the circumssances attending the crucifixion down to the burial of Christ, he says nothing about the darkness, the veil of the temple, the earthquake, the rocks, the graves, or the dead men.

While reading the account of these wonderful events, we can hardly realize the intense excitement they must have occasioned, or the deep impression they must have made on the public mind, at the time of their occurrence. No one, therefore, can think that, if they had been true, as the writer of Matthew's gospel relates them, they would have escaped the notice of the other evangelists. As faithful historians an account would have been given by all of them: the names of the saints restored to life would have been recorded; the fact of their whereabouts stated after they were first seen; whether they went back into their graves, or remained among the living, and in what place their abode was fixed; what they said or did; and how long they remained before going back to their graves.

Now, let the reader understand that we have full faith in the crucifixion of Jesus, and that he was apparently dead when he was taken down from the cross, but that he was not really dead. Nor can we see that it makes the least difference as to the atonement, after he had suffered on the cross, whether suspended animation lasted a longer or a shorter time; and in no other cases than such as we refer to do we believe in the resurrection of the body. Thousands of cases have been witnessed where, to even the practiced eye of a physician, death had, to every appearance, taken place, and yet, hours, and sometimes days, afterward, life was found still to remain in the body, and the fact ascertained that the supposed dead were not dead. Faith in a spiritual resurrection is a proper and reasonable thing, while to us the resurrection of the body entire appears unreasonable and improbable. Not a shade of doubt ought to exist in the mind of any one as to the spiritual resurrection of Jesus, or that his spirit did not, at the time of his crucifixion, or subsequently, ascend to God, his Father and our Father. Of this we have spoken elsewhere.

CHAPTER VII.

INSTRUCTION, DIRECTION, AND ADMONITION.

If the reader has concluded that we are inimical to the New Testament, we desire to say again that we are disposed to take it for what it is, rather than for what our better judgment tells us it is not. Our faith in God is as strong as it can be; so is our belief and faith in Jesus of Nazareth, and in a holy spirit—these three: so far we are Trinitarians. This is as far as we can honestly go.

We have no doubt that Jesus was sent into the world by God, his Father and our Father; and not only he, but others, with inferior powers, yet sent by God. So we see that the whole world is full of God, who is manifesting himself continually, through his inspiration, teaching us the way of truth and life. These manifestations may not be visible every moment, but they have come, are coming, and will come. The power of God is acting without intermission, directing and enlightening. Were we so disposed, we might have more of this regenerating force, we might have more of God and his spirit. This, we are aware, is a repetition of what has been said frequently before, but we desire to keep it before our readers, to prevent their misunderstanding our views.

The following are some of the many particular portions of the New Testament that we desire to notice. They are so plain that comments on most of them are superfluous. The Sermon on the Mount (Matt. v–vii) is given entire; for though this and other things which we quote are readily found in the Bible, we deem it proper to insert them here to the extent we do, and hope none will complain on that account:

1. "And seeing the multitudes, he went up into a mountain: and when he was set, his disciples came unto him:

2. "And he opened his mouth, and taught them, saying,

3. "Blessed are the poor in spirit: for theirs is the kingdom of heaven.

4. "Blessed are they that mourn: for they shall be comforted.

5. "Blessed are the meek: for they shall inherit the earth.

6. "Blessed are they which do hunger and thirst after righteousness: for they shall be filled.

7. "Blessed are the merciful: for they shall obtain mercy.

8. "Blessed are the pure in heart: for they shall see God.

9. "Blessed are the peacemakers: for they shall be called the children of God.

10. "Blessed are they which are persecuted for righteousness' sake: for theirs is the kingdom of heaven.

11. "Blessed are ye when men shall revile you, and persecute you, and shall say all manner of evil against you falsely, for my sake.

12. "Rejoice, and be exceeding glad: for great is your reward in heaven: for so persecuted they the prophets which were before you.

13. "Ye are the salt of the earth: but if the salt have lost his savor, wherewith shall it be salted? it is thenceforth good for nothing, but to be cast out, and to be trodden under foot of men.

14. "Ye are the light of the world. A city that is set on an hill cannot be hid.

15. "Neither do men light a candle, and put it under a bushel, but on a candlestick; and it giveth light unto all that are in the house.

16. "Let your light so shine before men that they may see your good works, and glorify your Father which is in heaven.

17. "Think not that I am come to destroy the

law, or the prophets: I am not come to destroy, but to fulfill.

18. "For verily I say unto you, Till heaven and earth pass, one jot or one tittle shall in no wise pass from the law, till all be fulfilled.

19. "Whosoever, therefore, shall break one of these least commandments, and shall teach men so, he shall be called the least in the kingdom of heaven: but whosoever shall do and teach them, the same shall be called great in the kingdom of heaven.

20. "For I say unto you, That except your righteousness shall exceed the righteousness of the scribes and Pharisees, ye shall in no case enter into the kingdom of heaven.

21. "Ye have heard that it was said by them of old time, Thou shalt not kill; and whosoever shall kill shall be in danger of the judgment:

22. "But I say unto you, That whosoever is angry with his brother without a cause shall be in danger of the judgment: and whosoever shall say to his brother, Raca, shall be in danger of the council: but whosoever shall say, Thou fool, shall be in danger of hell fire.

23. "Therefore, if thou bring thy gift to the altar, and there rememberest that thy brother hath aught against thee;

24. "Leave there thy gift before the altar, and

Instruction, Direction, and Admonition. 331

go thy way; first be reconciled to thy brother, and then come and offer thy gift.

25. "Agree with thine adversary quickly, whiles thou art in the way with him; lest at any time the adversary deliver thee to the judge, and the judge deliver thee to the officer, and thou be cast into prison.

26. "Verily I say unto thee, Thou shalt by no means come out thence, till thou hast paid the uttermost farthing.

27. "Ye have heard that it was said by them of old time, Thou shalt not commit adultery:

28. "But I say unto you, That whosoever looketh on a woman to lust after her hath committed adultery with her already in his heart.

29. "And if thy right eye offend thee, pluck it out, and cast it from thee: for it is profitable for thee that one of thy members should perish, and not that thy whole body should be cast into hell.

30. "And if thy right hand offend thee, cut it off, and cast it from thee: for it is profitable for thee that one of thy members should perish, and not that thy whole body should be cast into hell.

31. "It hath been said, Whosoever shall put away his wife, let him give her a writing of divorcement:

32. "But I say unto you, That whosoever shall put away his wife, saving for the cause of fornication,

causeth her to commit adultery: and whosoever shall marry her that is divorced committeth adultery.

33. "Again, ye have heard that it hath been said by them of old time, Thou shalt not forswear thyself, but shalt perform unto the Lord thine oaths:

34. "But I say unto you, Swear not at all; neither by heaven; for it is God's throne:

35. "Nor by the earth; for it is his footstool: neither by Jerusalem; for it is the city of the great King.

36. "Neither shalt thou swear by thy head, because thou canst not make one hair white or black.

37. "But let your communication be, Yea, yea; Nay, nay: for whatsoever is more than these cometh of evil.

38. "Ye have heard that it hath been said, An eye for an eye, and a tooth for a tooth:

39. "But I say unto you, That ye resist not evil: but whosoever shall smite thee on thy right cheek, turn to him the other also.

40. "And if any man will sue thee at the law, and take away thy coat, let him have thy cloke also.

41. "And whosoever shall compel thee to go a mile, go with him twain.

42. "Give to him that asketh thee, and from him that would borrow of thee turn thou not away.

43. "Ye have heard that it hath been said, Thou shalt love thy neighbor, and hate thine enemy:

44. "But I say unto you, Love your enemies, bless them that curse you, do good to them that hate you, and pray for them which despitefully use you, and persecute you;

45. "That ye may be the children of your Father which is in heaven: for he maketh his sun to rise on the evil and on the good, and sendeth rain on the just and on the unjust.

46. "For if ye love them which love you, what reward have ye? do not even the publicans the same?

47. "And if ye salute your brethren only, what do ye more than others? do not even the publicans so?

48. "Be ye therefore perfect, even as your Father which is in heaven is perfect."

Matthew vi:

1. "Take heed that ye do not your alms before men, to be seen of them: otherwise ye have no reward of your Father which is in heaven.

2. "Therefore, when thou doest thine alms, do not sound a trumpet before thee, as the hypocrites do in the synagogues and in the streets, that they may have glory of men. Verily I say unto you, They have their reward.

3. "But when thou doest alms, let not thy left nand know what thy right hand doeth:

4. "That thine alms may be in secret: and thy Father which seeth in secret himself shall reward thee openly.

5. "And when thou prayest, thou shalt not be as the hypocrites are: for they love to pray standing in the synagogues and in the corners of the streets, that they may be seen of men. Verily I say unto you, They have their reward.

6. "But thou, when thou prayest, enter into thy closet, and when thou hast shut thy door, pray to thy Father which is in secret; and thy Father which seeth in secret shall reward thee openly.

7. "But when ye pray, use not vain repetitions, as the heathen do: for they think that they shall be heard for their much speaking.

8. "Be not ye, therefore, like unto them: for your Father knoweth what things ye have need of, before ye ask him.

9. "After this manner, therefore, pray ye: Our Father which art in heaven, Hallowed be thy name.

10. "Thy kingdom come. Thy will be done in earth, as it is in heaven.

11. "Give us this day our daily bread.

12. "And forgive us our debts, as we forgive our debtors.

13. "And lead us not into temptation, but deliver us from evil: For thine is the kingdom, and the power, and the glory, forever. Amen.

14. "For if ye forgive men their trespasses, your heavenly Father will also forgive you:

15. "But if ye forgive not men their trespasses, neither will your Father forgive your trespasses.

16. "Moreover, when ye fast, be not, as the hypocrites, of a sad countenance: for they disfigure their faces, that they may appear unto men to fast. Verily I say unto you, They have their reward.

17. "But thou, when thou fastest, anoint thine head, and wash thy face;

18. "That thou appear not unto men to fast, but unto thy Father which is in secret: and thy Father which seeth in secret shall reward thee openly.

19. "Lay not up for yourselves treasures upon earth, where moth and rust doth corrupt, and where thieves break through and steal:

20. "But lay up for yourselves treasures in heaven, where neither moth nor rust doth corrupt, and where thieves do not break through nor steal:

21. "For where your treasure is, there will your heart be also.

22. "The light of the body is the eye: if, therefore, thine eye be single, thy whole body shall be full of light.

23. "But if thine eye be evil, thy whole body shall be full of darkness. If, therefore, the light that is in thee be darkness, how great is that darkness!

24. "No man can serve two masters: for either he will hate the one, and love the other; or else he

will hold to the one, and despise the other. Ye cannot serve God and mammon.

25. "Therefore I say unto you, Take no thought for your life, what ye shall eat, or what ye shall drink; nor yet for your body, what ye shall put on. Is not the life more than meat, and the body than raiment?

26. "Behold the fowls of the air: for they sow not, neither do they reap, nor gather into barns; yet your heavenly Father feedeth them. Are ye not much better than they?

27. "Which of you by taking thought can add one cubit unto his stature?

28. "And why take ye thought for raiment? Consider the lilies of the field, how they grow; they toil not, neither do they spin:

29. "And yet I say unto you, That even Solomon in all his glory was not arrayed like one of these.

30. "Wherefore, if God so clothe the grass of the field, which to-day is, and to-morrow is cast into the oven, shall he not much more clothe you, O ye of little faith?

31. "Therefore take no thought, saying, What shall we eat? or, What shall we drink? or, Wherewithal shall we be clothed?

32. "(For after all these things do the Gentiles seek): for your heavenly Father knoweth that ye have need of all these things.

33. "But seek ye first the kingdom of God, and his righteousness; and all these things shall be added unto you.

34. "Take, therefore, no thought for the morrow: for the morrow shall take thought for the things of itself. Sufficient unto the day is the evil thereof."

Matthew vii:

1. "Judge not, that ye be not judged.

2. "For with what judgment ye judge, ye shall be judged: and with what measure ye mete, it shall be measured to you again.

3. "And why beholdest thou the mote that is in thy brother's eye, but considerest not the beam that is in thine own eye?

4. "Or how wilt thou say to thy brother, Let me pull out the mote out of thine eye; and, behold, a beam is in thine own eye?

5. "Thou hypocrite, first cast out the beam out of thine own eye; and then shalt thou see clearly to cast out the mote out of thy brother's eye.

6. "Give not that which is holy unto the dogs, neither cast ye your pearls before swine, lest they trample them under their feet, and turn again and rend you.

7. "Ask, and it shall be given you; seek, and ye shall find; knock, and it shall be opened unto you:

8. "For every one that asketh receiveth; and he

that seeketh findeth; and to him that knocketh it shall be opened.

9. "Or what man is there of you, whom if his son ask bread, will he give him a stone?

10. "Or if he ask a fish, will he give him a serpent?

11. "If ye, then, being evil, know how to give good gifts unto your children, how much more shall your Father which is in heaven give good things to them that ask him?

12. "Therefore, all things whatsoever ye would that men should do to you, do ye even so to them: for this is the law and the prophets."

21. "Not every one that saith unto me, Lord, Lord, shall enter into the kingdom of heaven; but he that doeth the will of my Father which is in heaven.

22. "Many will say to me in that day, Lord, Lord, have we not prophesied in thy name? and in thy name have cast out devils? and in thy name done many wonderful works?

23. "And then will I profess unto them, I never knew you: depart from me, ye that work iniquity."

This sermon, as a rule of action, a guiding chart to lead men in the path of duty, to live happily here and to secure a blessed hereafter, has, as a whole, no equal. With no other direction than that here given none would go far astray, if their aims and desires were right. God will lead us into all truth if we are willing to be led by him.

Whole pages might be filled with commendation of this superhuman production; for no man could utter such words unaided by the express inspiration of God, the working of his spirit, the outpouring of his divine force and power.

Matthew ix:

9. "And as Jesus passed forth from thence, he saw a man, named Matthew, sitting at the receipt of custom: and he saith unto him, Follow me. And he arose, and followed him.

10. "And it came to pass, as Jesus sat at meat in the house, behold, many publicans and sinners came and sat down with him and his disciples.

11. "And when the Pharisees saw it, they said unto his disciples, Why eateth your Master with publicans and sinners?

12. "But when Jesus heard that, he said unto them, They that be whole need not a physician, but they that are sick.

13. "But go ye and learn what that meaneth, I will have mercy, and not sacrifice: for I am not come to call the righteous, but sinners, to repentance."

Now, there is high authority for saying that this book of Matthew was written by him, or by his dictation, not later than A.D. 68. If it was compiled by him, why does he speak of himself as he does in the 9th verse? Does it not show that the stories and detached portions of what now constitute the book were gathered up and put in such form as the compiler deemed proper, as near as he could ascertain, a long time after Matthew? Far be it from us to accuse the writers of the New Testament of intentional wrong. They considered the writings of priceless value to the world, and so do we.

These few words express, with great force, the inestimable value of the religion of Jesus (Matt. xi):

28. "Come unto me, all ye that labor and are heavy laden, and I will give you rest.

29. "Take my yoke upon you, and learn of me; for I am meek and lowly in heart: and ye shall find rest unto your souls.

30. "For my yoke is easy, and my burden is light."

Matthew xvi:

24. "Then said Jesus unto his disciples, If any man will come after me, let him deny himself, and take up his cross, and follow me.

25. "For whosoever will save his life shall lose it; and whosoever will lose his life for my sake shall find it.

26. "For what is a man profited, if he shall gain the whole world, and lose his own soul? or what shall a man give in exchange for his soul?

27. "For the Son of man shall come in the glory of his Father with his angels; and then he shall reward every man according to his works.

28. "Verily I say unto you, There be some standing here which shall not taste of death till they see the Son of man coming in his kingdom."

We may say, in respect to this passage, that it shows plainly there is something to be done in the way of duty to entitle us to be called Christians. Evil must be overcome, wicked thoughts driven out of the mind. Jesus must be followed not only in word, but in deed; not in talk alone, but in action. It will be readily seen from the 28th verse that a strong expectation was cherished that the new kingdom was soon to be set up by Jesus. The same impression is obtained from many other passages.

Matthew xx:

20. "Then came to him the mother of Zebedee's children with her sons, worshiping him, and desiring a certain thing of him.

21. "And he said unto her, What wilt thou? She saith unto him, Grant that these my two sons may sit, the one on thy right hand, and the other on the left, in thy kingdom.

22. "But Jesus answered and said, Ye know not what ye ask. Are ye able to drink of the cup that I shall drink of, and to be baptized with the baptism that I am baptized with? They say unto him, We are able."

From the above extracts it is also evident that a kingdom was expected to be established by Jesus, and that his most faithful and zealous followers expected to occupy high positions in it here on the earth.

Matthew xxiii:

13. "But woe unto you, scribes and Pharisees, hypocrites! for ye shut up the kingdom of heaven against men: for ye neither go in yourselves, neither suffer ye them that are entering to go in.

14. "Woe unto you, scribes and Pharisees, hypocrites! for ye devour widows' houses, and for a pretense make long prayer: therefore ye shall receive the greater damnation.

15. "Woe unto you, scribes and Pharisees, hypocrites! for ye compass sea and land to make one proselyte, and when he is made, ye make him twofold more the child of hell than yourselves."

23. "Woe unto you, scribes and Pharisees, hypocrites! for ye pay tithe of mint and anise and cummin, and have omitted the weightier matters of the law, judgment, mercy, and faith: these ought ye to have done, and not to leave the other undone.

24. "Ye blind guides, which strain at a gnat, and swallow a camel.

25. "Woe unto you, scribes and Pharisees, hypocrites! for ye make clean the outside of the cup and of the platter, but within they are full of extortion and excess.

26. "Thou blind Pharisee, cleanse first that which

is within the cup and platter, that the outside of them may be clean also.

27. "Woe unto you, scribes and Pharisees, hypocrites! for ye are like unto whited sepulchers, which indeed appear beautiful outward, but are within full of dead men's bones, and of all uncleanness.

28. "Even so ye also outwardly appear righteous unto men, but within ye are full of hypocrisy and iniquity.

29. "Woe unto you, scribes and Pharisees, hypocrites! because ye build the tombs of the prophets, and garnish the sepulchers of the righteous,

30. "And say, If we had been in the days of our fathers, we would not have been partakers with them in the blood of the prophets.

31. "Wherefore ye be witnesses unto yourselves, that ye are the children of them which killed the prophets.

32. "Fill ye up, then, the measure of your fathers.

33. "Ye serpents, ye generation of vipers, how can ye escape the damnation of hell?

34. "Wherefore, behold, I send unto you prophets, and wise men, and scribes: and some of them ye shall kill and crucify; and some of them shall ye scourge in your synagogues, and persecute them from city to city:

35. "That upon you may come all the righteous blood shed upon the earth, from the blood of righteous

Abel unto the blood of Zacharias son of Barachias, whom ye slew between the temple and the altar.

36. "Verily I say unto you, All these things shall come upon this generation.

37. "O Jerusalem, Jerusalem, thou that killest the prophets, and stoneth them that are sent unto thee, how often would I have gathered thy children together, even as a hen gathereth her chickens under her wings, and ye would not!

38. "Behold, your house is left unto you desolate.

39. "For I say unto you, Ye shall not see me henceforth, till ye shall say, Blessed is he that cometh in the name of the Lord."

In many respects these quotations are entitled to serious contemplation. And it may be well to have the reader understand that the term "scribe" was applied to those who adhered with great tenacity to the law—a lawyer, an expounder of the Jewish law. Pharisaism took its rise B.C. 145. Speaking after the manner of our time, they were a High-Church party—great sticklers for forms and special observances, who looked particularly to keeping the outside of the cup and platter clean. Above all others they were denounced by the meek and lowly Jesus, as, we fear, many deserve to be who have come after them.

The destruction of the temple, according to the record (Matt. xxiv), is foretold by Jesus, and his disciples inquired of him the time it would happen, and also of the signs that should be given of his second coming. In connection with the admonition contained in this chapter, let us see how well some other portions will bear critical examination. Before it takes place—that is, the destruction of the temple at Jerusalem, and the sacking of the city, which happened about A.D. 70, some thirty-five years after the crucifixion—the writer represents Jesus as saying:

Matthew xxiv:

14. "And this gospel of the kingdom shall be preached in all the world for a witness unto all nations; and then shall the end come."

What end was this? Surely not the end of the world, for that exists yet; though it is plain enough that the more enthusiastic and zealous of Jesus' followers anticipated wonderful changes, not only in spiritual but in temporal matters, involving the end of old religious rites and dogmas, and the setting up of the Messianic kingdom. In the year A.D. 70 the Christian gospel was not preached in all the world, nor is it now in half the world. That part of the prediction has not been fulfilled, nor has the event happened which is stated in verse 27:

27. "For as the lightning cometh out of the east, and shineth even unto the west; so shall also the coming of the Son of man be.

28. "For wheresoever the carcase is, there will the eagles be gathered together.

29. "Immediately after the tribulation of those days shall the sun be darkened, and the moon shall not give her light, and the stars shall fall from heaven, and the powers of the heavens shall be shaken:

30. "And then shall appear the sign of the Son of man in heaven: and then shall all the tribes of the earth mourn, and they shall see the Son of man coming in the clouds of heaven with power and great glory.

31. "And he shall send his angels with a great sound of a trumpet, and they shall gather together his elect from the four winds, from one end of heaven to the other."

Can any one say that the above prediction has been verified?

34. "Verily I say unto you, This generation shall not pass till all these things be fulfilled.

35. "Heaven and earth shall pass away, but my words shall not pass away.

36. "But of that day and hour knoweth no man, no, not the angels of heaven, but my Father only.

37. "But as the days of Noe were, so shall also the coming of the Son of man be.

38. "For as in the days that were before the flood they were eating and drinking, marrying and giving in marriage, until the day that Noe entered into the ark,

39. "And knew not until the flood came, and

took them all away; so shall also the coming of the Son of man be."

Nor is this true about Noe, or Noah, who preached about the flood one hundred and twenty years before it came, and, according to the account, was many years in constructing the ark; so it was a matter of public notoriety. Strange that any sane man should interpret this xxivth chapter as referring to the final end of the world! Yet there are those who insist that this is its meaning, just as they contend that everything in the Bible is the inspired word of God, an infallible record. None too much disposition is shown to get at the truth, and for that reason, and from relying on the learned doctors who would have us think they are infallible teachers of an inspired record, many remain in ignorance. Why not adopt our ground, that all men are in a measure inspired for themselves? God is the true light, who lighteth every man that cometh into the world. We know this, whether we read it in the Bible or not.

Matthew xxv:

31. "When the Son of man shall come in his glory, and all the holy angels with him, then shall he sit upon the throne of his glory:

32. "And before him shall be gathered all nations: and he shall separate them one from another, as a shepherd divideth his sheep from the goats."

Here we have a brief account of what is construed

by many as a general judgment, but which we are told in xxiv, 34, was to take place during the generation then on the earth, and during the lifetime of some of those who heard the prediction. Yet this, like many other portions of Scripture, is by some deprived of its true meaning.

Mark ix:

1. "And he said unto them, Verily I say unto you, That there be some of them that stand here which shall not taste of death till they have seen the kingdom of God come with power."

At the time calculated for the verification of this prediction Jesus was on the earth, and during that generation there was no such coming as this passage indicates, and no great events took place except Jesus' crucifixion and the destruction of Jerusalem.

Mark xi:

12. "And on the morrow, when they were come from Bethany, he was hungry:

13. "And seeing a fig-tree afar off having leaves, he came, if haply he might find anything thereon: and when he came to it, he found nothing but leaves; for the time of figs was not yet.

14. "And Jesus answered and said unto it, No man eat fruit of thee hereafter forever. And his disciples heard it."

The peculiarity of this quotation should be noticed. We are at a loss to understand what reason there

Instruction, Direction, and Admonition. 349

was for cursing the fig-tree, when "the time of figs was not yet," and are disposed to doubt its historical truth.

Luke i:

1. "Forasmuch as many have taken in hand to set forth in order a declaration of those things which are most surely believed among us,

2. "Even as they delivered them unto us, which from the beginning were eye-witnesses, and ministers of the word;

3. "It seemed good to me also, having had perfect understanding of all things from the very first, to write unto thee, in order, most excellent Theophilus,

4. "That thou mightest know the certainty of those things wherein thou hast been instructed."

We should not fail to notice how Luke begins his gospel. He tells us plainly that he was not an eye-witness; that what he wrote were simply historical sketches, and bits of history gathered from various sources which he believed reliable.

Luke x:

25. "And, behold, a certain lawyer stood up, and tempted him, saying, Master, what shall I do to inherit eternal life?

26. "He said unto him, What is written in the law? how readest thou?

27. "And he answering said, Thou shalt love the Lord thy God with all thy heart, and with all thy

soul, and with all thy strength, and with all thy mind; and thy neighbor as thyself.

28. "And he said unto him, Thou hast answered right: this do, and thou shalt live.

29. "But he, willing to justify himself, said unto Jesus, And who is my neighbor?

30. "And Jesus answering said, A certain man went down from Jerusalem to Jericho, and fell among thieves, which stripped him of his raiment, and wounded him, and departed, leaving him half dead.

31. "And by chance there came down a certain priest that way: and when he saw him, he passed by on the other side.

32. "And likewise a Levite, when he was at the place, came and looked on him, and passed by on the other side.

33. "But a certain Samaritan, as he journeyed, came where he was: and when he saw him, he had compassion on him,

34. "And went to him, and bound up his wounds, pouring in oil and wine, and set him on his own beast, and brought him to an inn, and took care of him.

35. "And on the morrow when he departed, he took out two pence, and gave them to the host, and said unto him, Take care of him; and whatsoever thou spendest more, when I come again, I will repay thee.

36. "Which now of these three, thinkest thou, was neighbor unto him that fell among the thieves?

37. "And he said, He that shewed mercy on him. Then said Jesus unto him, Go, and do thou likewise."

Very plainly we can see by this that one may live near us and yet be anything but a neighbor. When we talk about neighborly acts we mean something performed. Godliness is in all things active. Away, then, with all lazy religion!

Everywhere in the teaching of Jesus we find the same prominent sentiment: that it is not those who do well for the sake of a reward that obtain credit, but those who do their duty because it is a duty, and who consider that in doing well they have only acted up to their own innate sense of obligation. In this there is a great reward.

Luke xvi:

1. "And he said also unto his disciples, There was a certain rich man, which had a steward; and the same was accused unto him that he had wasted his goods.

2. "And he called him, and said unto him, How is it that I hear this of thee? give an account of thy stewardship; for thou mayest be no longer steward.

3. "Then the steward said within himself, What shall I do? for my lord taketh away from me the stewardship: I cannot dig; to beg I am ashamed.

4. "I am resolved what to do, that, when I am put out of the stewardship, they may receive me into their houses.

5. "So he called every one of his lord's debtors unto him, and said unto the first, How much owest thou unto my lord?

6. "And he said, An hundred measures of oil. And he said unto him, Take thy bill, and sit down quickly, and write fifty.

7. "Then said he to another, And how much owest thou? And he said, An hundred measures of wheat. And he said unto him, Take thy bill, and write fourscore.

8. "And the lord commended the unjust steward, because he had done wisely: for the children of this world are in their generation wiser than the children of light.

9. "And I say unto you, Make to yourselves friends of the mammon of unrighteousness; that, when ye fail, they may receive you into everlasting habitations."

Making friends with the mammon of unrighteousness in the way spoken of, if it secured favor in this world, could not in the next.

Luke xxi:

5. "And as some spake of the temple, how it was adorned with goodly stones and gifts, he said,

6. "As for these things which ye behold, the days will come, in the which there shall not be left one stone upon another, that shall not be thrown down.

25. "And there shall be signs in the sun, and in

the moon, and in the stars; and upon the earth distress of nations, with perplexity; the sea and the waves roaring;

26. "Men's hearts failing them for fear, and for looking after those things which are coming on the earth: for the powers of heaven shall be shaken."

31. "So likewise ye, when ye see these things come to pass, know ye that the kingdom of God is nigh at hand.

32. "Verily I say unto you, This generation shall not pass away till all be fulfilled.

33. "Heaven and earth shall pass away: but my words shall not pass away."

From the most reliable accounts of those who have examined the walls of the temple at Jerusalem we learn that some portion of the old wall is still remaining, though the destruction was in reality total. Whether that destruction was foreknown to Jesus by prophetic vision, is a matter which we do not feel called upon to settle. We would not deny or support the position. The statement is again made here that its destruction would take place during that generation, which in one or two other places is coupled with the end of the world.

John i:

1. "In the beginning was the Word, and the Word was with God, and the Word was God.

2. "The same was in the beginning with God.

3. "All things were made by him; and without him was not anything made that was made.

4. "In him was life; and the life was the light of men.

5. "And the light shineth in darkness; and the darkness comprehended it not."

John iii:

14. "And as Moses lifted up the serpent in the wilderness, even so must the Son of man be lifted up:

15. "That whosoever believeth in him should not perish, but have eternal life."

They had only to look at Moses' serpent. So, in the case of Jesus, we are only required to believe in him, not as the Son of God, but as a Messiah. Very few there are in the Christian world who do not believe in Jesus as a redeemer—a purifier in some sense.

John vi:

44. "No man can come to me, except the Father which hath sent me draw him: and I will raise him up at the last day.

45. "It is written in the prophets, And they shall be all taught of God. Every man, therefore, that hath heard, and hath learned of the Father, cometh unto me.

46. "Not that any man hath seen the Father, save he which is of God, he hath seen the Father.

47. "Verily, verily, I say unto you, He that believeth on me hath everlasting life."

Instruction, Direction, and Admonition. 355

If God does not draw us, how can we come? If he does draw us, how can we avoid coming?

John xii:

12. "On the next day much people that were come to the feast, when they heard that Jesus was coming to Jerusalem,

13. "Took branches of palm trees, and went forth to meet him, and cried, Hosanna: Blessed is the King of Israel that cometh in the name of the Lord.

14. "And Jesus, when he had found a young ass, sat thereon; as it is written,

15. "Fear not, daughter of Sion: behold, thy King cometh, sitting on an ass's colt.

16. "These things understood not his disciples at the first: but when Jesus was glorified, then remembered they that these things were written of him, and that they had done these things unto him."

Here is another evidence that the Jews, and the people generally, expected a king: not the King of Heaven, as many now think Jesus was, or the king of saints, but a king to rule like David—a temporal king to reign over Israel.

John xiv:

1. "Let not your heart be troubled: ye believe in God, believe also in me.

2. "In my Father's house are many mansions: if it were not so, I would have told you. I go to prepare a place for you.

3. "And if I go and prepare a place for you, I will come again, and receive you unto myself: that where I am, there ye may be also.

4. "And whither I go ye know, and the way ye know.

5. "Thomas saith unto him, Lord, we know not whither thou goest; and how can we know the way?

6. "Jesus saith unto him, I am the way, the truth, and the life: no man cometh unto the Father, but by me.

7. "If ye had known me, ye should have known my Father also: and from henceforth ye know him, and have seen him."

This second coming none of the disciples thought, at the time, would be far off. The expectation of the followers of Jesus was in a new Jerusalem coming down from heaven, and Jesus coming in the clouds of heaven, escorted to earth by holy angels. Time has rolled on, and still there is no indication of a city paved with gold and adorned with pearls.

John xviii:

15. "And Simon Peter followed Jesus, and so did another disciple: that disciple was known unto the high priest, and went in with Jesus into the palace of the high priest.

16. "But Peter stood at the door without. Then went out that other disciple, which was known unto

the high priest, and spake unto her that kept the door, and brought in Peter.

17. "Then saith the damsel that kept the door unto Peter, Art not thou also one of this man's disciples? He saith, I am not.

18. "And the servants and officers stood there, who had made a fire of coals; for it was cold: and they warmed themselves: and Peter stood with them, and warmed himself.

19. "The high priest then asked Jesus of his disciples, and of his doctrine.

20. "Jesus answered him, I spake openly to the world: I ever taught in the synagogue, and in the temple, whither the Jews always resort; and in secret have I said nothing.

21. "Why askest thou me? ask them which heard me, what I have said."

Much is said now about the sin of denying Jesus, and justly, as we see by this account. This statement is confirmed by other writers, who, further, say that Peter began to curse and to swear. And yet, with all this perfidy, we are told that he holds the keys of heaven, and can reject whom he will. If this be so, is he not a very undesirable man for such a responsible office?

It seems, from what he wrote and put on the cross, that Pilate had some fear that Jesus would in time act as king of the Jews, though the chief priests were only willing to allow that Jesus said he was king of the Jews:

John xix:

19. "And Pilate wrote a title, and put it on the cross. And the writing was, JESUS OF NAZARETH THE KING OF THE JEWS.

20. "This title then read many of the Jews: for the place where Jesus was crucified was nigh to the city: and it was written in Hebrew, and Greek, and Latin.

21. "Then said the chief priests of the Jews to Pilate, Write not, The King of the Jews; but that he said, I am King of the Jews.

22. "Pilate answered, What I have written I have written."

The statements of the excited people who visited the sepulcher do not agree at all:

John xx:

6. "Then cometh Simon Peter following him, and went into the sepulcher, and seeth the linen clothes lie,

7. "And the napkin, that was about his head, not lying with the linen clothes, but wrapped together in a place by itself.

8. "Then went in also that other disciple, which came first to the sepulcher, and he saw, and believed.

9. "For as yet they knew not the scripture, that he must rise again from the dead.

Instruction, Direction, and Admonition. 359

10. "Then the disciples went away again unto their own home.

11. "But Mary stood without at the sepulcher, weeping: and as she wept, she stooped down, and looked into the sepulcher,

12. "And seeth two angels in white, sitting, the one at the head, and the other at the feet, where the body of Jesus had lain.

13. "And they say unto her, Woman, why weepest thou? She saith unto them, Because they have taken away my Lord, and I know not where they have laid him.

14. "And when she had thus said, she turned herself back, and saw Jesus standing, and knew not that it was Jesus.

15. "Jesus saith unto her, Woman, why weepest thou? whom seekest thou? She, supposing him to be the gardener, saith unto him, Sir, if thou have borne him hence, tell me where thou hast laid him, and I will take him away.

16. "Jesus saith unto her, Mary. She turned herself, and saith unto him, Rabboni; which is to say, Master.

17. "Jesus saith unto her, Touch me not; for I am not yet ascended to my Father: but go to my brethren, and say unto them, I ascend unto my Father, and your Father; and to my God, and your God.

18. "Mary Magdalene came and told the disci-

ples that she had seen the Lord, and that he had spoken these things unto her."

Some allowance should be made for the lack of harmony in this relation, as it was evidently made by one who was not an eye-witness. In verse 12 two angels are spoken of, both of whom in verse 13 are talking to Mary, while in verse 15 there is only one angel, or spirit, whom Mary supposed to be the gardener. We do not see that this story can be of much service in proof of a bodily resurrection, or anything else in particular. Mary Magdalene reported the occurrences as she understood them in her affrighted state.

John xxi:

12. "Jesus saith unto them, Come and dine. And none of the disciples durst ask him, Who art thou? knowing that it was the Lord."

About this resurrection there is something singular. If Jesus was really dead (there are some who think he was not), and his disciples saw only what we call a ghost, how could he dine with them? If he was raised in material and earthly form and substance, why should we say that others have not come out of their graves? Can flesh and blood inhabit heaven? Now, we contend that Jesus' death made no atonement for sin, and, hence, whether he came to life after being nailed to the cross, or not, is, in our opinion, of no importance. We have no faith in a vicarious atonement.

The disciples are still anxious about the restoration of the kingdom:

The Acts, i:

1. "The former treatise have I made, O Theophilus, of all that Jesus began both to do and teach,

2. "Until the day in which he was taken up, after that he through the Holy Ghost had given commandments unto the apostles whom he had chosen:

6. "When they, therefore, were come together, they asked of him, saying, Lord, wilt thou at this time restore again the kingdom to Israel?

7. "And he said unto them, It is not for you to know the times or the seasons, which the Father hath put in his own power."

The Acts, v:

1. "But a certain man named Ananias, with Sapphira his wife, sold a possession,

2. "And kept back part of the price, his wife also being privy to it, and brought a certain part, and laid it at the apostles' feet.

3. "But Peter said, Ananias, why hath Satan filled thine heart to lie to the Holy Ghost, and to keep back part of the price of the land?"

As to Ananias, he did not lie any more than Peter did; whether he did or did not drop down dead, is not important. To tell the truth squarely and fearlessly, under any circumstances, is always better than to seek to evade it. Let all remember this, and act accordingly. Peter might have thought how he lied a little while before.

The Acts, vii:

28. "Wilt thou kill me, as thou diddest the Egyptian yesterday?

29. "Then fled Moses at this saying, and was a stranger in the land of Madian, where he begat two sons.

30. "And when forty years were expired, there appeared to him in the wilderness of mount Sina an angel of the Lord in a flame of fire in a bush.

31. "When Moses saw it, he wondered at the sight; and as he drew near to behold it, the voice of the Lord came unto him,

32. "Saying, I am the God of thy fathers, the God of Abraham, and the God of Isaac, and the God of Jacob. Then Moses trembled, and durst not behold."

In the history we have of the Acts there is a constant lugging in of Old-Testament matters, and a great many things are represented as being found there which are not in the Bible at all as it now stands. In this case (verse 32) we are told about the God of Abraham, Isaac, and Jacob, and the question arises in our minds whether he was or was not the Jehovistic God.

The Acts, ix:

1. "And Saul, yet breathing out threatenings and

slaughter against the disciples of the Lord, went unto the high priest,

2. "And desired of him letters to Damascus to the synagogues, that if he found any of this way, whether they were men or women, he might bring them bound unto Jerusalem.

3. "And as he journeyed, he came near Damascus: and suddenly there shined around about him a light from heaven:

4. "And he fell to the earth, and heard a voice saying unto him, Saul, Saul, why persecutest thou me?

5. "And he said, Who art thou, Lord? And the Lord said, I am Jesus whom thou persecutest: it is hard for thee to kick against the pricks."

Saul was a brave man, and, while he thought he was doing God service in persecuting the Christians, was really the most ardent and zealous of any; he was equally zealous in supporting the Christian Church.

The Acts, xi:

1. "And the apostles and brethren that were in Judea heard that the Gentiles had also received the word of God."

In apostolic times the matter was under constant discussion as to the right of Jews and the Gentiles to admission into the new fold. A subject so broad, that has nothing in it of any particular importance in connection with our train of reasoning, will not be touched upon.

The Acts, xiii:

1. "Now, there were in the church that was at Antioch certain prophets and teachers; as Barnabas, and Simeon that was called Niger, and Lucius or Cyrene, and Manaen, which had been brought up with Herod the tetrarch, and Saul."

It appears from chap. xiii there were prophets in the first century, though we have no account of what they said.

We have the following account (chap. xiii) of Paul's defense after his arrest. He prefaces his remarks with a summary of Hebrew history, doubtless with the twofold purpose of pleasing the Jews and keeping in favor with the Christians. None can read this account of Paul's defense without being impressed by his great tact and shrewdness, as well as by his ability:

16. "Then Paul stood up, and, beckoning with his hand, said, Men of Israel, and ye that fear God, give audience.

17. "The God of this people of Israel chose our fathers, and exalted the people when they dwelt as strangers in the land of Egypt, and with an high arm brought he them out of it.

18. "And about the time of forty years suffered he their manners in the wilderness.

19. "And when he had destroyed seven nations

in the land of Canaan, he divided their land to them by lot.

20. "And after that he gave unto them judges about the space of four hundred and fifty years, until Samuel the prophet,

21. "And afterward they desired a king: and God gave unto them Saul the son of Cis, a man of the tribe of Benjamin, by the space of forty years.

22. "And when he had removed him, he raised up unto them David to be their king: to whom also he gave testimony, and said, I have found David the son of Jesse, a man after mine own heart, which shall fulfill all my will.

23. "Of this man's seed hath God according to his promise raised unto Israel a Savior, Jesus."

This is another speech or defense of Paul's, going somewhat into particulars of his personal history and what is called his conversion:

The Acts, xxii:

1. "Men, brethren, and fathers, hear ye my defense which I make now unto you.

2. "(And when they heard that he spake in the Hebrew tongue to them, they kept the more silence: and he saith,)

3. "I am verily a man which am a Jew, born in Tarsus, a city in Cilicia, yet brought up in this city at the feet of Gamaliel, and taught according to the

perfect manner of the law of the fathers, and was zealous toward God, as ye all are this day.

4. "And I persecuted this way unto the death, binding and delivering into prisons both men and women.

5. "As also the high priest doth bear me witness, and all the estate of the elders: from whom also I received letters unto the brethren, and went to Damascus, to bring them which were there bound unto Jerusalem, for to be punished.

6. "And it came to pass, that, as I made my journey, and was come nigh unto Damascus about noon, suddenly there shone from heaven a great light round about me.

7. "And I fell unto the ground, and heard a voice saying unto me, Saul, Saul, why persecutest thou me?

8. "And I answered, Who art thou, Lord? And he said unto me, I am Jesus of Nazareth, whom thou persecutest.

9. "And they that were with me saw indeed the light, and were afraid; but they heard not the voice of him that spake to me."

The Acts, xxiii:

1. "And Paul, earnestly beholding the council, said, Men and brethren, I have lived in all good conscience before God until this day."

6. "But when Paul perceived that the one part were Sadducees, and the other Pharisees, he cried out

in the council, Men and brethren, I am a Pharisee, the son of a Pharisee: of the hope and resurrection of the dead I am called in question.

7. "And when he had so said, there arose a dissension between the Pharisees and the Sadducees: and the multitude was divided.

8. "For the Sadducees say that there is no resurrection, neither angel, nor spirit: but the Pharisees confess both."

Romans viii:

12. "Therefore, brethren, we are debtors, not to the flesh, to live after the flesh.

13. "For if ye live after the flesh, ye shall die: but if ye through the Spirit do mortify the deeds of the body, ye shall live.

14. "For as many as are led by the Spirit of God, they are the sons of God.

15. "For ye have not received the spirit of bondage again to fear; but ye have received the Spirit of adoption, whereby we cry, Abba, Father.

16. "The Spirit itself beareth witness with our spirit, that we are the children of God:

17. "And if children, then heirs; heirs of God, and joint-heirs with Christ; if so be that we suffer with him, that we may be also glorified together.

18. "For I reckon that the sufferings of this present time are not worthy to be compared with the glory which shall be revealed in us.

19. "For the earnest expectation of the creature waiteth for the manifestation of the sons of God.

20. "For the creature was made subject to vanity, not willingly, but by reason of him who hath subjected the same in hope,

21. "Because the creature itself also shall be delivered from the bondage of corruption into the glorious liberty of the children of God."

Much encouragement may be derived from this portion of Paul's Epistle to the Romans. How important that we should seek to be led by the spirit of God! for it is certain that just in proportion as we do this we become his children. What higher motive for action can we have? How the 21st verse pleads for the imperfection of our nature! All are imperfect, all are of the earth, earthy; but God knows all this, and he knows when we strive to do our duty.

Romans xii:

1. "I beseech you, therefore, brethren, by the mercies of God, that ye present your bodies a living sacrifice, holy, acceptable unto God, which is your reasonable service.

2. "And be not conformed to this world: but be ye transformed by the renewing of your mind, that ye may prove what is that good, and acceptable, and perfect, will of God.

3. "For I say, through the grace given unto me, to every man that is among you, not to think of him-

self more highly than he ought to think; but to think soberly, according as God hath dealt to every man the measure of faith.

4. "For as we have many members in one body, and all members have not the same office:

5. "So we, being many, are one body in Christ, and every one members one of another."

10. "Be kindly affectioned one to another with brotherly love; in honor preferring one another;

11. "Not slothful in business; fervent in spirit; serving the Lord;

12. "Rejoicing in hope; patient in tribulation; continuing instant in prayer;

13. "Distributing to the necessity of saints; given to hospitality.

14. "Bless them which persecute you; bless, and curse not.

15. "Rejoice with them that do rejoice, and weep with them that weep.

16. "Be of the same mind one toward another. Mind not high things, but condescend to men of low estate. Be not wise in your own conceits.

17. "Recompense to no man evil for evil. Provide things honest in the sight of all men.

18. "If it be possible, as much as lieth in you, live peaceably with all men.

19. "Dearly beloved, avenge not yourselves, but

rather give place unto wrath: for it is written, Vengeance is mine; I will repay, saith the Lord.

20. "Therefore, if thine enemy hunger, feed him; if he thirst, give him drink: for in so doing thou shalt heap coals of fire on his head.

21. "Be not overcome of evil, but overcome evil with good."

What beautiful ideas are contained in this quotation! With this instruction alone, well considered, all can have a sure guide. The whole is so perfectly good that no attempt ought to be made at discrimination.

I Corinthians:

This book contains less of deeply-interesting matter than some of Paul's other epistles, and hence our notice of it will be brief. With our views of broad inspiration, we could not fail to speak of the deep inspiration of Paul, who was of such a vigorous temperament that nothing less powerful than a flash of lightning could turn him from his work of persecution; and that is what many think he was struck with at the time of his so-called conversion. Be this as it may, the work was none other than that of God, who chose this means to carry out his purposes, and to raise up for the Church one of its greatest advocates and defenders. And here let us say that Paul was full of inspiration. Can any one suppose that he could have said and done so much without the spirit and power of God to move him? We should look at the history of Paul as a whole, and by so doing cast a veil over his faults, foibles, and eccentricities. He calls on the people to do their duty and wait for the coming of Jesus (x, 7), which he intimated was near at hand, and that those he addressed would live to see. This idea seems to have been constantly before them, a ruling thought. They did not expect to wait long for the promised coming of Jesus.

Paul has much to say in this epistle concerning the matrimonial relation. We are not told that his own marriage was particularly unhappy, and he says that in some cases it is better to marry, though, as a rule, when a great work is to be performed by a man, he ought not to be encumbered with a wife. All that Paul says on this subject shows plainly that his mind was imbittered, from some cause. When a man advanced in life talks as he does about an institution ordained of God, and so well calculated, when entered into understandingly and properly, to add to the happiness of both parties, there is some reason for it which does not appear on the surface. Jesus was born of a woman who was the lawful wife of Joseph. Looking back on the great and good men who were born in wedlock, we are at a loss to account for Paul's condemnation of marriage. Fornication and licentiousness he is none too severe upon. Widows are allowed to marry, provided a proper opportunity offers.

Circumcision, as a ceremonial, Paul scouts and treats as of no importance. It may be unimportant; to say the least, it seems like a foolish performance, and was borrowed from some of the earlier nations, though the Jews regarded it as a covenant of grace. The reasons for its adoption have been surmised, that is all. Idolatry is denounced in unmeasured terms; which leads us to conclude that some of the Corinthians were addicted to it. Idolatry and adultery were the great besetting sins of the Hebrew race. All their efforts to conquer these tendencies only served to keep them in check for a season.

Great labor was bestowed by Paul on the subject of the Resurrection. If he was able to settle the matter in his own mind, to his own satisfaction, all who read what he says are not so fortunate. There is quite a difference between a bodily resurrection and a future spiritual life. Going back to a period long before Christianity and Hebrew history, we find that faith in a future life was entertained, to some extent. Not until the crucifixion of Jesus, or, really, until some time after, was the idea entertained that our bodies of earthy matter, of flesh and blood, could be admitted to the presence of God and glorified spirits. Christians who are so anxious to believe all that is believable can, with an eye of faith, see Jesus as he appeared on earth, sitting at the right hand of the Eternal Jehovah. Jesus' death and restoration to life again are called the first fruits of this bodily resurrection—a doctrine entirely at variance with sound sense and true logic.

I Corinthians, xiii:

Among all the good things in that good book the Bible, what is contained in this quotation is the most comprehensive and beautiful:

1. "Though I speak with the tongues of men and of angels, and have not charity, I am become as sounding brass, or a tinkling cymbal.

2. "And though I have the gift of prophecy, and understand all mysteries, and all knowledge; and though I have all faith, so that I could remove mountains, and have not charity, I am nothing.

3. "And though I bestow all my goods to feed the poor, and though I give my body to be burned, and have not charity, it profiteth me nothing.

4. "Charity suffereth long, and is kind; charity envieth not; charity vaunteth not itself, is not puffed up,

5. "Doth not behave itself unseemly, seeketh not her own, is not easily provoked, thinketh no evil;

6. "Rejoiceth not in iniquity, but rejoiceth in the truth;

7. "Beareth all things, believeth all things, hopeth all things, endureth all things.

8. "Charity never faileth: but whether there be prophecies, they shall fail; whether there be tongues,

they shall cease; whether there be knowledge, it shall vanish away."

13. "And now abideth faith, hope, charity, these three; but the greatest of these is charity."

I Corinthians, xv:

14. "And if Christ be not risen, then is our preaching vain, and your faith is also vain."

Before the crucifixion of Jesus and his restoration to life again, what was the fate of the devout Hebrews? If the doctrine of the resurrection of the material body had its beginning with Jesus, we have no information to that effect till some time after that notable event. What was not found in the true account of things in relation to Jesus' death was, we are inclined to think, supplied, to make the story sufficiently wonderful. Man was made to be, or not to be, immortal before the death of Jesus or his so-called resurrection from the dead. The change that took place was moral, not physical. No law of our nature suffered a change, nor did any moral law undergo a modification. Right was right; and wrong, wrong. Sin was the same in its effects: it brought a guilty stain, and merited a just punishment. God will in nowise clear the guilty. They must suffer here, if not hereafter. The death of Jesus could not take away the effect of sin. That follows naturally and surely. May God speed the time when all will see that every man must bear his own sin, and not depend upon another to do it for him. We cannot sin by proxy, neither can we obtain forgiveness by proxy.

35. "But some man will say, How are the dead raised up? and with what body do they come?

36. "Thou fool, that which thou sowest is not quickened, except it die:

37. "And that which thou sowest, thou sowest not that body that shall be, but bare grain, it may chance of wheat, or of some other grain:

38. "But God giveth it a body as it hath pleased him, and to every seed his own body."

After calling his supposed questioner a fool, which is a term forbidden in the Bible, Paul gives us to understand that if bodies are buried there may come up an entirely different thing, or "another kind of grain" than that which had been planted. Paul was not a fool, but he talked in a very strange way, sometimes. This subject of corporeal resurrection will be dropped; for it is one that we do not understand, and we very much doubt if any human being does or ever will understand it. We are strongly established in the faith of a future life, and that in a future state God will give us such a body as he pleases. About this resurrection and future state there is a wide difference of opinion among those of equal talent and research. They cannot be right on both sides of the question, as to whether our new bodies will be in fact the old ones, though nominally new, or whether they will be spiritual bodies clothed with a consciousness of the old life and all its recollections.

II Corinthians, v:

1. "For we know that if our earthly house of this tabernacle were dissolved, we have a building of God, an house not made with hands, eternal in the heavens.

2. "For in this we groan, earnestly desiring to be clothed upon with our house which is from heaven:

3. "If so be that being clothed we shall not be found naked.

4. "For we that are in this tabernacle do groan, being burdened: not for that we would be unclothed, but clothed upon, that mortality might be swallowed up of life."

18. "And all things are of God, who hath reconciled us to himself by Jesus Christ, and hath given to us the ministry of reconciliation:

19. "To wit, that God was in Christ, reconciling the world unto himself, not imputing their trespasses unto them; and hath committed unto us the word of reconciliation."

In chap. xii Paul speaks somewhat of himself, and also says that he knew a man, fourteen years before the time he was writing—whether he was in the body or not he could not tell—who was caught up into Paradise and heard things he could not utter. He does not say who it was, whether himself or some one else. The relation sounds odd enough.

Hebrews xi:

In this chapter we have a long list of things that were done by faith: by faith the worlds were made; Abel's offering was accepted; Enoch was translated; Noah built the ark; Abraham was about to offer up Isaac; and by faith Sarah herself conceived.

The Revelation:

Of this book we will not undertake to speak. There are so many who doubt its authenticity, and, among the great mass of intelligent people, so few who understand it, that we will attempt no explanation. According to chap. i, 3, it seems the expectation was that all things spoken of were shortly to take place.

PART III.

RELIGIONS SINCE CHRISTIANITY.

CHAPTER I.

MOHAMMEDANISM, OR ISLAM.

Mohammed, the founder of Islamism, was born in Arabia about the end of the sixth century of our era. His father died young, leaving his widow and infant son in destitute circumstances. Five camels and an Ethiopian slave constituted their entire property. The infant Mohammed was cared for by his uncle, who early trained him to the life of a merchant. He visited Syria when he was thirteen. In time he became the factor of a rich widow of noble birth, who took him for her husband, and placed him on an equality with the richest in Mecca. Being now freed from the necessity of personal exertion, he formed the scheme of establishing a new religion, or, to use his own expression, of replanting the only true and ancient one—that professed by Adam, Noah, Abraham, Moses, Jesus, and all the prophets—by destroying the idolatry into which his countrymen had generally fallen, and weeding out the corruptions and superstitions which he thought the Jews and Christians had introduced into their religion. His aim was to elevate it to its original purity, which consisted chiefly in the worship of one God.

He retired to a cave in Mount Hira, where he unfolded the secret of his mission to his wife, Khadijah, and told her that the angel Gabriel had appeared to him with the information that he was appointed to be the Apostle of God. Khadijah received the declaration with great joy, swearing by him in whose hands she was that Mohammed would be the prophet of his nation. At her instance, Warakah Ebu Newfal, a Christian and cousin, who could write Hebrew and was tolerably versed in the Scriptures, adopted her opinion, and said the angel who had appeared to Moses was the same one that had appeared to Mohammed. The first overture the prophet made was in the month of Ramadan, in the fortieth year of his age, usually called the year of his mission. He began cautiously, and his advance was slow. His first proselytes were those under his own roof. He secured the co-operation of Abdallah, surnamed Abu-Beer, a man of great authority among the Koreish, and one whose interest he knew would be of great service to him. This was followed by the addition of several others of high repute in Mecca. Of these, six were his chief companions; to which three more were added in the space of three years.

Mohammed, believing that he had support to warrant an open promulgation of his views, gave out that God had commanded him to admonish his near relations; and in furtherance of this design he directed that an entertainment be prepared, where he intended to open his mind to them. To this invitation about forty responded; but Abu Laheb, one of his uncles, caused the company to break up before Mohammed had an opportunity to speak. A second invitation was given for the next day, when he made them a speech by saying: "I know no man in all Arabia who can offer his kindred a more excellent thing than I now do to you. I offer you happiness both in this life and in that which is to come. God Almighty has commanded me to call you unto him. Who, therefore, among you will be assistant to me herein, and become my brother and my vicegerent?"

His followers at the present time are estimated at one hundred and fifty to two hundred millions; and, like Christianity, Mohammedanism has missionaries scattered over a great portion of the globe, and for hundreds of years has maintained its supremacy over the sacred places in Palestine, so dear both to Jew and to Christian.

Mr. Clodd says that the term Islam comes from a word meaning, in the first instance, "to be at rest, to have done one's duty, to be at perfect peace," and is commonly held to mean submission to the will and commandments of God. Muslim, or Moslem, comes from Islam, and signifies "a righteous man." What we know about some of the earlier religions is so mixed with fable and legend that it is difficult to separate the false from the true; but nearly all the incidents of Mohammed's life are too well authenticated to leave much room for doubt, their truthfulness being supported by thousands who knew him for many years. It is also because it is the youngest of the great religions of the world that we are able to know so fully about Mohammedanism, and to see how its first simple form became overlaid with legend and foolish superstition; and it enables us to learn how, in like manner, myth and fable crept into more ancient religions.

Although Christians can see very plainly that all the miracles about Jesus' birth were beyond a doubt really such, they cannot believe there was anything wonderful connected with the birth of Mohammed—one legend about whom is that angels took him from the arms of his nurse, drew his heart from his bosom, and then squeezed from it the black drop of sin which is in every child of Adam. Mohammed never claimed to be a perfect man; he did not undertake to foretell future events or to work miracles. He said his miracle was the Koran, which should remain forever. He spoke of the sun, the moon and stars, the day and the night, and various other of God's works, as constant miracles before our eyes. Though he made no such pretense himself, his followers claimed for him the greatest of all impossible wonder-workings: how he rode, by night, upon the lightning to Jerusalem, and then, ascending to heaven, passed through the dwellings of the prophets into the presence of the Unseen. This he himself said was only a dream. When he died, the people would not believe it. Thus it has been with others who were esteemed prophets of the Most High.

Mr. Clodd says Mohammed has suffered much from friends as well as from foes. When the former asked him for a sign, as the Jews asked Jesus, they readily believed all that was told of him; the latter thought nothing too vile or too bad could be said of him. Martin Luther, among others by whom Mohammed was disliked, called him a horrid devil, and to this day most Christians believe him one of the worst of impostors. Few, if any, unprejudiced religious students would say he was free from sin; but he was no cheat who tried to cover it up. His strong belief in one God has never been questioned, nor has he ever been accused of polytheism. Though poor, he was of noble birth.

In his boyhood Mohammed was sickly, and subject to fits, with which he was troubled in after years. He sought lonely places for meditation, caring little for company. He could neither read nor write, having no way to gather knowledge but by his eye and ear. Although sweet-natured and truthful, he was, perhaps owing to the bad state of his health, oftentimes cast down and gloomy; but in his bright moments he was gleeful and happy, playing with children and telling them extravagant tales. All his habits of living and dress were simple in the extreme. As age advanced, his gloomy turns became more frequent and severe. Strange revelations came to him, and he thought he heard the voice of the angel Gabriel: who of us can say he did not hear a voice not human?

That Mohammed benefited the Arabs in many ways is very certain: he gave them a better religion than they had before, gave them more correct ideas of God, and elevated their thoughts. The Jews settled among the Arabs at an early day, and hence their religion prevailed to some extent.

Mr. Clodd says the Arabs are to-day what they were hundreds of years ago: lovers of freedom, temperate, good-hearted; but withal crafty, revengeful, dishonest. They are very fond of music and poetry. Not much is known about their religion before Islam, for until the advent of Mohammed their history is almost a blank; though they had in their early existence many gods, and worshiped the sun and moon, trees, stones, and numerous other things, especially the "black" stone of the Kaaba, around which were placed three hundred and sixty-five idols. Travelers tell us this stone is an aerolite (or "air-stone," as the word means, which has fallen from space to the earth), said to have been one of the precious stones of Paradise, and to have dropped to the earth with Adam; once white, it has become black from the kisses of sinful men, or through the silent tears which it has shed for their sins. The tradition also is that the building which incloses it was erected by Abraham and Ishmael. To the place where it stands the Moslems all over the world turn five times every day in prayer to God.

At the time when Mohammed appeared there were societies of Jews and Christian sects in Arabia which had sought refuge in the desert lands from the cruel power of Rome. The Christians wasted their strength in foolish wrangling. The pure, sweet spirit of Christianity which they ought to have kept fled from them. Still earlier than these came the sun-worshipers from Chaldea and the Zoroastrians from Persia. These and other varied beliefs found a home in Arabia, so that many Christian and Jewish ideas became mingled with Islam. Men before Mohammed preached against pagan creeds, but they were only forerunners of the mightier prophet.

Mohammed did not claim to have a new religion or a new faith, but the religion of Abraham, who, he said, was neither a Jew nor a Christian, but pious and righteous, and not an idolator, and whom he places among the six chief prophets chosen by God to make known his truth. Mohammed said that these were Adam, Noah, Abraham, Moses, Jesus, and himself. Though Mohammed had but little knowledge of Jesus—and this obtained from hearsay and the Apocryphal books, which had been discarded by the Christians—he never uttered aught against him or those who claimed to be his followers. Moslems have not treated Christ and his followers as we have treated them and their leader. In the mosque at Medina a grave is kept open, beside that of the Prophet, for the burial of Jesus, who, they believe, will one day return to earth to establish everywhere the religion of Mohammed.

Much was borrowed from the Jews by Islam: the belief in good and bad angels, the ordinances relating to marriage, fasting, etc., etc. So far as the pagan customs could be improved, they were, and in many of them the worst forms were entirely abolished. The frightful practice of killing female children ceased with the establishment of Islam. There is, to this day, however, a great lack in the respect paid to the family tie. Mohammed permitted the worship of the Kaaba stone to be continued. In like manner, the Roman Catholic missionaries, when they emigrated to Northern Europe, made use of the old Teutonic religion, and worked parts of it into their own, intending to reject the bad and use the good features. In this way the development and growth of all religions may be traced—new stock being grafted into the old tree. The great religions of the world have each their good and poor points. None of them can long be kept perfectly pure, as systems, even though they may have been so at first. Where the sacred trees of the Teutons had stood, the Catholics raised crosses; where holy wells had been dug, they built churches and abbeys; where love and piety had named flower and insect after the Lady Freyja (goddess of plenty), they put the Virgin Mary in her stead.

We may say here that the Arabs have a tradition that Mecca was a place of great note long before the time of Mohammed, and that it was the birthplace of their tribes.

The Mohammedan faith was not destitute of good points and ennobling ideas. It counseled men to live a good life, and to strive after the mercy of God by fasting, charity, and prayer, which its founder called "the Key of Paradise." One of the many passages in the Koran calling to prayer is as follows: "Observe prayer at sunset, till the first darkening of the night, and the daybreak reading—for the daybreak reading hath its witnesses.... And watch unto it in the night.... and say, 'O my Lord, cause me to enter [Mecca] with a perfect entry, and to come forth with a perfect forthcoming, and give me from thy presence a helping power."

There is (says Mr. Clodd) preserved a sermon on Charity, said to have been preached by Mohammed, which is so beautiful that it deserves a place beside the apostle Paul's sweet words in I Cor. xiii, while in reading it we think of that touching saying by Jesus as to the Eye that sees with approval a gift to the thirsty, although that gift be but a cup of cold water:

"When God made the earth, it shook to and fro till he put mountains on it to keep it firm. Then the angels asked, 'O God, is there anything in thy creation stronger than these mountains?' And God replied, 'Iron is stronger than the mountains, for it breaks them.' 'And is there anything in thy creation stronger than iron?' 'Yes, fire is stronger than iron, for it melts it.' 'Is there anything stronger than fire?' 'Yes, water, for it quenches fire.' 'Is there anything stronger than water?' 'Yes, wind, for it puts water in motion.' 'O, our Sustainer, is there anything in thy creation stronger than wind?' 'Yes, a good man giving alms: if he give it with his right hand and conceal it from his left, he overcomes all things. Every good act is charity; exhortation to another to do right is charity; your smiling on your brother's face, your putting a wanderer on the right road, your giving water to the thirsty, is charity. A man's true wealth hereafter is the good he has done in this world to his fellow-men. When he dies, people will ask, What property has he left behind him? But the angels will ask, What good deeds has he sent before him?

This is very good for a Mohammedan; and, after a careful and candid examination of the Koran and all it contains, of the life of Mohammed and his teaching, though the whole is far inferior to the New Testament and the teaching of Jesus, we can but own that there is some good in the former as well as in the latter; that Mohammed did a vast deal for his country and nation—for all who embraced his faith and lived up to his requirements. At his death he left many millions of people far in advance of what he found them, in all that constitutes greatness, in all that comprises goodness and nobleness. Their ideas of God, we may remark, were quite as well developed as could have been expected, considering the point from which they started. By this method of reasoning we should examine all the great religions, and not condemn them in such unmeasured terms, in all respects, as many have done. Thus shall we find that the great leader of this faith and his followers were honest, that they acted up to the full measure of light that was given, and are to be judged accordingly. The great truth they strove to realize was, that God is one; they considered it infidelity to believe in three Gods, or to think that the God they believed in was only a third of a God. Some may laugh at the crudeness of the notions they entertained about a trinity, but it is not to be denied that they were sincere. If Trinitarians were called upon to explain the strange doctrine to which they pretend to adhere, more difficulties than they imagine would surround them.

When Mohammed began to teach in Mecca, as well as in other places, attacks on him were so bitter that he was obliged to leave the city. On his return his wife died; he also suffered the loss of his property; and in the midst of his affliction a conspiracy was formed to take his life, and he was obliged to leave Mecca again, and started for Medina. The Moslems date their years from the prophet's flight to Medina, just as we date history from the birth of Jesus. On Mohammed's arrival at Medina a glad welcome greeted him, and he at once became ruler and lawgiver. Soon, however, he ceased to be a preacher, and became a warrior. Having drawn the sword, he offered idolators and Jews either death or conversion to Islam. His followers were urged to fight bravely, and in case of death he promised their immediate entrance into Paradise. So they rushed to the combat without fear, for it was God's battle against the wicked. The vengeance of Mohammed was particularly furious against the Jews, whom he had tried hard to win over to his side. He admitted their religion to be divine, and adopted many of their rites and doctrines, making Jerusalem the Kiblah, or place toward which men were to turn in daily prayer. For all this, strange to say, the Jews ridiculed him, so that to the day of his death he was their bitter foe. His victorious armies overran the whole of Arabia and other portions of country, conquering kings and princes, and demanding that they submit to Islam.

Toward the tenth year after his flight Mohammed went on his last pilgrimage to Mecca, at the head of forty thousand Moslems. On his return to Medina, feeling that death was near, he took up his residence near the mosque, that he might be in attendance as much as possible at the public prayers. After calling the people together, he asked them, as did Samuel, if he had wronged any one, or if he owed any one, and then, after reading some verses from the Koran, went home to die. His death happened in the sixty-second year of his age. Mr. Clodd justly says he was a great and good man, and the religion which he set forth met the needs of men in the East as no other religion ever did, and it is not likely to cease its hold upon men, or give place to any other, for a long time to come, if ever. Nearly two hundred millions of people who have the strongest possible belief in God, admitting that they have wild and extravagant notions, are not blotted out in a long course of years. We ought not to blame Mohammed for many of the sad errors and vices mixed up with Islam, any more than we should blame Jesus for the evils which have crept into Christianity. He waged wars, and so did the Jewish leaders; the latter's wars, too, were the most cruel and relentless. The earth was crimsoned with the blood they shed. And we all know that the most awful and distressing wars have been carried on by the Christians.

Hopes are entertained that brighter days are now dawning upon us, and that religious wars may soon cease, so that neither Christian, Mohammedan nor any other religious people will again endeavor to spread their faith by the use of the sword. True religion never leads men to fight, except in self-defense. It is the lack of it which incites to war. Human progress has been too rapid, human intellect has become too much expanded, for one portion of mankind to say to another portion, If you will not adopt our religion we will kill you. Moslems believe that, in different ages, God has made his will known to prophets, through scriptures, of which all but four are lost, to wit: the Pentateuch, the Psalms, the Gospel, and the Koran; the Koran only being perfect. They also believe that many strange events will happen; that there will be a resurrection and a final judgment, when the souls of both good and bad will have to pass quickly over a bridge laid across hell, which the souls of the good will be able to cross, but that the wicked will fall in.

The success of Islam was astonishing. In one hundred years after the death of the Prophet it had been embraced by half the then known world, and its green flag waved, to a greater or less extent, from China to Spain. In many instances Christianity gave way before it, and has never regained some of the lost ground. Islam is still making advances in Africa and elsewhere. Why should it not be so? We cannot say that Islam is idolatry, or that it is not vastly preferable to it. Mohammedans are not fighting against Christianity. May we not hope, therefore, that what they believe is best for them, with the light they have, and that they will finally accept the truth?

Along the northern coasts of Africa and nearly to the equator, from Turkey to within the borders of China, and among the larger islands of the East, the faith of Islam spreads; like the Christian religion, it is divided into sects, numbering in all, as we have stated, from one hundred and fifty to two hundred millions. From every mosque the blind *mueddin*, or crier, proclaims at daybreak: "There is no God but God, and Mohammed is his prophet. Prayer is better than sleep; come to prayer." Who shall dare to say that God does not accept the prayer of the pious Moslem when he falls on his face in the holy city? **To say that, with all the false notions common to Islam, there is nothing good in it, would be gross injustice.**

The term Arab has long been used to indicate a people debased, quite destitute of the higher qualities. This is entirely wrong. The Arabs have done much for Europe in the diffusion of learning. When astronomy was neglected in other places, it found a home in Arabia, and the same is true of many other branches of learning. Christian Europe and Christian America must not assume too much. To say of anything that it is as false as the Al-koran, is taken by many Christian people, to mean that it is entirely untrue. This Mohammedan Bible contains much that has no reference to religious precepts. The Moslems tell and believe many absurd stories about their Koran, and disbelieve much that we Christians tell about our religion; and they as honestly think that our errors are numerous as we think that theirs are.

They believe the Koran to be entirely the inspired work of Mohammed. It consists of 114 *surahs*, or chapters, which were dictated by him to a scribe, and the copies thus made were placed in a box, but were imperfectly preserved. About a year after Mohammed's death such portions as remained were collected "from date-leaves, tablets of white stone, bones, parchment-leaves," and memories of men, and copied, without order of time or subject.

The titles of the chapters, says Mr. Clodd, are taken from some chief matter in them, but are generally unmeaning. The headings seem odd enough; as, for example, "The Lion," "Thunder," "The Fig," etc. The form of beginning is the same in each chapter: "In the name of God, the Compassionate, the Merciful." The place where the revelation was made to Mohammed is also stated. The writing is in the purest Arabic. The oneness of God is prominently taught in the Koran. There are also many stories, legends, laws, and counsels, mixed in with Jewish history and lore. Large portions of it seem utterly meaningless, while other parts are beautiful and impressive tributes to God's majesty and purity. The Moslems never touch it with unwashed hands, or hold it below the girdle about their waist, and they are greatly troubled to see it in the hands of an unbeliever.

The following brief chapter is valued highly:
"Say there is one God alone,
God the eternal:
He begetteth not, and he is not begotten,
And there is none like unto him."

The following surah, named "The Folding Up," thus describes the last day:
"When the sun shall be folded up,
And when the stars shall fall,
And when the mountains shall be set in motion,

And when the she-camels with young shall be neglected,
And when the wild beasts shall be huddled together,
And when the seas shall boil,
And when the souls shall be joined again to their bodies,
And when the leaves of the Book shall be unrolled,
And when the heavens shall be stripped away like a skin,
And when hell shall be made to blaze,
And when Paradise shall be brought near,
Every soul shall know what it has done."

The following is a passage from another surah, and one of the latest in point of time:

"God! There is no God but He, the Living, the Eternal. Slumber doth not overtake Him, neither sleep; to Him belongeth all that is in heaven and earth. Who is he that can plead with Him but by His own permission? He knoweth that which is past, and that which is to come unto them, and they shall not comprehend anything of His knowledge but so far as He pleaseth. His throne is extended over heaven and earth, and the upholding of both is no burden unto Him. He is the Lofty and Great."

CHAPTER II.

HEGELIANISM AND OTHER SYSTEMS.

We quote first from Appleton's Cyclopædia, as follows: "George William Frederic Hegel was born at Stuttgardt, 1770, and died at Berlin, in the flush of his fame, Nov. 14, 1831. A philosopher whose power and renown remind one of traditions concerning Pythagoras, for he created a school not only numbering in its ranks his most distinguished contemporaries, but exciting a whole people: the influence of Hegel diffused itself through the politics and religion, as well as through all the speculation, of Germany. The principles on which this remarkable thinker constructed his system are two-fold: First, his discovery, or alleged discovery, of a universal law, according to which thought unfolds itself — the fundamental and sole law of dialectics. Every thing or notion, says Hegel, exists to the mind because it has, or seems to have, *a contradictory;* or, in other words, there is some other thing or notion standing outright against it, and by opposition marking it off or defining it. A notion and its opposite, or contradictory, are two elements essential to every act of thinking; and as soon as these are realized a third act or movement supervenes, viz.: the effort to reconcile the two contradictories, to find some third, and, of course, higher, notion in which they unite or blend. Three elements, therefore—a notion, its contradictory, and the solution of the contradiction; a thesis, its anti-thesis, and the synthesis of the two—represent a complete act of logic, or one movement of dialectic; and on the type of this movement Hegel undertook to explain the entire course of action of thought in its efforts to comprehend the universe. It were not easy to overestimate the surprising skill with which a task so novel and arduous has been executed; in this respect, indeed, the 'Encyclopædia of Philosophical Sciences' will ever be a marvel."

Prof. Stowe says: "The influence of this philosophy extends far beyond the circle of its professed disciples. It invades Christian, even orthodox, pulpits; does not exist alone as a speculation, but proceeds immediately to action." He makes no attack on the founder, who, he says, was one of the noblest of men, with a fine physical organization, a prodigious intellect, and a generous heart, and among the first to protest against atheism. What a pity that many who dote on their orthodox faith did not possess the same noble traits!

Thought is presented to the astonished reader, rising up from its barest expression, through a gigantic scheme of ascending triplets, until, comprehending every possible form of knowledge, it reaches the absolute and infinite. This absolute he deemed an essence, the notion of God. No obscure residuum could remain. Prof. Stowe says this philosophy of Hegel consisted of three shades, or divisions, which he calls the religious, the non-religious, and the anti-religious; and that Marheinecke was of the first order; that he was a clear-headed, sound-hearted Christian theologian and preacher; one of the best historians, one of the most accurate reasoners, and one of the strongest Hegelians.

Goschel was another ardent Hegelian, and, Prof. Stowe asserts, a truly pious man; and he declared Hegel, Goethe and Dorner the best of Christians, and we cannot think his authority is to be questioned.

Thus we have the strongest of orthodox evidence in favor of free thought, and that the declaration or honest opinion is no sin, nor the least impediment to the enjoyment of Christian religion. Of all men, we dislike most the narrow-minded bigot who thinks heaven will be pretty well filled when he and his friends, with all their church and denomination, get there. If anything is devil-born, such thoughts and ideas are.

Religion is the consciousness of the infinite; it is and can be nothing but man's own consciousness of his inward being. It is a delusion to suppose the nature of man is a limited nature. The religious object is within us. God is man's revealed inner nature, his pronounced self. Religion is the solemn unveiling of the concealed treasures of humanity, the disclosure of its secret thoughts, the confession of its dearest secrets. The Christian religion is the relation of man to his own being, as to another being; the dream of the human soul. Here, says Prof. Stowe, is the New-Testament doctrine of the Logos, the God-man, God-revealed, and the Holy Ghost; the inner nature of man reacting upon itself; the spiritual influence which all good men crave and pray for.

David Frederic Strauss comes in for severe criticism at the hands of Prof. Stowe. His labors began to influence the thinking world in 1836, and he, the Professor avers, made the most severe attack on the credibility of the Gospel history, or its divine inspiration, that had ever been made. This influence is now spreading, and his works are read with great avidity.

Strauss contends that the Jews expected a national Messiah, as they thought the Old Testament predicted. When Jeschuah (or Jesus) and John began to preach, the former conceived the design of the regeneration of his countrymen; and, being influenced by the supernatural prejudices of the times, imagined that God would help him re-establish the kingdom of David. Jeschuah gradually became reconciled to this thought. Having no means and no political influence, he saw that the priest-party was daily more incensed against him. Some passages in the Old Testament, he began to think, indicated a suffering and dying Messiah; so he anticipated a violent death, which he finally suffered. As to miracle: when the first shock of his terrible end was past, this idea of suffering and death began to be started; the Old Testament was again ransacked for fresh predictions of a Messiah; and his followers concluded that the Messiah, though departed, was not lost, but had gone to glory, had gone into his heavenly kingdom, and must naturally love and care for all who had known him on earth; and, finally, they began to imagine they had seen him after his burial, and so declared; at which all were much excited, and also imagined they had seen him on several occasions, amid the mountain fog, or in the gray twilight.

In this way the great miracle of the Resurrection was generated, and found foothold in the world, and became the fruitful parent of other miracles. The expectation was for miracles, and if there were none, then they had no Messiah. As he had told his disciples they should be fishers of men, there should be a miraculous draught of fishes; he had said the unfruitful tree should be cut down, and so was the fig-tree. Miracles having thus been set to growing, we soon find an abundant crop.

The Messiah could, of course, heal leprosy as well as Moses and Elijah did. Jordan in the Old Testament had healing powers, and Siloam in the New; as Elijah struck men with blindness in the Old Testament, so Christ cured blind men in the New; as Jeroboam's withered hand was restored in the Old Testament, so Christ healed withered hands in the New; as Moses divided the Red sea, so Christ stilled the Galilean sea; as Moses turned water into blood, so Christ turned water into wine: and so all the miracles of the Old Testament find parallels in the New.

This was all deemed necessary by the sacred historian, who endeavored to show that Christ was the son of God, or he could not have performed such miracles. If miracle-working proved Christ a God, why not Moses also? and did it not make gods of those who pretended to work wonders, and to possess the gift of healing? This power, though so strongly promised, did not amount to much after Christ's death, and very soon died out altogether. As with the doings of Christ, so it is with his sayings: those which stand recorded are amplifications from brief hints of his remembered apothegms.

Thus we have the material for the Gospel story, which, after a while, is worked up by different writers into a connected narrative, as we have it in the four gospels of Matthew, Mark, Luke, and John. This, Prof. Stowe says, is the opinion of Hegel, Strauss, and men of that school: all of whom, Mr. Stowe affirms, were most exemplary men, with all the good qualities that adorn humanity. He also pays a high compliment to M. Wiesse, an older man than Strauss, a sound philosopher and metaphysician, and the author of a work on the idea of God as a system of æsthetics, published in 1838.

M. Wiesse says there lived in Palestine, during the reign of Tiberius, a good man, one Jesus of Nazareth, who, among other gifts, possessed the magnetic power of healing—in fact, a full-charged galvanic battery, ready at any touch to be discharged. He went about Galilee preaching and collecting disciples. Applying his magnetic power to the healing of diseases and quieting demoniacs, he very naturally gained the affection of the Galileans; they recognized him as the Messiah, and desired to make him king. Though he felt his Messiahship, he had no political ambition, seeking rather the moral elevation of the people, and to this end uttered many parables. The blessed effects of his ministry he represented by the descent of a dove from the opening heavens; the strength of faith, in the parable of a Canaanitish woman asking help of a Jew; the judgment to come, by the barren fig-tree, cursed and withered; the regeneration of the world, by his turning water into wine. He caused great excitement by awakening a woman who had fallen into a swoon, and was supposed to be dead. He visited Jerusalem but once, and then at the feast of the Passover, when he was apprehended and crucified.

We have no reason to believe that he prayed aloud the night before his apprehension, or that he said when they were nailing him to the cross, "Father, forgive them, for they know not what they do." During his crucifixion there was an accidental obscurity of the heavens, which occasioned much comment. He was buried, and his body remained in the tomb, but his nervo-magnetic spirit once appeared to his disciples, and then passed up into the clouds. After his death his parables were turned into stories, and men thought them actual occurrences. These stories were not propagated by the apostles, but were told by others, who, as they found ready believers, kept on telling more stories, from every trivial circumstance. Once, after Jesus' death, the apostles, being at supper, became greatly excited, and hence came the story that Christ himself had instituted the Lord's Supper.

These writers of strange books, as Prof. Stowe would have us take them to be, are, he says, all men of profound learning, sound in logic, and of most exemplary lives

Aug. Gfroerer was the writer of a Church history in 1845, a work of great merit. Like all the others spoken of in this connection, he was the contemporary of Strauss. The gospel of John he believes to be genuine, but the other three gospels he considers spurious and mythical. The books of Mark and Luke, he says, owe their origin to the influence of the writings of Philo and other Jews. Many ideas are derived directly from the Talmud, the fourth book of Esdras, the book of Enoch, and other apocryphal writings, which he considers older than the Gospels by many centuries. The Jews held fire to be a necessary accompaniment of revelation; hence the tradition that John declared that Jesus should baptize with fire. The doctrine of the Trinity is of Rabbinic origin.

Ernest Renan has a high standing as a writer of many volumes, most of which can be found on the shelves of every well-appointed library, and require no comments at our hands.

David Schenkel.—Professor Schenkel, a German writer who is among the ablest of the present generation, also wrote a life of Jesus, or "The Character of Jesus Portrayed." He says Christ made but one journey to Jerusalem, which terminated in his death. John the Baptist did not recognize Jesus' Messiahship, nor testify of him, nor urge any disciple to follow him. Jesus could not possibly have said, "Not one jot or tittle of the Old Testament law should pass away." He could not have referred to his resurrection before his death, for he was not raised; and if he had been he could not have known it beforehand.

Of a suffering Messiah the Old Testament knows nothing. He considers Mark the most accurate of all the gospel writers, but thinks that many things which are not trustworthy have been added to his narrative by another hand. The book of Matthew, he says, was written by a Jewish disciple, and much of it should be rejected. Luke must be carefully winnowed. He places little reliance on John's gospel, since it contradicts the historical order by representing Jesus as having a distinct conception of his work from the beginning.

F. C. Bauer.—This writer says the original Gospels were written for the express purpose of deception, and to sustain the theology of Paul against that of Peter, or the theology of Peter against that of Paul. Since their first appearance these Gospels have been so modified and smoothed over that all traces of their controversial character have disappeared. According to Bauer, the Gospels had their origin in church feuds and dissensions, and were written for a purpose. This controversy dates from the time of the apostles, and lasted until the middle of the second century. It was a contest between those who viewed Christianity as Judaism and the Lord as the Messiah, and those who viewed Christianity as a new principle, by which both Judaism and heathenism were to be transformed into a new system. The strife was obstinate. The life of Paul was passed in a struggle for recognition as one of the apostles, for perfect equality of Jew and Gentile converts, for emancipation from the law.

The books of the New Testament are partisan writings, on one side or the other of these questions, or else they are later productions, intended to conceal these differences and to unite all Christians upon one common ground. Most of the books are of this latter class; hence it follows that they are not the genuine productions of those whose names they bear. The lateness of St. Mark's gospel is inferred from the absence of all controversial matters, as well as on other accounts. St. Luke's gospel had originally a strong Pauline and anti-Jewish tendency, but in the later edition this was much modified. St. Matthew's gospel in its original form was very different from the one we now possess—more decidedly Judaic in tendency; while the Greek, as we have it, is in general character with the other two gospels.

Prof. Stowe sums up, under the general head of "Hegelians," the main points of all the authors referred to, by saying that they consist of two parts: 1. Objections to the historical truth of the Gospels derived from the narratives themselves; and, 2. Hypotheses to account for the existence and influence of the Gospels, supposing them to be historically untrue. He then goes on to say—what many who think they have a large share of Christianity will object to—that the

Gospels are not, and do not profess to be, complete histories; that they are simply detached memoirs, or select anecdotes, intended solely to illustrate the character and teachings of Christ; to show what kind of a teacher he was, and to give an idea of the substance and manner of his teaching.

This the writers themselves affirm, in so many words. Says John, at the close of his narrative: "There are also many other things that Jesus did, the which, if they should be written every one, I suppose that even the world itself could not contain the books." John must be either grossly misrepresented in this matter, or else he was an ignorant enthusiast. Christ's ministry was very short—varying in duration, according to different writers, from two and a half to three years: had he talked all the time, and had all his hearers commented upon, elaborated and amplified every sentence he uttered, the writing out of the whole, even in the clumsy style of that day, would have come far short of filling up the world. This ridiculous assertion illustrates the extravagant style of writing in that age. Assuming that all of these biblical writers meant to be correct, their great zeal and the fanatical tendency of the times in which they lived would be sure to lead them to exaggerate the facts that formed the basis of what they described.

THE APOCALYPSE.— Nepos, a pious and learned bishop of Arsinoe, in Egypt, about the year A.D.

230 published a book in regard to the millennium, or the thousand years of Christ's reign on the earth. Dionysius, A.D. 255, wrote a book in which he expressed doubts as to the divine authority of the Apocalypse, stating that many before his time had rejected the book, alleging that it was altogether dark, entirely without sense or reason, and ascribed it to the heretic Cerinthus. He said he could not understand the book, that it was written by a man named John, but not the apostle John; and he did not know what John. The ancients were by no means agreed as to the time when John saw the Apocalypse, but it is generally conceded to have been in the reign of Nero. The learned bishop Eusebius says that Dionysius, like other pastors of his time, did at first receive the work as genuine, but rejected it afterward on the ground that it was not written by John at Ephesus.

CHAPTER III.

THE BOOK OF NATURE.

In a former volume we had something to say about that blessed open book in the heavens, and we cannot resist the temptation now to make a few extracts from one of the ablest scholars and divines of our age. Doubtless there are those who will not agree with us in all that we call Science, if by any possibility it conflicts with the Bible. The Old Testament contains things which we consider quite as much out of place as what we introduce here, and they are certainly less essential to a knowledge of the power of God. When we are asked to believe that the contents of a book are the sacred, inspired revelation of God, merely because a portion of the world calls them so, we naturally turn to that great book in the heavens, and try to read that. Before the invention of printing, which dates back only a few hundred years, books in manuscript were frequently falsified or interpolated, which could not have been the case if the scribes who copied them had been inspired. When we come to the printing of books, this danger exists substantially the same, for the translator and the printer are not inspired either.

To say that the Bible was written by God's own finger, as some do who claim to be divines, is an assertion which cannot be proved by the Bible itself, by any other book, or in any possible way.

There are those who honestly think that, if they attain to a thorough knowledge of all there is in the Old and New Testaments, they know about as much as is necessary. What is denominated Science they will say may be studied, though it is a matter of small account to know whether the sun revolves around the earth, or the earth around the sun; whether the earth is flat, like a trencher, or of a globular form; whether our world is the center of created matter, and the sun so fixed as to go down under it and pop up every twenty-four hours, with a bit of moon and some stars set up in the heavens to give a faint light when he is out of sight; or whether the earth and sun, with all the other planets of our system, constitute a very small part of our astral system, and that entire system only a little fraction of the universe, instead of being the whole or a large part.

There are quite too many people who never stop to think that moral and religious light has been breaking forth for many millions of years, and will continue to shed new effulgence for millions of years to come. Not to realize this fact is to loose the foundation for the vast thoughts and conceptions by which we are distinguished from the lower orders of animal creation. Going back to the early, crude notions in regard to astronomy and geology would appear to some ridiculous, but not to all. Those who never heard of any theory but the old, worn-out, obsolete theories, and were satisfied that they were right, would naturally desire no better. People of this stamp would readily swallow all the fables and legends in the front part of the Old Testament as the inspired word of God, an infallible record, written by God's own finger —or anything else you might ask them to. Many people nowadays will tell you that the Jews were inspired for themselves and for all the world beside, and that God began at a certain time to pour out this inspiration, and when the term was up he ceased. They will also tell you that at a certain period after the birth of Jesus the age of miracle set in, during which time the dead were raised, even after decomposition had commenced; that all diseases could be cured, mountains taken from their solid beds and cast into the sea. In short, anything could be done: seas dried up, the furious waves stilled, or, if necessary, instead of a whale's swallowing one man, he might have taken them down by the dozen. Only let a thing be found in the Bible, and why should not credulous people believe it? If it be not true, why did the Lord let it be put in the Bible at all?

Let us consider a moment, lest some one should say that we deny the Bible. There are certain truths constantly before our eyes. The most essential moral and religious truths may be read *everywhere:* first, and most important, they are printed indelibly on every human heart, where they must be read; they are impressed on all we see and feel. Books are well enough; but, above all things, intelligent mortals never ought to worship a book, though it may be called the word of God.

W. A. Stearns, President of Amherst College, had the independence to come out, in the face of deep-rooted prejudice, in favor of critical investigation, and say to the world around him, Let us reason together; give up your foolish ideas, and take sound sense and correct notions instead. The title of his book is *Ecce Cœlem*. He says:

"The great book of Nature is the heavens, which it is a joy and an exaltation to peruse: such a natural and truthful book—one that is so acceptable to all, not a part. Its outspread pages invite study by day and by night. It is now an interpreted book. The interpretations were hard. Great men, persevering men, and many of them, have been engaged in the work for long ages. The results are before the world.

Once men could not see an eclipse or a shooting-star without inferring some dire calamity. Now humanity does not tremble at the signs of heaven. The progress of astronomical science has freed us from our superstitious terrors. We leave such foolish things to centuries long past and the ignorant heathen. To the science of the stars we owe the safety and audacity with which unlimited canvas now stretches on the widest seas in the darkest nights. Scarcely a branch of business or knowledge, however humble or high, but is debtor, in one way or another, to astronomical investigations.

"A large and generous culture of the mind is indispensable to the achievement of great things, to solidity of understanding, elevation of thought, and glow of imagination."

Mr. Stearns goes on to say:

"This science is worth more than all the fictions and poems the world has ever seen. The chief theorems of astronomy are more lofty than Milton or Homer. It is a poem as well as a science—the best example of polished completeness, and the noblest specimen we have of an epic poem. Look at the mighty secrets that men have wrested out of that starry page above us! That ancient sentiment should be often repeated, 'An undevout astronomer is mad.' None can tell us how ancient astronomy is as a science. Neither history nor tradition carries us back to its beginning. We can learn nothing of its founder or founders, their names being lost in the darkness of primeval ages. The first clear view of it dates back about three thousand years before Christ. Some claim Chaldea for its birthplace; others, Egypt; and some, India—the latter having the most ancient of astronomical tables.

"Thales, Pythagoras, Hipparchus and Ptolemy are names not soon to be forgotten; nor the glory of that famous Alexandrian school founded three hundred years before Christ, which, with its library, continued till the sack of Alexandria in the seventeenth century. That terrible vandalism, that destroyed the wisdom of so many centuries, suppressed astronomical culture for nearly a thousand years; and the cast-away science found a home among the Arabs at Bagdad, where knowledge was gathered from every quarter of the world. While in Europe it was midnight darkness, light was poured forth from Arabia. Spreading into Spain, it started afresh in Europe in the fore part of the sixteenth century. Up to that date the real amount of discovery in the heavens by all nations was comparatively small.

"Copernicus, of Prussia, cast away the old theories, and soon began his triumphant career. Then followed Tycho Brahe, Kepler, Galileo, and Newton, who made prodigious strides; since which there has been an incessant and vigorous pressing onward. The light has shone from every direction. The French have particularly distinguished themselves. Claivant, La Grange, La Place and Arago are among the most conspicuous of French astronomers. Flamstead, Halley, Bradley, Mackelyne and the two Herschels adorn the English page. For Germany and Russia are the great names of Bessel, Argelander, Struve, and Maedler."

From A.D. 600 to 1500 no other suggestion than the one made by Thales, that the earth goes around the sun, and not the sun around the earth, is known to have been made. Archimedes tells us that Aristarchus, about 280 B.C., held to the opinion that the earth revolved around the sun. This was not believed to be true by Archimedes, and nothing is said of it in the only book Aristarchus ever published. Some have given Pythagoras credit for teaching, 500 B.C., that the earth goes around the sun, but apparently without good reason. Be this as it may, the world itself did not believe any such thing until the time of Copernicus, a priest who was born in 1472, a few years before a still more celebrated reformer—Luther. For a long time astronomers refused to believe Copernicus any more than they believed Aristarchus.

CHAPTER IV.

PRAYER.

Much is said, and believed, about prayer, its propriety and efficacy; and lest some may think we have no faith in such a thing, we would say that, in our opinion, prayer is beneficial in many respects; but in regard to its influence on the orderings of Providence —as to God's doing or not doing according to the requests of mortals, and changing his purposes—we have no faith; and we consider that those who entertain such a belief labor under a great delusion. If, during a time of drought in any particular place, all the ministers and all the laity should unite in prayer for rain, and ask God to send it, for his own sake and for that of a suffering people, does any one suppose it would rain one day sooner than it would if no prayer had been offered, any more than the course of nature would be altered so as to cause a river to run back toward its source? When we come to look thoughtfully at the probability of prayers being answered in a particular sense, our faith must be greatly lessened, if not wholly destroyed; for such a thing would be like an ordering of the laws of the universe by mortals, which could not fail to result in confusion, instead of the beautiful order and harmony which we enjoy. It rains now when it will rain, not when man desires it to.

Some prayers may be low-minded and selfish. Many want favors for the advancement of worldly plans, the accumulation of property, and a thousand things which, could they have by asking, would occupy a large share of the time of the Being who is supposed to be able to grant them. To contemplate a universe peopled with beings capable of praying, and all of them continually sending up to God each a separate, a particular, petition for what he wanted or imagined he wanted, might afford to all a joyous satisfaction, but no person in his senses can believe that the Lord would attend to all their wants, and answer the whole fully and satisfactorily.

When a battle is impending between two armies, one side may be more deserving of victory than the other; but how far the powers of heaven will interpose to settle the matter is another thing. The force of circumstances, the degree of preparation, strategy, and bravery, have much to do with the matter. The days of Moses, Aaron, Joshua and Gideon are gone.

The miracles claimed by them as being wrought by God in answer to prayer, even if they were then substantial realities (which we do not believe), are not likely to be repeated.

True merit and sincere godliness may constitute a well-founded claim to the favor of heaven, and yet such favor may not be given us on that account. The good do not always share God's blessing in the highest degree. The practically and vitally good often suffer the severest afflictions. Tempests sweep and floods overwhelm them. Many go to the ocean's bottom uttering as sincere a prayer as mortal ever breathed. If the prayers of good men would save from drowning, shipwrecks would be few. The saint (if there be such a thing here) and the sinner share the same fate, so far as we can discern. For God to rain on the just and not on the unjust is hardly possible. Therefore we do not see how God can give especial answers to particular prayers, any more than he can or will create a series of especial providences for all those who ask him. Prayers and expectations of this kind may be uttered and calculated upon, if comfort and consolation can be gained thereby, but this is all they will amount to. And yet prayer is a becoming acknowledgment of the power and goodness of God, and of our own weakness and dependence. To say that God can and does bless us without our asking is no argument against the performance of duty.

The shortest and best prayer ever made was that offered by the publican, who, feeling so debased that he could not even raise his eyes toward the open heavens, cried out in agony, "God be merciful to me a sinner." Going to his own house, looking into his own heart, from whence the prayer came in all sincerity, not only forgiveness, but justification, came, as a matter of course. He made no vain boasting that, in the use of some dead form of prayer, or by some meritorious act, he had earned a blessing and merited forgiveness. Knowing his need of mercy, he implored God to grant it. No roundabout way was taken; the words used were plain and direct. All who ask in this spirit, in whatever temple or place they may be on the broad earth, whether Christian, Mohammedan, or Jewish, will have peace and pardon. Like all religious duties, prayer, to be of any avail, should be emphatically a matter of heart-work. Lip-service will gain nothing.

Prayer is alike proper for individuals, families, and churches, as well as on occasions of public interest. As one person often speaks to the edification of many, so one may often enliven the spiritual feelings of a large circle. Spiritual emotion may at times be dormant, only to be awakened by the spiritualizing power of some one capable of warming it into life. Lack of outward exhibition does not prove that it may not be stirred up in every heart. Influences are all the time at work to develop what may properly be called inspiration—a working of the divine Spirit; the power of Omnipotence leading and directing us. Without this, who can think and act as they ought?

An electric chain, a spiritual connection, extends, in a greater or less degree, through creation, binding soul to soul, leading matter to embrace matter, closely in some cases and almost imperceptibly in others. Beginning with God, it must extend through all his works. Let it not be said that we are opposed to, or think lightly of, prayer, or doubt its efficacy within reasonable bounds.

THE UNIVERSAL PRAYER.

Father of all! in every age,
  In every clime, ador'd,
By saint, by savage, and by sage,
  Jehovah, Jove, or Lord!

Thou Great First Cause, least understood,
  Who all my sense confin'd
To know but this, that thou art good,
  And that myself am blind;

Yet gave me, in this dark estate,
  To see the good from ill;
And, binding Nature fast in Fate,
  Left free the human will.

What conscience dictates to be done,
  Or warns me not to do,

This, teach me more than hell to shun,
   That, more than heaven pursue.

What blessings thy free bounty gives
   Let me not cast away;
For God is paid when Man receives,
   T' enjoy is to obey.

Yet not to Earth's contracted span
   Thy goodness let me bound,
Or think thee Lord alone of Man,
   When thousand worlds are round:

Let not this weak, unknowing hand
   Presume thy bolts to throw,
And deal damnation round the land
   On each I judge thy foe.

If I am right, thy grace impart,
   Still in the right to stay;
If I am wrong, oh, teach my heart
   To find that better way!

Save me alike from foolish pride,
   Or impious discontent
At aught thy wisdom has denied,
   Or aught thy goodness lent.

Teach me to feel another's woe,
   To hide the fault I see;
That mercy I to others show,
   That mercy show to me.

Mean though I am, not wholly so,
   Since quicken'd by thy breath;

Oh, lead me wheresoe'er I go,
  Through this day's life or death!

This day, be bread and peace my lot:
  All else beneath the sun
Thou knowest if best bestow'd or not,
  And let thy will be done.

To thee, whose Temple is all space,
  Whose altar, earth, sea, skies,
One chorus let all Being raise!
  All Nature's incense rise!

—POPE.

INDEX.

A.

	PAGE
Abraham, his low and high traits of character	178
" the account of his interview with the Lord probably mere legend	178
" his ideas of theology	177
" father and leader of the Hebrew race	173
" his crime of fornication, remarks on	180
" Mohammed's opinion of	386
Acts, the, i, v, comments on	361
" " vii, ix, " "	362
" " xi, " "	363
" " xiii " "	364
"Aditi," definition of	70
"Ahura-Mazda," meaning of	100
"Air-Stone," tradition of	385
Alexander, founder of Alexandria, his acts of toleration	121
Alexandria, the oasis in the moral world	122
Ammon, king of all the gods, and the especial god of the Egyptians	118
Antoninus, Marcus Aurelius, his character	158
Antioch, its importance, wealth, vices, and disasters	211
Apollo, oracle of at Delphi, facts concerning	145
" " " " officiating priestess of	145
Apocalypse, the, opinions of various learned men concerning	408
" " the only one of the New Testament writings which affirms its own inspiration	313
" " Martin Luther's ground for rejecting	314

Apostles, the, difference of views of on important subjects..284
" " a great modification in their notions worked
by the death of Christ...................286
Arabs, the, Mr. Clodd's description of.....................384
" " their history a blank until the advent of Mo-
hammed 385
" " their gods....................................385
Arabia, the home of astronomical science...................415
Arimanius, god of darkness................................ 98
"Aryan," meaning and use of name....................... 21
Aryan tribes, the, and their descendants................... 20
Aryana-Vaejo, supposed situation of.......................101
Aryans, the, earliest history of............................. 62
" " country peopled by........................... 21
Asia, Northern, singular change of climate in..............101
Astronomers, conflicting theories of early..................416
Atheism engendered by false notions of God............... 37
Atonement, the, origin of..................................315
"Augury," derivation and meaning of.....................155
Augurs, Roman, business of...............................155
"Authorized version" the, of New Testament, value of.....241
Avesta, the, discovered and published by Mons. du Perron.. 98
" " language of.............................. 99
" " the sacred book of a great Iranic religion...... 97
" " books contained in...........................105

B.

Babel, tower of, Chaldæan legend concerning.............. 22
Bacchus, mysteries of......................................144
Baldur, the mildest and wisest of the Scandinavian gods....167
Baptism, the form of given by Matthew not authorized by
Jesus..303
Bethany, where situated....................................306
Bethlehem, star of, its appearance explained.... 228
Bible, the, oldest manuscripts of transcribed at Alexandria..129
" " its inspiration considered.......................217
" " how it should be read..........................235
" " delusions into which ignorant minds are led by
its sole study....................................411
" " Tischendorf's zeal in collecting manuscripts of...244
" " its origin and character, as given by Mr. Clodd..215

Index. 427

	PAGE
Bigotry, God's detestation of	94
Birmese, the, excellent traits of character of	91
Blind men, curing of, discrepancy between the accounts of	298
"Book of the Dead," Egyptian, recently discovered	120
Bragi, the Scandinavian god of eloquence and poetry	169
Brahmanism, character and sacred books of	41
" the God of	61
" a singular combination of self-denial and indulgence	43
" and its offshoots, extent of	77
" and Hinduism, different sects of	58
" Mr. Clarke's definition of	59
Brahmans, their tendency to asceticism	72
Brahma, supreme god, the, different names of	78
Brahmana, the, extracts from account of Creation in	70
"Buddha," meaning of	89
Buddha, birth of	82
" his future greatness revealed in a dream	82
" his tendency to meditation	83
" vicissitudes attending the spread of his doctrine	83
" fable of	30
" death of, in his 85th year	85
"Buddhas of Confession"	93
Buddhism, origin and incidents of its inception	84
" council held to fix doctrines of	85
" what countries embraced by	89
" the state religion of India 4th century B.C.	89
" its numerous followers	81
" fundamental doctrine of	89
" rationality and humanity a part of its system	90
" a zealous, but not an intolerant, religion	91
" defined by Mr. Clarke as Eastern Protestantism	86
" the god of and prayers to	93
" truths and defects of	44
Buddhist and Roman Catholic customs, similarity between	86
" morality, Saint Hilaire's description of	92
" architecture, its singularity and beauty	82
Buildings, sacred, popular ideas regarding	26
Bundehesch, the, doctrine, promulgation and reliability of	110
" " its elaborate theories and results	111
" " Windischmann's translation of	110

C.

                                                                                           PAGE

Cæsarea, its extent, splendor, and importance..............206
Calendar, invention of by the Egyptians..................123
      "   old and new styles, facts relating to..............231
Calvary, its exact location not positively known..........206
Capernaum, location of...................................203
Cataline's conspiracy, remarkable debate concerning.......156
Charity, Buddhist and Christian contrasted................ 94
      "   a sermon on, said to have been preached by Mohammed.......................................388
Cheops, in Egypt, pyramid of..............................115
China, its antiquity, area, and population................ 47
      "   social and political equality in..................... 48
      "   three national religions of.......................... 49
      "   the state worship of................................. 48
Chinese, the, early enterprise and skill of............... 48
      "   " religious sects, relations existing between... 49
      "   " recognition of a Supreme Power............. 48
      "   " institutions and customs, permanence of..... 47
      "   " sacred books, names and character of........ 54
Chorazin, its assumed situation..........................203
Christ, the death and resurrection of, predictions concerning obscure and doubtful........................304
      "   his resurrection wholly unexpected by his disciples..306
Christ's Church, superstitions in........................147
Christian era, the, important events of first century....232
      "   virtues and proverbs, Egyptian origin of..........126
Christians, their uncharitable views of other religions... 35
Christianity, our knowledge of its early history imperfect..250
      "   all good not embraced in, alone.............. 94
      "   destined to develop into a universal religion.. 88
"Church," its origin and signification...................301
Church, Christian, the, delusion in at the time of the apostles.281
Cilicia, situation of....................................212
Cimbri, the, remarkable facts relating to................163
Circumcision, copied by the Hebrews from the Egyptians...124
      "   why adopted by Abraham......................180
"Codex," meaning of.....................................237
Codex Alexandrinus, account of..........................237
      "   Vaticanus, interesting facts relating to............237
      "   Sinaitic, its discovery by Dr. Tischendorf.........239

Index. 429

	PAGE
Confucius, birth of	49
" number of descendants of	49
" the great influence of his writings and teachings.	50
" his pure morality and lofty aims	50
" popularity of his doctrine among the masses	51
" his political and literary labors	51
" Mr. Clodd's characterization of system of	52
" autobiographical sketch of life and principles of.	53
" his whole life filled with commendable actions	54
" his ideas of heaven and an unknown power	56
" testimonials to his memory	54

Corinth, its wealth, luxury, and licentiousness..............211
I Corinthians, comments on.................................370
I   "   xiii, comments on.............................373
I   "   xv, comments on...............................374
Creation of the world, the, Eddas account of..............165
   "   the, account of in the Rig-Veda....................66
   "   "   order of in the Bundehesch...................105
   "   "   Mosaic account of possibly copied from the
             Bundehesch....................................119
"Creed of Christendom," the, extracts from................266
Crucifixion of Jesus, disagreement between the evangelists
   as to the time of and circumstances attending..........323
Customs borrowed from the Jews by Islam...................386
   "   heathen, adopted in part by Christianity..........127
Cyprus, island of...212

D.

Decapolis, the several cities composing...................204
Deluge, the, Chaldæan accounts of..........................22
Demoniacs, two, the healing of an exceedingly improbable
   story..298
Devil, the, idea of borrowed by Christians from older re-
   ligions..258
Devotion, an inward work, without regard to external show...76
Doctrines, four principal, common to Egyptian mythology
   and orthodox Christianity..............................128
Dogmas, Hebrew and Christian, promulgated thousands of
   years ago by the Egyptians.............................130
Dualism, Zend-Avesta and New Testament recognition of..44
Duty, meritorious only when conscientiously performed....351

E.

		PAGE

"Edda," meaning of 165
Eddas and Sagas, the, the chief source of our knowledge of
    the Teutonic race... 164
Egypt, situation, extent, and importance of.................. 113
    "   history of divided into three periods............... 126
    "   monuments in, their magnificence.................. 113
    "   funeral ceremonies in............................... 125
    "   an object of interest to the civilized world in all ages. 114
Egyptian priests, their functions and privileges............. 123
    "   prophets, a highly honored class.................. 124
    "   enterprise and skill, early evidence of.......... 114
    "   Ritual of the Dead................................. 125
Egyptians, their belief in a future life..................... 118
    "   sacred books of made known by Clemens Alex-
             andrinus... 119
    "   their religion and mythology..................... 116
Empedocles declares God to be the Absolute Being....... 138
Epictetus, character and noble life of........................ 158
Epicurus, his peculiar theories 141
Epistles, the, authenticity of.................................. 225

F.

Faith, different varieties of................................... 218
    "   in a spiritual resurrection reasonable; the resurrection
        of the body unreasonable........................... 326
Famine, the, in Canaan.. 181
"Flamens," the priests of particular Roman deities....... 155
Freyja, the most propitious of the Scandinavian goddesses.... 168

G.

Galilee, Sea of, or Tiberias................................... 203
    "   settlement and inhabitants of..................... 195
Galileans, why they were disliked by the Jews............ 195
Genesis, chapters xi, xii, comments on....................... 175
    "   chapter xiii, comments on........................ 177
    "   "   xv,   "   " 178
    "   "   xvii, "   " 180
Gennesar, its fertility and beauty............................ 202
God not a being of wrath and fury.......................... 186
    "   narrow-minded religionists' misinterpretation of....... 86

Index. 431

PAGE

God, man's first conception of..................... 25
" Buddhists' notion of an infinite.................. 44
God's constant care for all his creatures.................. 37
" law, books not necessary to a knowledge of........222
" recognition of our efforts to do our duty to the best
    of our ability......................................368
Gods, Egyptian, names and explanations of...............117
" Greek, names of derived from Egypt...............122
" of Greece, the, Homer's description of..............135
" the, Aryan idea of and names for.................. 23
Gospel, the, dispute among the apostles as to its contemplated
    mission 266
" " no reason for assuming that Jesus intended its
    spread outside the Jewish nation..........271
" fourth, the, discourses in not the utterances of Jesus...316
Gospels, original, the, written for the purpose of deception,
    according to Bauer... 406
" their correctness, as records of Christ's words, yet to
    be established...................................313
Greece, early history of................................132
" deities and gods of................................133
" its religion unlike all others in the human character
    of its gods......................................133
Greek religion, the, curious facts concerning..............141
" philosophy and nominal Christianity contrasted.....140
" sacrifices, character and mode of offering..........142
" priests, offices of..................................143
" philosophers and scholars prepare the way for the ad-
    vent of Christianity............................138

H.

"Heathen," New Testament translation of.... 38
Heathen, the, Jesus' recognition of....................... 38
" " Paul's charity for........................... 38
"Hebrew," derivation and meaning of....................173
Hebrew race, idolatry and adultery their great besetting sins..372
Hebrews, early, the, their faint conception of a God.....174
" the, God's promise to............................176
Hebrews xi, comments on................................377
Hegel, George William Frederic, his life and principles...397
Hegelianism, remarks of Prof. Stowe on................398

Hegelians, the, main points of summed up by Prof. Stowe...407
Heimdall, warder of the Scandinavian gods.................169
Hellenic tribes or groups, the.............................133
Hermes, description of the sacred books of................119
Hermon, Mount, and its surroundings........................205
Herod, his slaying of the children in Bethlehem a silly story..295
" " empire divided between his three sons, Archelaus,
   Herod Antipas, and Herod Philip..........194
Hindu race, the, vague antiquity of........................63
" code of laws, the....................................61
" philosophy, the three great systems of..............75
" nation and religious systems, Mr. Maurice's account of 77
Hindus, the, devotional feeling of.........................67
" their philosophy mixed with coarse superstitions....60
" " strange ideas of attaining felicity..........60
Hinduism, ancient and modern contrasted....................75
History, exaggerated statements in Jewish and other......188
" Jewish, prophetic period in..........................189
Holy Spirit, the, what was it?.............................273
Honest opinion, its declaration no sin.....................399
Hope in a life of future happiness a sufficient reason for
 leading an upright life...............................222

I.

Iconium, where situated....................................213
Iduna, the Scandinavian goddess of youth...................169
Incarnation and genealogy of Jesus, contradictory accounts
 of the...293
India, gods and festivals of...............................77
" a land of riches, relics, and mysteries..............59
Indra, the supreme god of the Hindus.......................69
" hymns to, their resemblance to the Psalms...........69
Inspiration, all men in a measure inspired for themselves..347
"Islam," origin and meaning of.............................382
Islam, its astonishing progress............................393
" " division into sects...............................393
" how Jewish and Christian ideas became mingled with.385
"Israelite," use of, facts concerning......................173
Italy, situation and boundaries of.........................148

J.

Janus, god, the, origin and characteristics of.............150

		PAGE
Jesus,	his genealogy, Mr. Greg's views	292
"	" birth variously stated	227
"	" mission, popular notions concerning	267
"	necessity of associating his name with that of David	255
"	his entry into Jerusalem, discrepancy in accounts of	297
"	" advent, popular theories concerning	230
"	the story of his being tempted by the devil incredible	257
"	marked discrepancy between Matthew and Luke as to the original residence of his parents	296
"	the new kingdom of	341
"	few who do not believe in him as a purifier in some sense	354
"	the religion of, its inestimable value	340
"	M. Wiesse's delineation of his life and character	403
"	Julius Africanus' unsuccessful endeavor to reconcile his genealogies as given in Matthew and Luke	261
"	the gospel of, sound sense the best guide in discriminating between the true and the fabulous in	291

Jesus' death no atonement for sin..........360
Jews, the, a Semitic race..........172
" " evidence that they expected a temporal king..355
John, his ancestry, life, and character..........263
" gospel of, pronounced by Origen to be the chief of all the gospels..........264
" either grossly misrepresented, or else he was an ignorant enthusiast..........408
John iii, comments on..........354
" xii, " "..........354
" xiv, " "..........355
" xviii, " "..........356
" xix, xx, " "..........358
" xxi, " "..........360
Joppa, its ancient importance, and interesting associations..207
Judaism, considered as a stepping-stone to Christianity..........183
Judea, the seat of the Jewish religion..........196
"Jupiter," derivation and meaning of..........151

K.

Kaiomarts, believed by Persians to have been both man and woman, whence came the first human pair..........108
"Karma," meaning of..........93

PAGE

Karnak, in Egypt, facts concerning........................115
Khordah-Avesta, the, extracts from........................103
"Kings," sacred books of the Chinese...................... 56
Koran, the, history and character of 394
   "   " erroneous ideas entertained of by Christians..394
   "   " Moslems' reverence for........................395
   "   " passage from..................................387
   "   " chapter from..................................395
   "   " passage from..................................396
K'ung-Foo-Tse, the patron saint of China.................. 49

L.

Lao-tse, his character and religious views................ 49
Legends, Jewish and Persian, strong likeness between...... 99
   " pointing to a common origin of all nations..... 29
Lessing presumes the existence of a number of fragmentary
   narratives of the sayings and actions of Jesus.........308
Logos, or Word, doctrine of maintained at Alexandria....129
   " the, New Testament doctrine of defined...........400
Lucretius declares all religion an unmitigated evil........157
Luke, his life and writings................................262
   " not to be implicitly trusted as a historian........274
   " chapters i, x, comments on........................349
   " chapter xvi,   "   " 351
   "   " xxi,   "   " 352

M.

Magians, worship of described by Herodotus B.C. 450.... 97
Magdala, the native place of Mary Magdalene..............205
Malchærus, interesting facts concerning...................200
Man, birthplace and early history of...................... 19
   " the account of his origin in Genesis not reliable...187
Manuscript, Egyptian, the oldest in the world.............127
Manuscripts, ancient, liability to errors in...............223
Manu, subjects treated of in.............................. 70
Mark, gospel of, where written............................261
   "   "   " chapter xvi, remarkable circumstance con-
                  cerning manuscript of.................245
Matthew, some account of his life before he was called to
             an apostleship.............................249
   " gospel of, difficulty in reconciling some portions of.256

Index.   435

| | PAGE |

Matthew, gospel of, different accounts as to when written....251
"   "   " in its early form intended for the Jewish
                          Christians in Palestine.............252
"   "   " variations in the supposed original copy..252
"   "   " Prof. Stowe's opinion of our present trans-
                          lation...............................253
"   "   " criticised by many learned men........254
"   "   " chapter ii, comments on...............260
"   "   "   "   xxiii, "   "..............342
"   "   "   "   xxiv, "   "..............345
Matrimony an institution ordained of God..................371
"Melchizedek," King of Salem, signification of............185
Melchizedek, our imperfect knowledge of...................178
Messiah, the, Strauss' conception of......................401
Ministry of Jesus, term of................................225
Miracle, the, of Christ's changing water into wine a clumsy
                          and manifest invention................317
"   not necessary to prove divine truth.............. 40
Miracles, origin of.......................................401
"   if the working of proved Christ a God, why not
                          Moses, also?............................402
"   ridiculous ideas of religious enthusiasts respecting..412
Mohammed, his birth and ancestors.........................379
"   forms the scheme of establishing a new religion.379
"   declares that he is appointed to be the apostle of
                          God....................................380
"   the opposition he encountered in establishing his
                          religion...............................390
"   ceased to be a preacher, and became a warrior...390
"   his bitterness against the Jews............... 391
"   the whole of Arabia overrun by his victorious
                          armies................................ 391
"   his death......................................391
"   Mr. Clodd's estimate of........................391
"   did not claim to be a perfect man............383
"   injustice done him by friends as well as foes.....383
"   his habits of living and dress.................384
"   the beneficent effects of his teachings upon his
                          country and people....................389
"   did not claim to have a new religion, but the
                          religion of Abraham...................386

Mohammed, his respectful treatment of Christians, and the
                injustice of the latter.....................386
    "   his followers at the present time............381
Mohammedanism, the youngest of the great religions of
    the world..382
Monotheism the foundation of the Mosaic laws...........190
    "   Christian, wherein differing from Jewish and
                Mohammedan.............................. 45
Moses, his silence on the subject of a future life.........190
    "   not the originator of all the laws sanctioned by him...191
    "   his contradictory peculiarities of character............189
"Muslim," or "Moslem," origin and meaning of..........382
Mythology common to all peoples and religions........... 28
Myths and folk-lore, subjects treated of in............... 28

N.

Nations, origin of.. 20
Nature, the great book of, remarks on by W. A. Stearns,
    President of Amherst College..........................413
Nazareth, the probable birthplace of Jesus.................197
New Testament, the, groundless opinion of high-church people
                        that it was all prepared under divine
                        guidance............................265
    "   "   " a careful study of, an imperative duty....235
    "   "   " books of, when collated..................216
    "   "   " mistakes in, by ignorance or design, of
                        translators............................214
    "   "   " collectively, a priceless gift from God to
                        man..................................214
    "   "   " when written in its earliest form.....226
    "   "   " opinions of Origen and Jerome on disputed texts in manuscripts............245
    "   "   " discrepancies unimportant to enthusiastic
                        believers............................247
    "   "   " alterations made before the books were
                        protected by Church authority.......248
    "   "   writings, by whom selected, history leaves in
                        doubt................................311
Nirvana, account of....................................... 93
Njörd, ruler of the winds................................167
Northmen, the most formidable among nations of their time..171

O.

               PAGE

Odin, the oldest of the Scandinavian gods.................166
 " remains of the religion of still existing in Norway......170
Old Testament, the, regarded as truthful, but not inspired,
        history............................184
 "   "   " what language written in.............174
Olympic games, character of..............................136
Omnipotent Power, an, a belief in, an incentive to the per-
  formance of every duty................................220
Omnipotence, man's lack of comprehension of............. 33
  "   the power of, all necessary to lead and direct us.421
Oracle, Delphic, meaning of..............................143
Oromazes, god of light................................... 98
Orpheus, mode of worship adopted by.....................144
Orphic doctrine, period and character of..................144
Osiris, god, the, legend of..............................118

P.

Palatine Hill, the home of the Latin gods................155
Palestine, boundaries of.................................193
Parliament and Congress, idea of originated from the Teutonic
  and Scandinavian assemblies............................161
Parmenides, his interpretation of God.....................138
Paul, his life and character, as persecutor and apostle....209
 "   " vision, the various accounts of..................288
 "   " deep inspiration.................................370
 "   " peculiar views on the matrimonial relation.......371
 "   " defense, the ability and shrewdness of..........364
Persia and Zoroaster, ancient religion of................. 96
Persian inscriptions, translations of some................ 97
Peter, the improbability of the story of his being the recipient
    of spiritual power, as related by Matthew.........302
 " his perfidy...357
Pharisaism, its rise and character........................344
Phœnicia, Mr. Coleman's description of...................268
Phœnicians, the, language of.............................183
Pilate, the reason of his presence at the Crucifixion......195
Pindar, the Theban, doctrine taught by...................135
Plato, his divine philosophy.............................139
Pliny, the elder, his view of religion...................158
Pontiff, the office of.....................................150

438 *Index.*

PAGE

Prayer, a becoming act, but no barrier against misfortunes....419
" the shortest and best ever made...................420
" oldest form of....................................... 25
" Universal, Pope's.......................... 421
Priests, origin of order of................................... 26
Priestcraft, its pernicious influences, as seen in Egyptian and
    Christian religions..131
Prophecies, pretended, concerning Jesus which have not the
        slightest reference to him......................293
" of the second coming of Christ, Mr. Greg on..310
Providence, the orderings of not influenced by prayer....417
"Puranas," when promulgated, and facts concerning...... 75
Purgatory, the Brahman's notions of....................... 79
Pythagoras, the beneficent results of his teachings........138

R.

Regia, the, seat of worship in the oldest Roman time.........154
"Religion," a definition of..................................222
Religion, supernatural, and mystery........................ 33
" Hindu, the, singular inconsistencies of........... 61
" much that is called new only a revival of old....... 80
" Christian, a portion of derived from Aryan religion. 28
" old stationary, Christian progressive.............. 45
Religions, ethnic and Christian, examination of............ 41
" pagan, not entirely ascribable to priestcraft..... 36
" old, advantage of a candid comparison of...... 40
" ethnic, or heathen...................... 32
" various, general survey of....................... 42
" Confucian and Roman Catholic, similarity between 44
" natural origin and growth of..................111
" denominational estimates of..................... 87
" crude, of antiquity not devoid of interest...... . 35
" different, how their development may be traced...387
" heathen, subsidence of condemnation of........ 40
Religious customs, similarity between Egyptian and Jewish...128
Resurrection, doctrine of older than the Hebrew race.....118
" bodily, an idea of comparatively recent origin..372
" the great diversity of opinion among learned
        men concerning.........................375
Revelation, the, remarks on.............................377
Rig-Veda, the, hymn from................................. 65

Rig-Veda, the, hymn from	67
" " " " "	68
Roman Catholic religion, the, composed in part of the old Teutonic religion	387
Roman nation, the, origin of	150
" Pantheon, the	151
" deities, classification of	152
" ceremonial worship, the	153
" priestly etiquette, arbitrary requirements of	154
Romans, the, much of their history before Christ unreliable	156
" " their religion	149
" " " funeral solemnities	156
Romans viii, comments on	367
" xii, " "	368
Rome, the mythical history and the true history of	148
" spirit of toleration displayed in	149

S.

Sacrifice the most ancient rite	25
" of human beings practiced in early Sweden	171
Salamis, city of	213
Salvation, John Calvin's strange theory of	219
Samaria, country and religion of	196
Sarah's connivance with Abraham to obtain posterity	180
Saul (Paul), his bravery and zeal	363
Scandinavia proper, location and boundaries of	161
Scandinavian mythology, its resemblance to that of Zoroaster	169
Scandinavians, a branch of the great Indo-European variety	161
" the, religion and gods of	162
" " cosmogony of	165
" " invasions and conquests made by	162
" " their religious beliefs and ceremonies	170
Science and the Bible	410
" astronomical, its influence in dispelling old superstitions	414
"Scribe," Scriptural meaning of	344
Seneca, his definition of the two principles of existence	157
Sermon on the Mount, the, and remarks on	328
Shem, the numerous descendants of	182
Sin, trying to find some excuse for its commission a too prevalent evil	186

PAGE

Sin, the taking away of by propitiatory sacrifice not reconcilable with human jurisprudence....................221
" its effects not removed by Jesus' death..............374
Socrates declared the basis of religion to be humanity........138
Soma, the juice of, a chief Hindu god........ 27
Soul, idea of its immortality first conceived by the Egyptians..123
" Hindu theory of the transmigration of the........... 79
"Speaking with tongues," account of largely mythical.....274
Sphinx, Egyptian, the..115
Stoics, the, doctrine of......................................140
Strauss, David Frederic, Prof. Stowe's criticism of........400
Superstition among the common people, evil effects of illustrated in Roman history................ 157
Supreme Being, a, original idea of....................... ... 64
" Power, a, reasons for believing in the existence of...187

T.

Temple of the Capitol at Rome...........................151
" at Jerusalem, destruction of......................353
Teutonic and Scandinavian race, Cæsar's description of....160
The life and character of Jesus, Prof. Schenkel on.......405
"The Way of the Two Destinies".......................109
The Bridge Chinevat...109
Theophany, belief of the Jews in.........................174
Ti-Ping Revolution, the, incidents and lessons of...... ... 56
Thor, mightiest of the Scandinavian gods..................166
" his famous mallet, belt and gauntlets...............167
Trachonitis, extent and location of.......................194
Tradition, Hebrew and Chaldæan, similarity between......... 23
Trinity, a, origin of the doctrine of..................... 78
" and Atonement, doctrines of assume form in Egypt long before Christianity......................129
Trophonius' Cave, oracles of, manner of preparation for consulting...146
Truth, to tell it squarely, under any circumstances, better than to lie, as Peter and Ananias did..................361
Tyr, the Scandinavian god of war..........,..............169

U.

"Unknown tongues," the, Paul's opinion concerning.......280

V.

Vedas, the, oldest work extant in Hindu literature......... 63

Index. 441

Vedas, the, regarded as inspired by Brahmans and Hindus.... 58
" " every Brahman student required to learn by heart 69
Vedic myths and legends................................... 29
" worshipers, the sincerity of their faith............. 65
" age, names and characters of gods of the........... 64
" " chronology of............................. 69
Vendidad, the, antiquity and genuineness of............. 98
Vesta, temple of..155

W.

War, a lack of religion which incites men to............392
" between Ormazd and Ahriman, gods of light and darkness...107
Water, use of as a symbol for cleansing from sin not original with the founders of Christianity.......................142
Wedding-ring, ceremony of derived from Egypt..........128
Well, Jacob's, where situated..........................201
Wilderness, the, facts concerning......................199
World, the, entire population of....................... 87
" " end of, prediction concerning...............345
Worship, baneful effects of formalism in on young minds..... 76
" early Brahman, false ideas of Christians regarding.. 76
" Indian and Christian compared................... 77
" Hebrew, beginning of..........................177
" the great business in ancient Egypt.............123

X.

Xenophanes and his followers............................138

Z.

Zend-Avesta, the, its connection with the ancient religion of Persia.. 96
" " " extracts from............................103
" books, language of................................. 99
Zoroaster, his life and character, Mr. Clarke on..........100
" and his precepts, Plutarch's account of......... 97
" little known with certainty of................. 99
" religion of copied in part from the Aryans.....100
" mentioned by Plato 400 years before Christ.... 97

UNUSUAL INDUCEMENTS
TO BOOKBUYERS.

REDUCTIONS.

The prices of most of our publications have been reduced from ONE-QUARTER to ONE-HALF, placing valuable works within every one's reach.

DISCOUNTS.

Generous discounts will be given to the trade and others, according to the nature and amount of the orders.

SAFETY.

Where there is reasonable evidence that any of our books are lost in the mails, we will duplicate them without extra charge, but losses very rarely occur.

Remittances should be by Postal Money Order, or Exchange on New York, to avoid loss.

POSTPAID.

Any publication sent free, by mail or express, on receipt of price.

THE COMPANION.

Any one ordering our books to the amount of $3 will receive our monthly free for one year.

Address all orders to

CHARLES P. SOMERBY,

Publisher, Bookseller, Importer and Printer,

139 EIGHTH STREET, NEW YORK.

Between Broadway and Fourth Avenue.

THE COMPANION.

DEVOTED TO THE

CULTURE, ENTERTAINMENT, AND BEST INTERESTS OF ALL.

Each number contains a choice variety of interesting and instructive Literature: Poems, Short Stories, Wit and Humor, Religious and Scientific Information, and General Miscellany.

An important feature of this journal is a selection of the literary gems and pearls of wisdom from the almost inexhaustible treasures of the Orient, lately opened to the Western World.

Philosophy, especially Sociology, will receive the attention its increasing importance demands.

A MONTHLY QUARTO. 16 pp., 50 CTS. PER YEAR.

Any one sending us $3 for our books will receive THE COMPANION free for one year.

CHARLES P. SOMERBY, PUBLISHER,

139 EIGHTH STREET, NEW YORK.

Between Broadway and Fourth Avenue.

THE MODERN THINKER.

SECOND EDITION.

Paper, 8vo, 160 pp., $1.

A REPLY

TO

DR. HITCHCOCK,

ON

SOCIALISM,

BY

A SOCIALIST.

12mo, 60 pp.; Paper, 25 Cts.; Flexible Cloth, 50 Cts.

SCRIPTURE SPECULATIONS:

WITH AN INTRODUCTION ON THE

CREATION, STARS, EARTH, PRIMITIVE MAN, JUDAISM, Etc.

BY HALSEY R. STEVENS.

"Where the Spirit of the Lord is, there is Liberty."

Extra Cloth, 12mo, 419 pp., $1.50. (Former price $2.)

EXTRACT.

"There rose not a prophet since like unto Moses, whom the Lord knew face to face." Now let us see the substantial truth of this claim of superior wisdom, superior illumination. If freedom is, as we all believe, essential to real manhood, if morality has hardly the ghost of a chance when a master's will is enforced by the lash, then the liberator in peace of millions of his brethren deserves even a higher place than any other emancipator in human history. For, had he deserted them because of their ingratitude, their fickleness, their cowardice, their superstition in the desert—and the thought came into his mind, for he is distinctly said to have rejected it with horror—had he gone back in honest indignation to the domestic peace of Midian, the Hebrew name would have been blotted out from history. And, more, the progress of humanity would have been unspeakably impeded. European civilization could not have come for ages. The sunny day of Christianity had not dawned. A republic of infinite promise would not have spread the banner of equal rights on these distant shores. Whether he was conscious of the fact or not, this intensely religious race had an element absolutely necessary to the progress of humanity—and for that they were the chosen of God. Other nations had other contributions to make: Greece with her art; Rome with her law; Egypt with natural science; the Orient with sacerdotal tradition: but from this bosom of a people clinging to the absolute unity of a supremely righteous Deity alone could come the Redeemer from all iniquity.

And how admirably was this people educated through their desert pilgrimage! They had no rallying point, not even the graves of their fathers. Moses gave them a present Deity represented in a portable shrine; so that "their fathers' God before them moved, an awful guide in smoke and flame." It was the Lord of Hosts who headed their host, cheered their battle, insured their victory as they were faithful, even screened their retreat when they disobeyed. They had no nationality—slaves never have—no country, no temple, no inviolable home, no hallowed grave, no certain future among those Nile brick-yards; so he binds them first of all around a common altar, brooded over by a present Deity, represented by the folding wings of Cherubim and the Shekinah light. Next, the fireside tie is sealed anew as exclusively theirs. The smile of heaven rested peculiarly on them. They were summoned to a glorious future. A noble country awaited their approach, to be their children's and that of their children's children through countless generations.

PRESS NOTICES.

This work may be called a running commentary on the text of the Scriptures. The author has no hesitation in expressing his opinions, but yet he does not transgress the limits of just criticism. He has no prejudice against the "sacred books," but he is unwilling that they should be reverenced without discrimination. "Faith," says he, "is excellent if founded on a noble life. We have no intention of setting at naught infinite wisdom or of treating eternal things with irreverence. The manly course for all writers is to say just what they think is just and true, and leave the event to God. Keeping back truth is a sin."—*Appleton's Popular Science Monthly.*

Many will admire the modest though independent spirit in which he pursues his speculations, his freedom from dogmatism, his learning, the acuteness of his remarks, his clear style, combined with his firm maintenance of all that leads to good works, enforces duty or serves in any way to make mankind happier, wiser or better. He writes with great candor and freedom, but with every appearance of giving us his honest convictions, saying that his intention has been "not only to increase the interest of plain persons like ourselves in the ancient Scriptures of Judæa, but to remove some stumbling-stones out of their path." And we think this will be the effect of his work.—*N. Y. Evening Mail.*

It is impossible to follow him without becoming enamored of the simplicity of his style, the clearness and candor of his statements, and the temperate, judicial spirit in which he writes.—*Brooklyn Argus.*

Mr. Stevens believes, like many others, that the time will eventually arrive when the greater portion of men will simply go forward in every Christian work according to honest convictions, humbly and thankfully looking upward for the true spirit—seeking sincerely after the pure waters of life.—*Chicago Times.*

Mr. Stevens has thought long and profoundly upon the subjects here treated. He has a vigorous, candid and disciplined mind. He writes like one who deeply loves the truth. The volume shows much erudition, and, being carefully indexed, it is quite valuable as a guide for Biblical students.—*Chicago Eve. Journal.*

As an exegetical and philosophical work it merits a place among those which have achieved an abiding reputation.—*Banner of Light* (Boston).

Mr. Stevens has gathered a mass of really valuable matter upon Creation, Astronomy, Primitive Man, Judaism, etc., independent of his Scripture discussion; he shows the Bible teacher where honest men are troubled in reading Moses and David; where, therefore, effort should be made to remove doubt and harmonize contradiction. He explains a great many obscure passages, does his best to strengthen the historic base of the sacred narrative, and exalts holy living as the supreme and holy revelation.—*Newburgh Telegraph.*

"Scripture Speculations" is a book deserving of more than one reading. It bears the impress of a writer evidently devout, in earnest, and strongly religious.—*Grand Rapids Eagle.*

ISSUES OF THE AGE;

OR,

CONSEQUENCES INVOLVED IN MODERN THOUGHT.

By HENRY C. PEDDER.

Everything that we now deem of antiquity was at one time new; and what we now defend by examples will at a future period stand as precedents.—TACITUS.

Extra cloth, beveled, black and gold back and side stamps, 12mo, 175 pp., $1. (Former price $1.50.)

CONTENTS.

Chap. I—Introduction. II—The Scientific Spirit and Its Consequences. III—Skepticism. IV—Ancient Faith and Modern Culture. V—The Supremacy of Law: Its Physical and Psychical Conditions. VI—The Doctrine of Human Progress. VII—Concluding Remarks.

PREFACE.

The contents of this volume being intended as a contribution toward the better understanding of modern thought, and the consequences which must necessarily result from the peculiar intellectual type of the age, it needs no exhaustive preface to explain the cause of its production. As a reason for its conception and birth, it is enough to say that it proposes to indicate rather than exhaust the nature of those problems of life and mind by which we are, in the present day, so abundantly surrounded. An uneasy, restless searching after something broader, deeper, and more satisfactory, is the predominant characteristic of the present age; and in view of this, it seems to us that it is the duty of every reflective mind to devote at least some attention to so important a subject. How far such a result may be accomplished in the following remarks, time and experience alone can determine. The *intention* is, however, a good one; and as such we can confidently recommend the following pages to those who are disposed to bestow an unprejudiced and thoughtful consideration on questions which are obviously of such vast importance: believing also that, although the searching analysis and skeptical spirit of the present age may cause many years' sojourn in the wilderness of perplexity and doubt, we are nevertheless certain in the end to enter the Promised Land and find peace.

In this view, therefore, should the accompanying thoughts answer the purpose of oases in what may seem to some a desert of negation and unbelief, they will amply have fulfilled their mission.

Lastly, we can only say, should it be found, as we think it will, that the ideas embodied in the different chapters deal with the silent depths of the soul, rather than the noisier but more superficial conditions of feeling, and also pertain to the serenity of intelligence, rather than the turmoil of irrational prejudice, it is hoped that they will, for this reason, be all the more welcome to those who, after many intellectual wanderings, have at last learned to realize a grandeur and usefulness in those transitional stages of thought and feeling which seem inseparable from the conditions of human existence, and which at the same time indicate so powerfully that man's destiny is progressive.

PRESS NOTICES.

The author of this volume has evidently kept company with many of the finer spirits of the age, until his mind has become imbued with the fragrance of their thought. He has excellent tendencies, elevated tastes, and sound aspirations.—*N. Y. Tribune.*

In the restless spirit of inquiry abroad, and the feverish excitement of doubt, he sees the returning glory of that intellectual empire which declined with Grecian culture. He has brought the fruits of a large culture and extensive reading, and a mind unusually calm and thoughtful, to bear upon the questions which are agitating the hour.—*N. Y. World.*

An admirably written, scholarly volume.—*N. Y. Graphic.*

An unprejudiced and thoughtful consideration of some of the most momentous questions that are now agitating the world, and will, no doubt, attract, as it deserves, the widest attention.—*N. Y. Commercial Advertiser.*

He presents a safe guide through the bewildering labyrinth of scientific, philosophical, and theological speculations, and evinces a thorough familiarity with most of the modern theories advanced.—*Jewish Times.*

The author is evidently a man of genuine literary taste. His book exhibits reflection and independence.—*N. Y. Eve. Post.*

A truly able discussion of the subjects which most vitally concern the higher nature and larger life of man.—*Chicago Evening Journal.*

His views are characterized by a broad catholicity and a depth of thought which do credit at once to his heart and his mind.—*Grand Rapids Democrat.*

Some of its chapters contain a power of analysis rarely surpassed. In many respects it is a valuable book for the student.—*St. Louis Dispatch.*

A work of much more than ordinary interest. It contains profound and impressive thoughts and sentiments.—*Buffalo Post.*

Its real merits can only be discovered by a perusal.—*Toledo Journal.*

"ADVANCEMENT OF SCIENCE,"

BEING THE

INAUGURAL ADDRESS

Before the British Association for the Advancement of Science, at Belfast, by the President, JOHN TYNDALL, D.C.L., LL.D., F.R.S., with Portrait and Biographical Sketch.

Also, a descriptive Essay, by Prof. H. HELMHOLTZ, with Sir HENRY THOMPSON and

PROFESSOR TYNDALL'S FAMOUS ARTICLES ON PRAYER,

together on heavy tinted paper, in extra cloth, 12mo, 105 pp., **50 cents.** The same, in pamphlet form, cheaper paper, **25 cents.** Inaugural and Portrait only, 69 pp., **10 cents.** (Former prices, $1, 50 and 25 cents.)

The Inaugural says: "The questions here raised are inevitable. They are approaching us with accelerated speed, and it is not a matter of indifference whether they are introduced with reverence or irreverence."

The N. Y. *Tribune* says: "PROF. TYNDALL CROSSES THE RUBICON.—It is the opening address of the President of the most important convention of scientific men in the world. Every line of it breathes thought, power, eloquence.....It is in many respects one of the most extraordinary utterances of our time."

The N. Y. *Commercial Advertiser* says: "Prof. Tyndall has inaugurated a new era in scientific development, and has drawn the sword in a battle whose clash of arms will presently resound through the civilized world."

The N. Y. *Graphic* says: "It will undoubtedly have great currency, and make a wide and deep impression."

G. W. Smalley, London correspondent of the N. Y. *Tribune*, says: "There can be but one opinion of the address as an example of intellectual power and of courageous sincerity rare in all times."

THE ESSENCE OF RELIGION.

BY L. FEUERBACH,

Author of "The Essence of Christianity," etc., etc.

TRANSLATED FROM THE GERMAN.

Cloth, 12mo, 75 pp., 50 Cts. (Former price 75 Cts.)

The spirit of the time is show, not substance. Our politics, our ethics, our religion, our science, is a sham. The truth-teller is ill-mannered, therefore immoral. Truthfulness is the immorality of our age!...My aim has been to prove that the powers before which man crouches are creatures of his own limited, ignorant, uncultured, and timorous mind, to prove that in special the being whom man sets over against himself as a separate supernatural existence is his own being.—*Extract*.

THE CULTIVATION OF ART,
AND ITS RELATIONS TO RELIGIOUS PURITANISM AND MONEY-GETTING.
By A. R. COOPER.

12 mo, 48 pp., Fancy Paper, 20 Cents.; Extra Flexible Cloth, 35 Cents.
(Former prices 50 and 75 cts.)

Mammon worship is the religion of our age and nation. What we call our religion is for the most part an affair of fashion and empty ceremony; our hearts are not in it, but our real religion is business. It is too much with us as Heine says it is with the merchant the world over: "His counting-house is his church, his desk is his pew, his ledger is his bible, his stock in trade the holiest of the holy, the bell of the exchange his summons to prayer, his gold his God, and credit his faith."....

The table, which in its primitive form was probably a block of wood, and only gradually came to be constructed as a piece of carpentry, at last attained to a marvelous execution in Florentine mosaic....Man's primitive bed was of course the soil of the spot which gave him birth. Instinct would lead him to seek shelter, and to heap up mosses, leaves, and soft materials upon which to take his rest with ease. But art, keeping pace with the general advance of civilization, now furnishes him with a palatial residence and a luxurious couch. Again, from the rude and simple pottery of the early man has come the wonderfully beautiful vases of ancient and modern times, and the china and glassware of our own days....The sculptor is but a sublimer workman in stone; painting had its origin in the use of color or outline drawing upon the walls of buildings. The grandest architecture is an evolution from the hut and cavern of primeval man, a glorified roof, as Ruskin expresses it. Sound, as expressed in music, is the analogue of a cry; and poetry is the beautifully impassioned utterance of the higher feelings.—*Extracts*.

PERCY BYSSHE SHELLEY
As a Philosopher and Reformer.
By CHARLES SOTHERAN.

Including an Original Sonnet by C. W. FREDERICKSON, Portrait of Shelley, and View of his Tomb.

Cloth, 8vo, 60 pp., $1. (Former price $1.25.)

"This work considers Shelley's love of freedom; anticipation of the theory of evolution; scientific scholarship; real belief in a Supreme Intelligence; Pantheism; faith in the true, though not the theological, Jesus; disbelief in miracles and the biblical account of Creation; appreciation of the allegorical truth hidden in all religions; hesitancy about a future state; love of virtue; sympathy with Ireland's oppression; advocacy of Queen Caroline; desire to see Protestant and Catholic parties united in humane efforts; defense of labor's rights; hatred of capital and commerce; devotion to free speech and rights of women; interest in dumb animals, and love for the United States."

THE HISTORICAL JESUS OF NAZARETH.
By M. Schlesinger, Ph.D.,
Rabbi of the Congregation Anshe Emeth, Albany, N. Y.

Extra Cloth, 12mo, 98 pp., 75 Cts. (Former price $1.)

EXTRACT.

The perfect harmony and fraternal feeling generally supposed to have existed between the founders and early propagators of Christianity are chimeras, which must be assigned to the place where they properly belong—that of mythology. The truth, which may be learned ever from those records which are in everybody's hands—the New Testament writings—is that there were lively contentions, bitter enmities, and intense hatred between the three great parties, the Jew-Christians, the Paulines, and the Gnostics, of whom each claimed to be in possession of the only pure and undefiled truth of Christianity.... Heathenism more and more absorbs the new religion; and those truths brought over from Judaism are soon lost sight of, for they are swept away, or buried under the deluge of Paganism. The new religion has no longer anything in common with Judaism, except whenever she takes her weapons, as her founder, Paul, always did, from the treasures of the sacred literature of the Jews, to turn them against those who furnished them.

PRESS NOTICES.

Dr. Schlesinger gives us the Jewish view of Jesus. Of course it is not the Christian one, but he concedes a great deal: that Jesus worked miracles, and by them, and the expectation and want of the people, was induced to assume the office of the Messiah—not at all of God. He thinks that Jesus never gave up this idea of his mission until he cried upon the cross, "Why hast thou forsaken me, my God?"—*The Inquirer* (N. Y.).

The first part of the work is a brief history of the origin and development of the Messianic idea of Israel before Jesus. This is the most valuable part of the work. The rabbi writes without any prejudice against Jesus. Indeed, he claims him as "a true son of his people," an "enthusiast who dies heroically for an idea." The book ought to be received as a token that the barriers of prejudice between Jew and Christian are falling, and that there are those in the Hebrew church who at least are studying the sources of Christian doctrine with a sincere desire to know the truth concerning them.—*Christian Register*.

Dr. Schlesinger gives an interesting and ingenious account of the development of the Messianic expectation among the Jews. At first and for ages it was not a personal Messiah that they looked for, he thinks. They thought that the people of Israel, by propagating their laws and religion among the nations, would become the saviour of the world. It was the offspring of the optimistic bend of the Hebrew mind. He thinks it was not until the reign of Herod that the national expectation took a personal form, and that Jesus of Nazareth was the first to claim the title and office—though it is thought by some scholars that he was not the first.—*N. Y. Graphic.*

The preface begins with a quotation from Draper: "In a matter so solemn as that of religion, all men whose temporal interests are not involved in existing institutions earnestly desire to find the truth." The amiable and learned Rabbi of the Synagogue of the "Men of Truth" does not only indulge in hypothesis—he chiefly deals with facts, which, through his hypothesis, are clearly grouped in a very instructive and readable book.—*The New Age* (Boston).

The book is interesting not only for its historical research, but as showing just how the Christian Saviour is looked upon by the descendants of those who put him to death.—*San Francisco Bulletin.*

The author occasionally deviates in his quotations from the Bible from King James' version, and resorts to the original Hebrew and Greek. A flood of light will fall upon many minds by its perusal.—*Boston Commonwealth.*

ANTIQUITY OF CHRISTIANITY.
By JOHN ALBERGER.
12mo, 61 pp.; PAPER, 25 Cents; EXTRA CLOTH, 50 Cents.
(Former price, paper, 35 cts.; cloth, 75 cts.)

CONTENTS.—Chapter I: Testimonies, Justin Martyr, Tertullian, Melito, Origen, A. Saccus, St. Clement, Eusebius, Constantine, Arnobius, Lactantius, St. Augustine, Faustus, Abulmerar, Orpheus, Mahistan, Egyptian Monuments. II: Christianity and the Church, The Slow Progress of the Church, The Means by which it Achieved its Victories, European Civilization due to the Introduction of Latin Pagan Works. III: Anima Mundi, The Philosophy of Pythagoras, of Socrates, of Aristotle, of Zeno, of Epicurus, of Plato. IV: Hindoo Mythology, Persian Mythology, Scandinavian Mythology. V: Divine Developments and Mutations, as Exhibited in the Christian and Pagan Mythology. VI: Divine Characteristics, Saviors, Logoses, Miraculous Conception, Phenomena, Incarnations of Divinity, Alarming Prophecies at the Birth of Infant Gods, Miraculous Escapes, Infant Miracles, Miraculous Voices, Divine Physicians, Divine Prophetic Power, Transfigurations, Divine Sufferings, Descent into Hell, Resurrection and Ascension. VII: Human Sacrifices, Trinity, Demons, Hell, Conclusion.

Extracts.—The origin of Christianity is involved in so much obscurity that the most distinguished Fathers of the primitive Church explicitly declared that it had existed from time immemorial...."In our time is the Christian religion, which to know and follow is the most sure and certain health, called according to that name, but not according to the thing of which it is the name; for the thing itself, the same which is now called the Christian religion, really was known to the ancients, nor was wanting at any time even from the beginning of the human race, until the time when Christ came in the flesh, from whence the true religion, not as having been wanting in former times, but having in later times received a new name."—*St. Augustine.*

The Childhood of the World.

A SIMPLE ACCOUNT OF MAN IN EARLY TIMES.

By Edward Clodd, F.R.A.S.

Cloth, 12mo, 91 pp., 50 Cts. (Former price 75 Cts.)

CONTENTS.

Part I.—Introductory; Man's First Wants; Man's First Tools; Fire; Cooking and Pottery; Dwellings; Use of Metals; Man's Great Age on the Earth; Mankind as Shepherds, Farmers, and Traders; Language; Writing; Counting; Man's Wanderings from his First Home; Man's Progress in All Things; Decay of Peoples.

Part II.—Introductory; Man's First Questions; Myths; Myths about Sun and Moon; Myths about Eclipses; Myths about Stars; Myths about the Earth and Man; Man's Ideas about the Soul; Belief in Magic and Witchcraft; Man's Awe of the Unknown; Fetish-Worship; Idolatry; Nature-Worship—Water-Worship, Tree-Worship, Animal-Worship; Polytheism, or Belief in Many Gods; Dualism, or Belief in Two Gods; Prayer; Sacrifice; Monotheism, or Belief in One God; Three Stories about Abraham; Man's Belief in a Future Life; Sacred Books; Conclusion.

PREFACE.

For the information of parents and others into whose hands this book may fall, it may be stated that it is an attempt, in the absence of any kindred elementary work, to narrate, in as simple language as the subject will permit, the story of man's progress from the unknown time of his early appearance upon the earth to the period from which writers of history ordinarily begin.

That an acquaintance with the primitive condition of man should precede the study of any single department of his later history is obvious, but it must be remembered that such knowledge has become attainable only within the last few years, and at present enters but little, if at all, into the course of study at schools.

Thanks to the patient and careful researches of men of science, the way is rapidly becoming clearer for tracing the steps by which, at ever-varying rates of progress, different races have advanced from savagery to civilization, and for thus giving a completeness to the history of mankind which the assumptions of an arbitrary chronology would render impossible.

As the table of contents indicates, the first part of this book describes the progress of man in material things, while the second part seeks to explain his mode of advance from lower to higher stages of religious belief.

Although this work is written for the young, I venture to hope that it will afford to older persons who will accept the simplicity of its style, interesting information concerning primitive man.

In thinking it undesirable to encumber the pages of a work of this class with foot-notes and references, I have been at some

pains to verify the statements made, the larger body of which may be found in the works of Tylor, Lubbock, Nilsson, Waitz, and other ethnologists, to whom my obligations are cordially expressed. E. C.
133 BRECKNOCK ROAD, LONDON.

OPINIONS.

Extract from a letter from Professor Max Müller to the author: "I read your book with great pleasure. I have no doubt it will do good, and hope you will continue your work. Nothing spoils our temper so much as having to unlearn in youth, manhood, and even old age, so many things which we were taught as children. A book like yours will prepare a far better soil in the child's mind, and I was delighted to have it to read to my children."

E. B. Tylor, F.R.S., in "Nature," says: "This genial little volume is a child's book as to shortness, cheapness, and simplicity of style, though the author reasonably hopes that older people will use it as a source of information not popularly accessible elsewhere as to the life of Primitive Man and its relation to our own. ....This book, if the time has come for the public to take to it, will have a certain effect in the world. It is not a mere compilation from the authors mentioned in the preface, but takes its own grounds and stands by and for itself. Mr. Clodd has thought out his philosophy of life, and used his best skill to bring it into the range of a child's view."

The Boston *Daily Globe* says: "We have never seen the subject of Primitive Man better set forth: the author first delineates the progress of our race in natural things, and then goes on by natural steps to explain the gradual modes of advance from lower to higher civilization."

THE ANONYMOUS HYPOTHESIS OF CREATION.
BY JAMES J. FURNISS.

EXTRA FLEXIBLE CLOTH, 12MO, 55 PP., 35 CTS. (Former price 50c.)

CONTENTS.—Introduction. Genesis—Chapter I: Remarks on Verse 1; Darkness on the Face of the Waters; Creation of Light; The Waters Divided; Dry Land Appears; First Appearance of Vegetation; The Orbs of Space; Beginning of Animal Life; Creation of Man. Genesis—Chapter II: Conclusion of First Account of Creation; Second Account of Creation Begins; First and Second Accounts Compared; Interpretation of the Mosaic Narrative, Literal or Allegorical? Theories in Support of Inspiration Doctrine, and Concluding Remarks.

INTRODUCTION.—In offering the following pages, the author lays no claim to originality so far as the subject-matter is concerned, for, perhaps, everything that he has there written has been more forcibly and more fully dealt with by others already; but his object has been to present the subject as concisely as practicable, for the benefit of those who have not the time or the inclination to peruse the more voluminous works. The author's purpose has been accomplished if he has succeeded in affording any assistance, however small, to the inquiring beginner.

THE
REIGN OF THE STOICS.

By Frederic May Holland.

Read the philosophers, and learn how to make life happy, seeking useful precepts and brave and noble words which may become deeds.—SENECA.

With Citations of Authorities Quoted from on Each Page.

Extra Cloth, 12mo, 248 pp., $1.25.

CONTENTS.

CHAP.		PAGE.
I.	HISTORY	11
II.	RELIGION	57
III.	MAXIMS OF SELF-CONTROL	83
IV.	MAXIMS OF SELF-CULTURE	123
V.	MAXIMS OF BENEVOLENCE	151
VI.	MAXIMS OF JUSTICE	183
VII.	PHILOSOPHY	195